THE THIRD KIND OF KNOWLEDGE

ALSO BY ROBERT FITZGERALD

Robert Fitzgerald. Photograph © Kelly Wise; used by permission.

Robert Fitzgerald

THE THIRD KIND OF KNOWLEDGE

Memoirs &
Selected Writings

EDITED BY

PENELOPE LAURANS FITZGERALD

A NEW DIRECTIONS BOOK

Grateful acknowledgment is made to the editors and publishers of the journals, magazines, and individual volumes in which many of these essays first appeared. Details of first publication are given on the opening page of each essay.

Manufactured in the United States of America
First published clothbound by New Directions in 1993
New Directions books are printed on acid-free paper.
Published simultaneously in Canada by Penguin Books Canada Ltd.

Library of Congress Cataloging-in-Publication Data

Fitzgerald, Robert, 1910–1985
    The third kind of knowledge : memoirs & selected writings / edited by Penelope Laurans Fitzgerald.
      p.   cm.
    ISBN 0–8112–1056–1
    1. Fitzgerald, Robert, 1910–1985.   2. Poets, American–20th century–Biography.   3. Translators–United States–Biography.
4. Poetry–Translating.   5. Greek language–Translating into English.   6. Latin language–Translating into English.   7. Classical poetry–History and criticism.   I. Fitzgerald, Penelope Laurans.
II. Title.
PS3511.I922Z477 1993
811'.52–dc19
[B]   88–1377
                                                  CIP

New Directions Books are published for James Laughlin
by New Directions Publishing Corporation,
80 Eighth Avenue, New York 10011

FOR
WILLIAM
MAXWELL

"Atque in perpetuum, frater, ave atque vale"

ACKNOWLEDGMENTS

For help with different matters in the preparation of this manuscript I am grateful to Marie Borroff; Cornelia Cook; Kai T. Erikson; Christine Froula and John Austin; Dana Gioia; Robert Giroux; Barbara and John Hersey; Donald Kagan; Robert Kiely; Sanford Kreisberg; the late Ann Laughlin; R. W. B. Lewis; Charles Long; Jonathan Lear; John Frederick Nims; Emily Maxwell; Richard Strier; Maria Tatar; Betty and Alan Trachtenberg; Dorothy Robinson and Philip Bouwsma; Judith Perkins; and for the publisher, Peggy Fox, Griselda Ohannessian, and Peter Glassgold.

William Maxwell and James Laughlin acted with generosity and waited with patience for a book that the author wished to be theirs.

Contents

Sections of photographs follow pages 28, 104, and 164.

. . . A man, this man,
Bred among lakes and railway cars and smoke,
The salt of childhood on his wintry lips,
His full heart ebbing toward the new tide
Arriving, arriving, in laughter and cries,
Down the chaotic dawn and eastern drift,
Would hail the unforeseen, and celebrate
On the great mountainside those sprites,
Tongues of delight, that may remember him—
The yet unborn, trembling in the same rooms,
Breakfasting before the same grey windows,
Lying, grieving again; yet all beyond him,
Who knew he lived in rough Jehovah's breath,
And burned, a quiet wick in a wild night,
Loving what he beheld and will behold.

Robert Fitzgerald
from "History"

Introduction

I first met him in 1964 in a windowed garret atop a classroom building at Mount Holyoke College, where he was spending a semester as visiting professor. He was fifty-four and had lived through many adventures, as journalist, naval officer, poet, translator, teacher. He had spent the past ten years living with his wife and family in Italy, six of those years translating his widely acclaimed version of the *Odyssey*. He numbered among his mentors T. S. Eliot and Ezra Pound, and among his close friends Flannery O'Connor, James Agee, and John Berryman. The class, almost all gathered by the time I arrived that afternoon, was seated around a long table, one intimidating young woman calmly puffing away on a pipe. He came forward to me, as he did to everyone who came to class that day, and formally shook my hand, bending slightly in my direction and saying kindly, "I'm Robert Fitzgerald."

Out the window over the distant hills of the Connecticut valley that semester the world turned increasingly leafy and green, and inside the classroom the pleasures that could be derived from a formal understanding of English prosody came magically to life before our eyes. Attention to detail was paramount, the largest effects often visible in the smallest details of a line, and he would show us these on a blackboard, putting his cigarette aside for a moment and patiently chalking the words in an elegant spidery handwriting. When he found a prosodic effect he admired in one of our own poems, he would read it to us, look up, and then—pausing—click his tongue against his cheek in appreciation. The highest grade he awarded was NAAB (Not At All Bad). The few people in the class who merited that accolade even once felt that their entire semester had been a success.

Students thought he looked the part of a writer and that his eyes told of a deep life. He was of medium height and build, with a classical profile, the most distinctive feature of which was a sharp Grecian nose. During his years in Europe he took to wearing a beret, a habit which he continued on his return to America in the sixties, and which seemed perfectly suited to him. At Mount Holyoke, as in Cambridge in the sixties and seventies and New Haven in the eighties, he was a recognizable figure in his tan raincoat and black beret with a green bookbag slung over his shoulder, making his way from office to library to classroom. He had courtliness, the courtesy of gesture and manner that made him immediately stand out and earned him deference and respect. Even people who didn't know him—a taxi driver in Cleveland or a shopkeeper in a small village in Maine—would call him "Professor," since he carried that air and that authority around with him. Yet he was completely without affectation, and the combination of his obvious refinement yet complete naturalness may be why people instinctively liked him. Perhaps it was his witness to suffering in early life that gave him inherent humility and made him benevolent, so that even when he was applying his rigorous standards to their creative work people always felt they were being justly and kindly treated.

His most striking characteristic was his way of speaking. He was born in 1910 to Irish-Catholic parents who had met while performing in a touring morality play called *The Sign of the Cross,* and although he was not an actor in the narrow sense, this theatrical heritage did manifest itself in his life. He was a supremely fine talker, one whose relaxed, measured, cultivated discourse was enhanced by a charming and expressive voice. He knew, remembered, told, and relished funny stories, and in the telling of them he displayed an actor's sly awareness of audience. His translations, of course, were themselves great stories, and an actor's instinctive sense of pace and control must have helped contribute to his grasp and transmission of them. In the classroom as well as in more informal situations, his authority came not from forceful gestures or declamation, but from his natural learning and distinction and from his elegant way of saying what he meant with such precision that listeners were held in rapt attention. He would hunch over the essay or the poem or the dinner table and make his points slowly, stopping to puff or stub out his cigarette, pausing much and harrumphing often, but every word that eventually came had its nuanced place in the sentences that he brought forth as if he were setting them on paper.

Illness and death were a part of his world from the beginning. When his parents married his father already was afflicted with the tubercular hip wound that would result years later in his death. As the searing memoirs in this volume tell, he lost his mother at five, his only sibling at seven, and his father at seventeen. It was no doubt this confluence of losses that made him aware of the sacramental nature of memory and fostered in him the belief that the sense of the past was an integral part of the religious conception of life he favored.

In fact, the power of the past in general is a subject that can be said to account for nearly all of his work. It is the central preoccupation of his poetry and of the memoirs and essays collected here. And it is at the heart of the act of translation itself. He believed, as he wrote in his essay "Generations of Leaves," that "the human gifts of piety and sense of the past weigh somewhat in the balance against the universal fact of mortality." All of his literary efforts were largely efforts, as he wrote in a notebook in the forties, "to transcend the sense of memory as evanescent and incomplete and take for wealth the actual recoveries that can be made: they cross the present continually and can be stilled."

A midwest childhood remained a deep part of him. Early photographs of him exist at ten years old, standing on the steps of the Springfield state house, a small figure next to the towering statue of Lincoln, whose prose remained a touchstone all his life. An unusually able and all-around student, he graduated from Springfield High School in 1928 with the highest ranking of any boy in his class, as the quarterback of the football team, and having gained a certain amount of local fame by attracting the attention and patronage of Vachel Lindsay, Springfield's native poet. Sent east to spend a year at Choate before going on to Yale, he met Dudley Fitts, the classical scholar and man of letters who was to become his first intellectual mentor and his collaborator in a number of translations, and whose influence and example changed his course from Yale to Harvard.

When asked to comment for a book of contemporary poetry that published some of his poems, he wrote: "I have been independent and trustful of my own powers. I hold by constructive beauty, energy of language, depth of life." Years before, in answer to a questionnaire for *Partisan Review*, he had said the same thing with different emphasis: "Groups, classes, organizations, regions, religions, and systems of thought have, like the starry universe, environed me since birth, and to those of my immediate environment I have paid whatever allegiance seemed appropriate or necessary, while still, I trust, remaining myself." An overview of his life would suggest that he was subject to powerful institutional influences, but that there was a part of him that did remain detached from them. This was true in the mid-thirties at the *Herald Tribune*, his first job, where he agonized through the long days to produce copy in a form and at a pace unsuitable to him, and where every spare instant of his waking life was given to his art. It was certainly true of his life in the late thirties and forties as a part of Luce enterprises, where, like his friend Jim Agee, he was a part of the stable of Luce's literati who managed to do their jobs on America's great newsmagazines while preserving an ironic distance from them. And it was true also of both his experiences at Harvard, where first as a student and later as a teacher he remained slightly aloof from an institution that so easily swallowed up others.

In his student days at Harvard, the savor of which is evoked in this volume in "Rousseau and Romanticism" as well as in his memoir of Agee, he learned Greek, studied with Babbitt, Parry, and Whitehead, took the lead role in the *Philoctetes* (he later said that having hundreds of lines of Greek on his tongue was instrumental in his sense of how to translate Homer), won the Bolyston Contest for Elocution (he later became Boylston Professor of Rhetoric and Oratory), and gave the Latin commencement oration. It was here that he met Eliot, who took some of his poems for the *Criterion*, and here that he made his close friendships with William Maxwell, James Laughlin, and James Agee. Something about the link between his first and second Harvard lives, or perhaps something about Harvard itself, can be gathered from his experience of arriving in a classroom in Seaver Hall in 1965, opening a desk to search for a pencil, and taking from it the fall term class list of Latin Poetry from 1932 with his own name on it.

In his second incarnation at Harvard in the sixties and seventies he held the Boylston chair, the fourth oldest at Harvard, the distinguished history of which made its incumbent among the most visible of many visible faculty figures. The chair had been empty since Archibald MacLeish retired, and when Robert assumed it he received national attention: *Time* did a story, and his former students at another college, having been misinformed by newspapers about the quaint prerogatives of the Boylston professor, sent him a cow to tether in Harvard Yard (he had to arrange for its removal to the country). His efforts in this position were large ones, and costly to him. He was a writer in an academic's gown. He had no taste for academic politics—he remained instinctively aloof from them—and he had no interest in being an administrator, although his natural authority allowed him, with Herculean effort, to perform administrative duties loyally and well. As Boylston professor he was the unofficial head of a writing program which included, among others, Robert Lowell and Elizabeth Bishop, a host of visiting elder statesmen, and a rotating group of distinguished younger poets and fiction writers—for all of whom, because he was known, loved, and trusted, he was often called upon to act as minister, guide, and defender.

In the meantime, while translating the *Iliad* he was also teaching his own courses, "Homer, Virgil, and Dante," and "Versification." The 1979 Harvard Course Evaluation Guide wrote of "Versification": "An opportunity to work with a consummate artist and a devoted teacher, this course is among the most highly praised of all courses evaluated." In 1988, three years after his death, twelve Harvard alumni of Versification—all young poets who had published books and achieved recognition in the world of poetry—gathered for an evening to read their poems and pay tribute to him. As he went from student of the great to teacher of the gifted, Harvard framed his life. In his last years, on the wall next to his worktable, near photographs of literary friends and mentors, hung two documents: the first, his admission letter to Harvard, typed out by the Dean of Admission, Henry Pennypacker, with a postscript warning him that he could not be enrolled for the A.B. degree until he passed an examination in Latin or Greek; and the second, the letter on his retirement conferring on him the title of Boylston Professor Emeritus.

Yet despite all of these large engagements—the *Herald Tribune, Time-Life-Fortune*, the Navy, Harvard—the happiest times of his life were certainly those when he was able to give undivided time and energy to his art. In Italy between 1953 and 1964, with the help of his second wife, Sally Fitzgerald, he had been able to live a life freely dedicated to family and poetry. Early on he had vowed that he would not under any circumstances rush the translation of the *Odyssey*, and he did not. He began by painstakingly writing out the Greek in big ledger notebooks, using the dictionary and making decisions about obscure passages as he went along. After that it was a matter, as he said, "of hurling myself at the expanse of Greek every morning, and maybe writing below the Greek lines tentative versions of the English verse which could later be typed up and worked on as drafts. . . . There were innumerable drafts." The venture took six years, interrupted only by occasional trips to the States for terms of teaching at colleges and universities which had proffered invitations.

It is possible to see the publication of the Fitzgerald translation of the *Odyssey* in 1965 as a turning point, not simply in the life of the translator, but in the life of American publishing as well, since in a sense it marked the coming of age of the paperback book for classroom study. From the first the translation had an enormous success in this country. His point about the great classical poems had been that "they were poetry when they first were conceived, they are poetry now, and if you think the time may come when they are not poetry, the burden of the argument rests with you." The Lattimore translation of the *Iliad*, rendered in an English approximation of dactylic hexameter, had led the way in suggesting that the Homeric poems could be rescued from those who thought of them as "prose narratives," or "novels." Now the Fitzgerald translation of the *Odyssey*, written in the loose iambic pentameter that was the staple of English poetry, seemed to many to complete the rescue. The happy years in Italy bore happy fruit.

Then again, in the four years between his retirement from Harvard and his death, he lived another kind of full and rich life in New Haven, Connecticut. After finishing the *Iliad* he had sworn he never would translate anything again. But under pressure from academic friends who thought a different translation of the *Aeneid* was needed, and in order to afford more time away from teaching for his own work, he undertook his third large effort of classical translation. During this period he also managed to compose the autobiographical memoirs in this volume, all of them written by someone whose lifelong habit of looking into the shadow of death gave him the habit of seeing things under the aspect of eternity. He enjoyed spending time in New Haven, making the full circle back to the school he had expected to attend when he was a boy. His favorite Yale story concerned walking behind two young women wheeling bicycles, and overhearing the wrath of one as she related to the other the curse she had just delivered to a former object of her affections: "And I said to him 'You know that part in the *Iliad* where Achilles drags Hector along behind the chariot? Well, I hope that happens to YOU.'" In the last year of his life, just before he accepted a year's stint as Poet at the Library of Congress, he reworked and published to universal critical acclaim the book entitled *Enlarging the Change*, his chronicle of the Princeton seminars in Literary Criticism between 1949–1951, a remarkable set of lectures and discussions by intellectual giants of that age, among them Jacques Maritain, Erich Auerbach, Francis Fergusson, Mark Schorer, Rene Wellek, and Erich Kahler.

He altered his own life dramatically twice. After the war, in which he spent the closing days on Guam on the staff of CINCPAC (he was to have been the naval historian at the landing on Honshu, had that happened), his ten-year marriage to Eleanor Green ended. He and Sarah Morgan were married in the Roman Catholic Church, and their faith became the foundation of their lives. Over the years, they had six children. During this period, especially in the late forties and through the fifties, the seriousness with which he took his faith was manifest in private and public ways; he and Sally Fitzgerald were active and visible in the Roman Catholic community. Then in 1972 he and Sally separated, and in 1982 he and I married.

Whatever Robert's specific religious beliefs at any time of his life, it is a fact that the life of the spirit always meant more to him than the life of the mind, and that this was obvious to all who knew him. In fact part of the secret of his personal charm may have been that in the brainy worlds in which he lived, the view of life he cherished and exemplified—when it is held with integrity, and people can always tell when it is—is especially pleasing and moving. In the end I would say he was someone who, for reasons that always remain inexplicable and mysterious, had a great effect on others. His own summation of what he had learned in a rich life appeared aptly enough at the end of his contribution to his Harvard College Fiftieth Reunion report:

> So hard at best is the lot of man, and so great is the beauty he can apprehend, that only a religious conception of things can take in the extremes and meet the case. Our lifetimes have seen the opening of abysses before which the mind quails. But it seems to me there are a few things everyone can humbly try to hold onto: love and mercy (and humor) in day-to-day living; the quest for exact truth in language and affairs of the intellect; self-recollection or prayer; and the peace, the composed energy of art.

* * *

The memoirs and essays printed in this volume were written over the course of a quarter of a century and at very different moments in the life of the author. With one exception, however, the autobiographical pieces were all written in the seventies and eighties. They are set in different geographic locations—Springfield, Illinois; Cambridge, Massachusetts; Cambridge, England; New York, New York—and they catch the spirit of different kinds of experience: Catholic family life in the Midwest; Harvard and Trinity, Cambridge, in the thirties; life at the *Herald Tribune* and *Time-Life-Fortune* in the thirties and forties—but they all have larger subjects too. Among these, "Notes on a Distant Prospect" and "Light from the Bay Windows," his pieces about his father, are those of the most consummate artistry. Some of the eloquent intensity of these early memoirs, and his gift for catching and conveying the quiddity of other people, is also visible in the next section in his ambitious efforts on his friends James Agee and Flannery O'Connor. "Gold and Gloom in Ezra Pound" was his discriminating labor in the early fifties to meet the formidable case of his old mentor and friend; T. S. Eliot wrote him that he thought the piece "simply excellent, a strikingly honest statement of your debt to Pound, and of your reservations." Taken as a whole, the pieces in these sections demonstrate their author's effort to challenge the erosion of time through memory and, as he says in "Generations of Leaves": "to pay homage, to bring an offering to the qualitative possibilities of existence."

Among the critical pieces, the postscript to the *Odyssey* is no doubt the best known since it stands in back of each of the over two million paperback copies of the *Odyssey* in print, and since it has in itself become a famous contribution to the discourse on translation. But all of the essays in this section are distinguished contributions of their kind; their author did not undertake such assignments lightly, and when he did, his efforts drew on the full range of his considerable abilities. Those most interested in intertextuality in the classical tradition may wish to turn to "Generations of Leaves," and those most drawn to the problem of classical translation to the trenchant introduction to Dryden's *Aeneid*. My own favorite among this group is the essay called "Mirroring the *Commedia*," which is not simply the critical appreciation of a translation, but the wonderful story of how the translation was made, a tribute to two men of utterly different character and temperament—Ezra Pound and Laurence Binyon—whose improbable collaboration gave the world this particular gift.

Of his life's work I would like to say one thing more. It is certainly true, as he himself sometimes thought, that if he had not, for a variety of reasons, done the classical translations he might have left a larger body of poetry. He might also have written more critical essays, like the discriminating examples in this volume, or given us more of the portraits that his studies of Agee and O'Connor exemplify, or more of the lyric meditations like the memoirs of his father. But it is also true that in his poetic translations all of his gifts—the capacity to divine character, to drive a narrative forward, to elect exactly the right word for the right context, to reimagine thought and action from one language into another, and to infuse at once directness and lyric power—combined to provoke and fit his special genius. Robert Fitzgerald's best-known accomplishment is likely to remain that of recovering for twentieth-century English poetry the great poems of another age. Nevertheless, his memoirs and essays, like his books of poems, are also works of distinction, and are presented here in the interest of wider appreciation. After considering them a reader may feel that what he said of his friend James Agee was also true of him: "What he was born to do, he did."

Penelope Laurans Fitzgerald
New Haven, Connecticut
January 1992

Prologue: Gifts from We Know Not Where

. . . As each of us is bounded by his or her own skin, so each of us has limits of other kinds, and the experience of living is to some extent a testing and determination of these. But the analogy of the skin breaks down because in fact some kinds of limit are very hard to establish. In mathematics, I surmise, each of us comes to a point beyond which he simply cannot go: but in the life of the imagination you never know what further reaches open up. Maybe in the timeless realm of abstract thought each one has a given capacity—like our bone structure and bodily limits, inalterably given. On the other hand for all that is bound up with time, all that is timeful, so to speak—the affective and aesthetic life and the work of the providing or making intellect—no given limit can be surely assigned. The term for the future in Thucydides, I remember, is often *tò aphanés*, the unapparent—in effect, the unforeseeable. Once you think of it as such you may perceive how vast and even unlimited it is. Oriented toward this, we are not so sure of our finitude. We may perhaps understand the immortal longings of which Shakespeare had Cleopatra speak, not to mention St. Augustine's great confession to God that our hearts are unquiet until they rest in him.

I make these points as a kind of premise for the only suggestion I have to offer, which is that a just expectation of life may include an expectation of moments that seem mysterious gifts from we know not where. These need not be full-scale epiphanies or blasts of revelation. As instances of what I mean, I may mention two incidents in my own life that were not hard to explain, in a way, but were at the same time teasing with implications far from ordinary. Both occurred during the several years when I worked at putting Homer's *Odyssey* into English verse. After I had lived with the poem for some time, I felt closely involved not only with Odysseus but with his patroness, the

From a commencement address given at St. John's College, Annapolis, May 1984.

goddess Athena, who now and then appeared to him in human guise to put heart into him in time of need. Once she even appeared as a little girl with braided hair. Then, one October, I had a chance to visit Greece for the first time, for a week or so. Thirty years ago smog was not yet a problem in Attica. On the contrary, the tawny land, the brilliant sun and limpid air at once seemed to me a divine brew, a medium from which a god might step at any moment.

While in Athens I took it into my head to fly over the Crete for a night and see the reconstructed Minoan palace at Knossos. The flight in the late afternoon at no great altitude took me over the lovely islands of the Cyclades, their beaches like gold foil in the late sunlight. A fine three-masted schooner was moored in the round little port of Melos. At Heraklion I found a room in a small hotel. I did not, and do not, understand modern Greek. They had no English at this hotel, so I had to get by in my poor French. I managed to have some dinner and then wandered out into the streets of Heraklion, where I felt more and more grievously that peculiar loneliness that comes of not knowing a soul and not speaking or understanding the local language. I found myself at last halted in front of a shoe shop, looking at the display, very disconsolate, when a voice said, "Good evening, sir!"

What a joy! My heart leaped with pleasure. I looked up and saw a little girl, eleven or twelve, with long pigtails, standing in the doorway and smiling. "Good evening to you!" said I. "How good it is to hear someone speak English! What's your name? And she said: *"Oh, I'm Athena."*

Well. Of course, it turned out that she had grown up in Camden, New Jersey, and had come over to help her grandmother run the shop, and had thought me an American because of my suit, and so on—all perfectly plausible. But did not the goddess always have a good story too? I still point out to myself that that girl didn't say her *name* was Athena—she said she *was* Athena.

The second incident occurred some years later when I was engaged on the second part of the *Odyssey*, which is set, you remember, on Odysseus' home island of Ithaca. I had contrived another brief visit to Greece in late July and decided to return to Italy by steamer from Piraeus, stopping over at Ithaca on the way. I stayed at a tiny hotel on the quay of the port of Vathi, run by a man who had worked for several years at one of the Horn & Hardart automats in New York. He introduced me to the mayor, with whom I got along in French, and the mayor produced an interpreter for me in the person of a fifteen-year-old boy who had grown up in South Africa. On the first day I visited the frame house where the Ithacans carefully kept things from the British archeological digs before the war. Some of these, votive offerings, showed that during the classical centuries there had been on this island a cult of Odysseus as a demigod. I had to think that over on the next day. On that day we took one of the decrepit Ithacan taxis to go up the island to the little cove where they say the Phaiakians put Odysseus ashore in his sleep. Here near the water there was a grove of tall eucalyptus trees with cicadas going like mad in the late July heat, and under the trees a few rickety tables at which some old locals sat in their shirt sleeves drinking soda pop. I walked up the shore a bit to take in the scene and then walked back toward the taxi. As I came abreast of the eucalyptus trees one old fellow got up and shuffled toward me. He stopped and spoke in perfect English, in Oxonian English. It might have been the voice of Sir Maurice Bowra. He said: "You know, *we* say that he never died. *We* say that he still turns up now and then, looking like a soldier or a sea captain . . . or . . . just a stranger." He paused and looked serenely at me. And there in the burning sun I shivered from head to foot. I could not say a word. I bowed my head and walked on.

Just a coincidence, of course—that an old Ithacan capable of saying that to me in my language, without any preamble, should have been there on that particular afternoon when for the only time in my life I came to that spot, and came from years of companionship, almost of identification with the hero whom he didn't have to name . . . But isn't that how the gods used to appear to mortals out of the radiant Aegean air, or how the messengers of heaven appeared to men in another mythical landscape?

THE THIRD KIND OF KNOWLEDGE

THAT STARRY COUNTRY

I ever after remembered that starry country

> From "Ecce Abstulistis Hominem
> De Hac Vita"

I understand your going back to Lincoln last year. I went back to Springfield one weekend in July in a rented Chevrolet, and I drove around the streets like the very ghost that was ahead of me on my bicycle forty years ago. The years intervening were like heavy plate glass between me and everything. The elms were gone, and the era, and the people. It is well that, as Yeats put it, all things remain in God.

> From a letter to William Maxwell

> This I make bloom for her
> As spring in her country;
> Praising the enemy,
> I give the dead their honor.

> From "Office for Easter"

Notes on a Distant Prospect

During my boyhood, from my eighth year to my eighteenth, my father lay all day in the next room. His left hipbone was tubercular, his thigh depressed by a suppurating wound like a bullet wound, and thick gauze dressings were taped on it morning and evening. He had a white bed in a second-story bedroom, not large, with bay windows under a maple tree, and he could look out over a quiet street toward a long slanting lawn where the afternoon sunlight lay, and beyond that to a grove of elms. There were days when his fever ran high. The doctor would then draw up to the curb in his black electric runabout—an old gentleman with gray mustaches who wore a wing collar and well-brushed derby and chesterfield. He would be shown upstairs, where he would fold up his snowy cuffs and wash his fine liver-spotted old hands three times before he proceeded to probe the wound, without anesthesia. On other occasions, when the sickroom was closed and nurses came and went, there was talk of "scraping the bone."

One night, when no one knew if my father would live, I woke up and saw for a long time a cigarette glowing and glowing again in the darkness where my aunt, for whom I had a passion, was sitting. My father's suffering was not so real to me as the death I understood to be tugging at him. I had a very good, direct sense of what it meant to die; it meant not to be there at all anymore. My mother had died when I was three, my younger brother when I was seven, and they had been removed as by a razor. Sometimes I lay awake at night, desolate with an exact and intimate foreknowledge of my own extinction. I was no more than eight or nine when it had come home to me that the fate of the breathing person was to be hurt and then annihilated.

Pain and danger I had met in the fresh world long before, in the first time I remember, before my father became bedridden: after my mother's death, when my grandmother gave him and his two small boys a home. I find that I am removed from my mother's room, there is a freckled nursemaid named Georgia, and sunny orange juice is being squeezed for

First published in *The New Yorker*, February 23, 1976.

3

the baby in a kitchen with a dumbwaiter. Then it is summer in another place near a calm blue lake, where they make up a bed for me outdoors on a porch swing, and I go to sleep in summer evening listening, for the first time that I will remember, to katydids and crickets, the grassy world in choir. The house then changes to the house known thereafter as ours. There is always, now, the short front yard falling away in a low terrace, the maple tree round which the buckling front walk divides, and the street down which will sometimes come, on his rattling wagon, a rag-man who has only holes where a nose should be. If we are playing outside we run and hide in the dusty cellar, and our hearts beat high in terror that the rattling noise may stop within our hearing. But that woe-ful death's-head is the only danger that haunts the street; all else is pastoral, accustomed. The reins passing through a slit in the front of the tall milk wagon are left slack, and while the milkman passes clinking behind the houses his old horse moves slowly along the curb, lipping the grass and tearing it with long yellow teeth. On hot and breathless eve-nings the wicker chairs are set out on the lawn, and we are allowed to sit up late as we drowse, watching the full moon rise over a low cottage and corn patch to the southeast. As dusk comes on the Fourth of July, Father props himself on his crutches in the street to pluck out the colored tissue-paper folds of a balloon, the last and most important of fireworks. A dim stout figure comes from across the street, our neighbor, and helps hold out the rustling pleated thing, all aglow within from the tiny bonfire lit on crosswires at its open base. When the tissue paper at last bells out firmly with heated air, the balloon is lifted between fingertips and let go; it floats up swinging above the treetops to drift away in a dark sky where there are others, dozens, of these luminous travelers.

A humorous and tender, lame personage, our father. He is a Sunday-afternoon friend who will take us to the park in Grandmother's electric and make us acorn pipes, sitting on the grass with his worn crutches beside him; or an evening friend who has a cigar cutter on a black silk ribbon, and tells us stories before bedtime—about Bronco Billy and his horse who came to his whistle, or Captain Ferguson the stagecoach driver, his Winchester across his knees, bringing the bags of gold dust safely to Fort Laramie. These weighty chamois bags! It amuses my father to get Charlie Chaplin costumes for my brother and myself—baggy trou-sers, tight little jackets, derbies, canes, and even black mustaches affixed with spirit gum—and, hanging on his crutches over his big Kodak, his shadow pooling at his feet, he will squeeze the rubber bulb with care to record this fantasy. He is attentive to the children's observances of Easter and Christmas, as well as the Fourth of July. The life of Santa Claus we learn from him in such elaborate detail that it will be years before the reindeer disappear from the winter sky. One Christmas Eve they become actually visible, jingling down the street between the snowdrifts to stop and toss their antlers in the starlight in front of our house. Then, sure enough, we see a portly figure get out of the sleigh, and we are so excited we can no longer bear to stay at the window; there is a thunderclap of laughter at the door, and Santa Claus in scarlet and white tosses a great armload of small packages and nuts and oranges into the room. I wonder if that apparition, staged with such professional art, predisposed me to faith in the mythical and magical.

But our father, in this earliest time, is sometimes another personage. How can I draw this one with accuracy and piety? His father, too, my grandfather, had been one of those Irishmen who when they drink go blindly under some wave that has been mounting inside them, or as if behind them, and are different men in the violence of the wave. There is, therefore, not often but often enough, a changed and redolent stranger of whom one has to be afraid. He comes out of mystery, for the child knows nothing of his early crippling in body and hope, of his later loss and blackness. All the child knows is that something shameful can overcome his father. I am sent to fetch him from what I sense to be degrading company—not very, in fact; only a few men playing poker in a shabby office downtown, with whiskey and syphon bottles beside them, old cronies who have not triumphed, clubbing together for small consolations. Or he does not come home, and I wake in the bluish-gray light before sunup and see my grandmother peering out between blind and window frame. There are three men loitering and talking at the corner of the driveway under the street lamp, and one of them has the outline of my father, though I do not see how my father can belong to this silent and sinister world of exhausted night. Then a whole spring season is filled with my grandmother's distress, for he has not made his Easter duty nor gone, for some time, to Sunday Mass. And one more image, to conclude: my father in a whiskey-fragrant reverie is putting us to bed in the glaring bedroom where the windowpanes are ink-black after dark and my little brother Monty has misbehaved in some way, so that in a groggy heartbroken voice my father says, "I'll kill him," and when in fear I beg him not to, he says, and repeats, "For your sake I won't."

Not until many years later could I get control of this nightmare in my mind. It began to make a kind of sense, insane enough, when I learned that my mother had died of puerperal fever after my brother's birth. I turned away then from imagining my father's misery, and could not imagine it now if I did not remember the mild, gay man—later so distinguished for fortitude and patience—gone crazed and sodden, cut off from himself. I remember, too, the terrible ambiguity in my own heart on the occasion, a satisfaction, mingled with my fear, in the favoritism shown to me. There should be a reticent surface to life, but I must allow phantasmata like these to break it if I am to make myself in any serious way intelligible. No general view of things would ever seem just to me unless it comprehended Heaven and Hell—a range in experience at least as great as that between my exaltations as a child and my glimpses of anguish and evil.

Our street was a short one, on a gentle rise, sloping to end at the west corner in an avenue beyond which were the level grounds and elms around the Edwards place, an old russet-colored house where Lincoln had been married. Eastward the street went down to cross the railroad. On the other side of the tracks there was another very old brick house with old low walls where the mortar was unchinking around a wild garden—a private school for girls. Midway in my childhood the Edwards place was torn down to make room for an enormous State building, a fortune in brickwork and cut stone and marble paving, and a clangorous Ford garage replaced the private school. But my small brother and I spent the early years in an old-fashioned country. The foliage of the tree at our window, dusky in summer or thrashing wet in summer storms, brought living nature into the room on which we closed and opened our eyes. Our white iron cribs with barred sides had been repainted unskillfully, so that drops of paint, still plastic, could be fingered on every bar. Close by was the smooth texture of wallpaper tinted with pale leaves and flowers. Downstairs the windows of the entrance hall, facing south, had panes of colored glass, and sumptuous lights of purple or red gold would be found brightening or fading here and there in the room. Outside there was the quietude of the street, shady or snowy, broken by wagons, by a rare automobile, and by the slow heavy meter of the freight trains clanking by at the corner, by day or by night—one of the great sounds the world made.

The world was not in fact bounded for us by our little street in the provincial capital town. My mother's family lived in the East, where people did not pronounce "r," and my father's pretty sister and her husband were in London or New York. Jaeger sweaters and winter caps, almost too warm and soft, came to the children for Christmas. In my sixth and seventh summers we traveled, a night and a day and another night—for my grandmother saved railroad fare by choosing inconvenient routes—from the cornland to the seashore. That was another world indeed, as I knew the evening I was first carried, half asleep, up to a strange veranda that faced high dunes and beyond them a low thunderous sound, deepening and then hushed at regular intervals. I would not forget that sound, nor the odor of brine in the night air and in the light blankets I went to sleep under. From our windows we then grew accustomed on waking to see beyond the sand hills the bulk of ocean, blue or gray or flecked with whitecaps or gun-colored under curtains of fog. Sand and rock, burning to the feet or wetted with foaming water, dune grass that seemed to cut and barnacles that did, profusions of seaweed streaming, crabs in the shallows moving in a slantwise silent scuttle—these took the place of the hot odorous grape arbors, bitter bark, cool roots and loam, the caterpillars and grasshoppers and ants of backyard play in the Midwest. At daybreak we watched the lobsterman in his dory making out to sea from the inlet, past the rock jetty where gulls were dipping and calling. Sails passed slowly on the sea's fine ultimate line. Once a battleship anchored offshore and a cutter came in to the beach; brawny sailors at the oars backed her in through the surf until two of them, barelegged, jumped out in the water and carried in on their shoulders a petty officer with a mailbag. It was 1917 or 1918, and once nearby at Newport and once farther south at New London Cousin Francis had his submarine, but for all our hopes we never saw that marvel.

The long coast of wild dunes curving to the south, the ocean ever moving and aloof, a light far out, flashing at dusk—these were the earth's visible frontier. Aside from the first star, and the enthralling full moon of harvest time, the heavens that achieved their glory after dark went unnoticed by the child. I think it was, above all, the daylong and nightlong traveling train that made me know the world's extent and mystery. Strange: strange—the word wears out its meaning, but it applies to a great part of the real at all times, as the eye of childhood perceives truly. The heavy blind at the window of the lower berth, gripping its runners at either end, would be pushed up an inch or two during midnight jars and couplings, and there to be spied upon would be empty stations, sidings, streets asleep under forsaken lamps in the great night, or a brakeman going by with a tiny flame in his lantern. Then at dawn the train is passing along a crest of country and I look out over a grand hollow in the world—later hauntingly named for me the

Lehigh Valley—where there are whole towns far away and smoky in the depth. Or dawn light is coming over farmlands and forests where no human being can be seen for mile on mile, only the earth and things of earth going about their cool business, quail rising, streams running, mist in pools on the fields. No thought or style would ever ring true to me unless I found within it somewhere the nerve of knowledge that I gained in this way—that other souls, and their ways and habitations, are very many and unknown, that the earth's body is vast to our humbling, and multiform in life indifferent to us.

One went out of oneself to know such things. Of oneself, my self, however, I knew and was accustomed to knowing how dependent it was—often in Grandmother's or someone's hands being shirted and shod, washed, fed, wiped, admonished; and how small—familiar with sidewalks and floors and the undersides of things, getting on tiptoe to look out of windows, subject to bloody abrasion of the forehead and knees. In the daydream of the self already there were effortless heroisms, feats of escape and conquest like those of Douglas Fairbanks, whom we had seen—our first movie—at Watch Hill. A long-barreled toy pistol felled in windrows all the Redskins or Germans of the bushes and the living air. While Grandmother at the tiller steered her beautiful electric homeward after calls on old lady friends, and while my brother and I sat together under the little glass vases and the black silken blinds that ran on cords, we were ourselves pilots of that airship passing over hostile terrains; we might hold our breath if the juice ran low and the massive craft went sluggishly or bucked. Imagination like a mercurial fluid ran where it would, as if to make up for the sense, minute and exquisite, of a physical reality implacably given, far beyond the child's power to understand or manage. Communication with grownups had to be laconic or sportive, since no language existed for the way things really happened, no means of learning what was common in experience and what was not. So the small creature pushing up concealed a kind of madness. The spirit that shivered alone in the wide world found other mysteries in its own being, and by these it could be isolated more forlornly still.

A tie of the flesh had been broken early for this child, and where there had been young sweet-smelling warmth to cradle it there were now the homely nursemaids and the kind old woman who fussed. When I was still in my crib I squirmed out of my nightclothes in the middle of summer nights for the diffuse erotic comfort of nakedness. A little later my passion for the young and dashing aunt whom I rarely saw was certainly erotic, a passion for her perfumed and rustling presence, her daring cigarettes, her cosmetics. I became aware of seductive display in the theater when we children were taken to Saturday matinées of vaudeville. We would sit in a box close to the rosily lit stage and watch the acrobats and jugglers whom we were meant to see; but there were also comedians in striped suits whose barking and leering dialogue would make everyone laugh, whereupon they would sing and shuffle and twirl their canes and doff their gay straw hats. In some of this they were assisted by light ladies with eyes like diamonds, and the quivering beauty of these actresses, so much of it bare and powdered, made the diaphragm ache. If others were affected by the carnal enchantment, it would not have occurred to me that anyone else could be so intoxicated as I. At times my own thin body clung to me like a sensuous shirt of Nessus; and in any reckoning with the flesh or estimate of its power I could not, afterward, disregard the helpless excitement at such times of that small figure, consumed by mirrors, furtive and flushed and horrified, in the savagely empty house in the warm afternoon.

Angry shame came over me often as I found out my gamut of weaknesses. I feared the rough boys I desperately fought. I feared the cold sea I breasted. I feared the shapes of the dark. I was self-conscious and hyperfastidious. Once we had a maid whose fingertips had cracked in cold weather and were covered by a tracery of black lines; I could barely force myself to eat what she had touched. Sometimes my brother and I would visit the watchman at the railroad crossing, a sad old man with a drop at the tip of his nose and a cap with earflaps, who sat by an iron stove in a little hut powdered with coal dust. When a train was coming he would take his big STOP sign off the nail and go slouching out to hold it up in the middle of the street. Once or twice he offered us bacon from his shiny lunchbox, and my brother would take it courteously but I had to refuse in an agony of distaste and self-dislike, trying not to look at the old man's black thumb. I felt myself cut off by timidity and squeamishness from all easy common life, but had no moral advantage to make up for it. I was proud with no reason for pride. On the contrary, I often lacked the stomach to stand out against crowds. One instance, the worst, would be like a lump in my body for years. There was a children's party in a big stuccoed ivy-covered house somewhere, at which a collection of many small children ran wild in strange passageways and stairs and bedrooms, and I went with a pack who scared and tortured my little brother by locking him in a closet. He was five years old. When we got home he had a fever, and a week or so later he died of influenza. My father woke me up in the middle of the night to tell me this, bending over sober and sad in the dim light reflected from the hall, and saying, too, that what had happened to Monty must happen to us all. I understood him well, but even then I think I wondered in my heart—as I would later wonder articulately—why I should go on living instead of my brother, who was a sturdier child and a braver and more open human being. A polished small coffin took the center of the parlor, and there the small boy lay, turned to pale wax, an utter stranger in his Eton collar. I do not remember the funeral Mass or what happened at Calvary Cemetery. One day not long afterward my father stayed home with a boil. Since it was not a boil but the sickness of the bone working outward, he never went back to his office, nor to any poker game, nor again to the church or cemetery—not, that is, until ten years later, stilled and blinded in his turn, he went.

These were the years of my going to school in that town while in the room next to mine my father lay, every evening my companion. He did not die when they thought he would, and after that there was a kind of adjustment or quiescence of illness when he even seemed to mend, so that invalid though he was he no longer had constant pain. My mother and my brother had been taken from me; now my father was given to me, and the gift was beyond estimation. He was freed now of his bitter demon, restored to himself and to patience, unconscious of his own courage, utterly without spiritual side. He had everything to impart, as I had everything to learn, of the discipline, humility, and humor proper to a man.

Light from the Bay Windows

Lying in bed, my father had before his eyes, across the room, a doorway into the bedroom that I shared with my uncle. This door was usually closed. On the wall to the left of it hung a large photograph in a plain gilt frame, a three-quarter-length portrait of my mother in her wedding dress of 1905. She was twenty-six. She stood erect, with hands clasped behind her, her dark eyes looking seriously and serenely directly into the camera, slender and at ease in her gown, with understated lace at her bosom. In a moment, perhaps, the warm pliant figure would resume swaying a bit on the balls of her feet. The universe at which we are at liberty to rage permitted her eight more years of life before high and terrible fever—childbed fever midway through my third year—drove her out. The photograph was paper. One other object in my father's bedroom recalled her: a light rocking chair that had been hers.

If I had got up on the wrong side of the bed, my father would tell me not to be a crosspatch; if I did something foolish or slovenly, not to be a goop. If I were laggard and unaccommodating, he would invite me to be a sport. These were terms, I divined, that he and my mother had used together. He would sometimes say, if I tried to pull his leg, "Don't kid the actors, old-timer." If it were a matter of sticking to something—piano lessons, for instance, over which after the first few weeks I lost heart utterly—he would say, "Be a trouper, Fitz," and I would hear the idiom of that life he and she had briefly led. I understood that in the theater no matter how you felt or how high your temperature, the show must go on. He would never have mentioned it, but day in and day out, in fact, he lived by this rule.

He could not lie on his left side, but he could and did turn on his right side at times to rest his back. As a young man he had been robust, but in invalidism he was thin, and it brings a kind of fury in me to call up in memory his pallid ribby back creased with bed wrinkles, his patience as he waited, resting on his side. When he made his short bathroom trips, swinging on his crutches, you saw that his left leg wasn't much use. It

First published in *The New Yorker*, December 18, 1978.

was shorter, and the dangling foot pointed outward, as though the old break in his hip had slightly twisted his leg. Long knowledge of his body as a burden, irreparably crippled, gave an edge to his concern for me.

The worst bodily anguish I can remember I endured at eight or nine. On the advice of a surgeon who thought it efficient, the family consented to my undergoing tonsillectomy, removal of adenoids, and circumcision, all on the same occasion. I found myself in an operating theater with figures in white masks around me, and then, pressed over my eyes and nose, a white sweet pungent cone that with a few inhalations became a spiral of light pulsing out of time. When time resumed, I awoke to a self wholly composed of pain. I asked at once that I please be shot, but no one would do me the favor. If anything could be what people later called traumatic, this experience must have been; a single, undifferentiated wound was what I felt myself to be.

But my usual illnesses, too usual at first for my father's peace of mind, were grippe and what my grandmother called "bilious attacks." These collapses filled my father with gloom and apprehension. My small brother, Monty, had died of a kind of grippe. In the heat of fever, I would keep turning the damp washcloth on my brow; if I let a corner hang down to my mouth, I could suck a little moisture from it. One of the appearances under which my father has come back to me most distinctly is that of his hovering at my bedside in his chenille bathrobe, on his crutches, transferring the right-hand crutch to be grasped along with the other by his left hand while he leans forward to feel my hot forehead. His face above mine is tender and woebegone. He will prepare the calomel and quinine prescribed by Dr. Taylor, crushing a tablet in a spoon with water, and will promise me a new silver dollar if I swallow the spoonful of gritty, bitter sludge.

Once, my grandmother took me calling on an old wife who remarked with cronelike insinuation on how "well formed" I was. Her report of this to my father provoked one of his rare angers. For some years, though, I must have seemed sickly and neurasthenic, and it became clear to me that he had my physical well-being steadily on his mind. On any fine spring or autumn day when he could persuade my uncle to take me to a golf course, he would keep me out of school and write a formal note of excuse, saying that I had missed school that day with his permission. He saw to it that I had a set of cut-down clubs for golf, the Bancroft racquet that I coveted for tennis, a Flexible Flyer sled, a well-made bow and arrows, hockey skates, a good football. One of the old friends who came to visit him occasionally was a professional baseball umpire of the

Three-I League, Matt McGrath, a grave, massive Irishman, always in worn and baggy blue serge, with a bullet head of closely cropped gray hair. Whenever he came, he brought me a pocketful of baseballs—three or four that had gone through a few innings of play. Apart from the grass stains, they were new: smooth unabraded white leather, smudged with green, tightly stitched in the interlocking tongue pattern that only a sphere could wear—cupped in my hand, authentic weights.

Before I started off to school in the morning, I would open my father's door, put down his window, put up his shades, and turn on his radiator. A faint sweet odor came from the empty jigger glass in which, late at night, always long after I had gone to bed, my uncle had given him his prescription whiskey to help him sleep. "Wake up, Dad," I would say. I would empty and rinse out his urinal. On weekend days I would help him wash and shave, bringing basins of warm water from the bathroom. On his dresser there was an oblong mirror, with a hinged stand that served as a handle, and my main job was to hold this steady as he lathered, squeezing Mennen's from a tube onto his shaving brush, and then used his straight razor. The room would be full of light from the bay windows. The word "shave" sounded exactly like the blade making clean panels in the half-mask of fine white foam and stubble. The maid brought his breakfast on a tray: grapefruit, toast, a boiled egg, a glass of milk. He had a way of holding a sip of milk for a moment forward in his mouth, supposing, I think, that the mineral content would benefit his rather worn and stubby teeth. After breakfast he would use his commode and would preferably attend to it himself, covering the enameled pail with its fitted lid and taking it down the hall to the bathroom. His right hand on the crutch handle would also hold the wooden handle of the pail.

The care of the wound or abscess in his hip involved the preparation with cotton and gauze of soft dressings perhaps six inches by three. One of these would be held in place by three strips of adhesive tape. Cotton soaked in benzene would be dabbed and pressed on the old tape until the attachment weakened and it could be stripped off; then the area of the wound would be cleaned with alcohol-soaked cotton, and the new dressing applied. Old dressings, stained more or less by the wound were kept in crumpled newspaper to be burned in the wire burn basket in the back yard, where I would linger to watch the gauze blackening, the cotton flaring, the adhesive tape curling in the flames. The change of dressing took place every morning after breakfast and every evening after supper. In the evening, regularly, I would help him, holding the roll of adhesive tape as he cut strips with his scissors.

The words concluded the Mass never ceased to amuse my father—"V: Go, the Mass is ended. R: Thanks be to God." He was a believing Catholic, as my mother had been, but life in the world and his own suffering, with reading and thinking, had made him practical and modest about it. He never took a preacher's tone. His rosary lay on his bedside table, and sometimes when I came home from school in the afternoon I would find him going through it in silence and would wait for him to finish. Later, I supposed it likely that he had committed sins of the flesh for which the Rosaries were penitential. Pensive and grave on his pillow, he fingered the black beads.

Sometimes there would be an errand I could do for him downtown. His favorite Harvester cigars, named after a great trotting horse pictured on the paper band of each, were to be had at a tobacco shop and magazine counter on Fifth Street across from the Majestic vaudeville theater. For dyspepsia he may require certain gray triangualr tablets that came in wooden containers like tiny casks with screw-on tops; for these I will walk to Ryan's Drug Store on the corner of Capitol Avenue and Sixth Street, carrying an extra dime for a Coca-Cola. This drink is stylishly made with a jet of syrup pressed into a glass of crushed ice, a released gush of carbonated water, a long jabbing and swirling spoon, a flourish as the dark-brown foaming glass is placed before me. It is blissfully cold on a hot evening, and pungent to the recesses of the nose.

If my father's carafe needs to be refilled, I take it down to the kitchen, where I use the icepick to remove chunks and slivers of ice from the block in the icebox, ensack these in a clean dish towel, and belabor the lump with a hammer on the sink board until I have enough cracked ice. Then I will help him remake his bed, smoothing and tightening the under sheet and putting the top sheet and plaid blanket in order. When all is ready for the night, I will get up beside my father on the bed, on the side of his good right leg, where he makes a place on the blanket for cards or checkerboard. On this side he has a round wicker table holding his gold watch, his gold Eversharp pencil, his Waterman fountain pen with the gold band, his carafe and glass. We play cards or checkers by the light of his bedside lamp.

I can now feel the texture of the wool blanket and see my father's pale, patient hands cutting the deck of cards. Those years are gone, and yet I can be there for this hour so many times repeated, when in casual talk he will recall things out of the past for me. After diphtheria in boyhood, on Dr. Ryan's advice, he was sent away to school in California, to Santa Clara College, south of San Francisco, where he went through his high-school years in the eighteen-nineties in that valley filled with orchards of plum trees. It amuses him to remember how the Jesuit teachers drilled Latin into a class, lining the boys up and having them recite, one voice after another without breaking the rhythm, conjugations and declensions: *hic, haec, hoc, huius, huius, huius* . . . Once he opens his pen and neatly makes the characters of the Greek alphabet for me. Xenophon and the frequent parasangs of the *Anabasis* remain in his mind as a schoolboy drollery.

Half a century later than these evenings with my father, I have found two photographs of him at Santa Clara. One is in an envelope with the legend, in my mother's hand, "Bob at age fifteen, taken in California." He is wearing pale trousers, a dark jacket, a pale hat, sitting with one leg over the other, a dim, smooth-faced, jaunty boy. The print is faded and so brittle it will crack to slivers unless I can do something to preserve it. The other photograph is less faded and printed on heavier card. It shows the Santa Clara football team of 1894 or '95. There are sixteen boys in turtleneck sweaters—a number, including my father, in the tight canvas sleeveless lace-up jackets they used then. His hair is parted in the middle, as always, and there is plenty of it, in the fashion of football players before they wore helmets. My father looks out quietly at the lens. There is no truculence in his capable look.

After California came the scene often alluded to as Ann Arbor—a beautiful place name to my ears. There my father helped to found the Comedy Club during his years at the law school, and lived in the Phi Kappa Psi house, as did his younger brother, my Uncle Art. In the attic of our house in Springfield I turned up copies of the *Michiganensian*, the university yearbook, for 1901 and 1902, in which there were photographs of my uncle in the Mandolin Club and my father as a slightly chubby young man, mugging merrily in Comedy Club productions. The most haunting thing remembered from Ann Arbor was a song, which the new radio (superheterodyne in a cabinet) one year brought back to my father from a banked stadium where thousands of voices were hushed and slowed in deference to one couplet:

> Yellow the fields where ripens the grain
> And yellow the moon on the harvest wane . . .

He sang this, as he sang everything, with a slight nodding vibration of the head—a habit I have inherited.

After we had played several hands of rum or two or three games of checkers, I would take up my book to read. My light came from the bulb in the frosted hood of the central chandelier. My mother's rocking chair was of dark cherry wood, with a seat of finely woven cane. I placed it under the light, near the foot of the bed, and reentered the world of Ivanhoe or Lord Greystoke or Renfrew of the Royal Mounted. My father would read his Womrath Library book or one of his magazines, the *Saturday Evening Post,* or *Collier's,* or *Cosmopolitan.* At the regular hour, he would remark that it was time for bed, and I would say that I had only a few pages to go to the end of the chapter.

As long as I was a small boy—until, that is, I had grown so much that it would have been embarrassing to us both—after washing and putting on my pajamas and brushing my teeth I would get into bed beside him and lie there warm for a while, with my head on his shoulder, talking a little or sometimes silent, and I knew that in my father's mind at those times my mother, too, was present; that just as when I occupied her chair but more distinctly now he felt that my physical presence was all that remained to him of hers. If I had an itch between my shoulder blades, my father would give me a gentle scratching, as to which it needed no saying between us that in this, too, my mother was being recalled, for she had liked him to scratch her back. I understand that on those occasions he had felt honored and amused that such a fine back had need of such homely service.

So my father and I shared my mother, although all I could bring to the sharing out of my own memory, even as a child, were a few faint sensations, far distant: one of her being with me at the top of a flight of stairs when in the dusk Big Bob appeared below and called up to Little Bob, while a church bell from nearby tolled some evening hour; another of her tallness and skirts near me during a catastrophe, when my ivory-headed cane fell through a downtown grating. By the time I was ten or twelve, even these sensations were a matter of remembering that I had at one time remembered them.

Poking around in my grandmother's room one day I found in the big drawer of her writing desk a letter to her in my mother's fine swift angular hand. The date must have been early in 1905, because in this letter my mother formally declared her attachment to my father and her wish to marry him. "I cannot live without Bob," said one of the sentences, and the force of that grownup passion startled and awed me. Did

I who owed my life to it understand it? It seems to me that I did then, essentially as well as I do now. Whether I knew it or not, I felt as she had felt: I could not live without my father, either. I had no words for this revelation, and I never told anyone about it.

No Castles, No Cathedrals

On my way to and from school with my short pace I passed through the nearby State House four times a day. In the lofty interior dusk there were gleams from polished marble floors crisscrossed by perforated rubber carpeting, and glints of varnish from canvas murals, huge and somber, showing episodes from frontier days, ceremonial meetings between feathered Indians and explorers in buckskins. At the center, four naves crossed and daylight came down from the dome. An odor of stale cigar smoke and cuspidors filled the place.

In good weather we sometimes saw the governor pass our house on foot on his way to his office in the State House. His mansion occupied a block on our street not far away, a big white house with a two-story pillared portico above a porte-cochere on a curving drive. The paunchy sauntering man in the Panama hat was Governor Len Small. According to a story I heard years later, at the close of his term of office he won from the *Illinois State Journal* a solicitous headline: DID YOU LEAVE ANYTHING, LEN? A small boy stood in some awe of this mythical figure, as of the great building he headed for, which dominated our neighborhood from the northwest.

At the end of a long rise you saw a façade of heavy piers and arches of gray limestone making a high loggia, on which rose a great porch of polished columns bearing an architrave and pediment. This mass of the forward or eastern wing was repeated in wings to left and right, south and north, and mansard roofs, each topped by two open cupolas, surmounted all three. The more slender central mass, as high again, in façades of more closely spaced columns, rose to a gaunt dome of weathered copper, lifting its lanterna at an enormous height above the city.

At twelve or so I cherished *The Beloved Vagabond* for brave mumming and wandering on the roads of France. What stirred me most in the novel was the vagabond's exploit of sketching, on a café table in Paris, a

---

First published in *Antaeus*, Spring/Summer 1982.

fantastic work of architectural genius, an affair of towers and domes that he called the *palais de dipsomanie*. I did not know what that meant, but I imagined something like our State House. The Chicago architect who designed it in 1868 had in fact modeled the porches on the temple of Jupiter Stator in Rome. He thought he had improved on St. Paul's and on the Capitol at Washington by omitting the peristyle, and the truth is that his impure and ungainly building had more height and majesty. It towered and bulked and cut off the winter sunset, the sheer cliff of it going aloft in arches and verticals in one great pile, to house the elect of Illinois and beyond that to represent the dignity of the Republic, heir to all ages and builders.

"No castles, no cathedrals, and no kings," wrote Emerson of America in 1833, "Land of the forest . . ." Well, here was our castle and our cathedral. As to the forest, all over that town the elm trees with small fine leaves and soaring trunks and boughs over streets and lawns cooled and darkened the summer air. A dozen years later, when my grandmother was dying in 1934, my aunt and I flew from New York to be with her. From Chicago in a Ford trimotor, made all of corrugated metal, we rose to what seemed then a great altitude, a couple of miles perhaps, and at that height we eventually looked down on Springfield for the first time from the air. On the pale expanse of prairie we saw many dark square miles of wooded land, and the dome of the State House in its clearing jutted up in that forest.

2

An architectural enchantment of a more general kind came over me with the discovery of perspective as an excitement of sense and spirit. Looking, say, from the State House eastward on a long avenue flanked by business buildings, on a clear day the masses withdrawing in sunlit planes and blue verticals of shade seemed subject to an exquisite astringent power, the magic of space itself that made things so beautifully and sharply dwindle. Then the eye could luxuriate in drawings or etchings of cityscapes and architectural monuments, especially etchings by Whistler and by Joseph Pennell. At the public library I chanced on Ruskin's little book on the art of drawing, so serenely didactic, and soon I spent hours with sketch pad and pencil. Not only buildings but figures and natural forms acquired a new beauty that could be studied in the hope of rendering it by line, and illustrators could be compared for veracity and style.

One picture never lost the power to terrify me: Kipling's drawing, in the last of the *Just So Stories*, of the giant animal that came out of the sea. The story had such charm that it tempted rereading, but I could not face the animal—a mountain of inspired bestiality—and closed my eyes to turn the page opposite which it appeared.

With some pleasures of the eye a boyish prurience began to mingle. *Redbook* magazine, for example, which I sometimes picked up for my bedridden father at a newsstand, published on several pages, in soft rotogravure, portraits of beauties whose deep decolletage dreamily bared their double rondure of bosom. Now and then there were fleeting exposures in movies. In *Kismet*, cameras in soft focus and careful cutting made the most of Mae Murray's white body and long ethereal hair in a harem bathing scene. For several years I concealed a passion for one unlikely movie figure, an actress named Thelma Todd, who appeared in comic shorts with Martha Raye of the capacious mouth. As a comedienne Thelma seemed to throw her beauty and sexuality away, but this only enhanced her power. Of all crushes of this kind, the most ineffable overcame me at a stage performance at the Majestic Theater of *Trelawney of the Wells,* John Drew's last touring vehicle. In many scenes of that play Miss Helen Gahagan performed twenty feet from my privileged seat, all sparkle and grace, all Edwardian silks and flounces and expanses of snowy bosom and shoulders, mighty and adorable, a true goddess.

There were excitements less dignified than these. In the Sunday supplement of the *Chicago Herald and Examiner*, regular attention in tones of scandal was given to the activities of libertines and chorus girls, Roman orgies of the rich, and at a certain stage these reports with their crude enticing illustrations became something that I waited and looked for, weakly fascinated, vaguely ashamed. Naked girls in champagne baths were a standby of those editors. One Sunday I had this supplement open on the floor in my bedroom while I pored, chin in hand, over the latest champagne-bath story, when a strange sympathetic process took place in my body, and in my disorientation afterward I both knew and did not know that it meant the passing of childhood.

3

Modest frame houses and lawns were the rule in our neighborhood. The front yard of our house ran thirty feet to a terrace that sloped to the cement sidewalk. Beyond the sidewalk there was again a plot of grass, perhaps four feet wide, bounded by the curb. The walk directly in front of the house divided to pass on either side of a maple tree whose branches shaded the front bedroom windows. On this walk fell tender maple keys in spring and the pointy yellow translucencies of maple leaves in autumn. In midsummer heat waves the light armchairs of wicker or woven straw on the porch would be carried to the lawn after supper and placed to catch any air that stirred, as the locust choir sawed away in the big trees.

The moon always rose over Mr. Brubaker's cornpatch, visible behind his white brick cottage across the street and down the block to the east. Beyond this place ran the Chicago & Alton Railroad tracks, south toward St. Louis and north toward Chicago. Since the crossing was only a few blocks from the C & A station, both incoming and outgoing trains would be going slowly as they passed, their wheels on the rail junctures making a sedate rhythm, clank clank . . . clank, clank. Sometimes with hissing of airbrakes and shock of couplings they would halt completely before jerking and moving on, flatcars or boxcars of the east and west—the Pennsylvania Railroad, the New York Central, the Wabash Railroad, the Burlington Route, the Chesapeake & Ohio, the Southern Pacific, the Atchison, Topeka & Santa Fe. When a passenger train went by you could often see, through open side doors of the mail car just behind the engine and coal car, canvas bags on long racks and light-blue-uniformed men sorting mail into them.

Our house was clapboard, painted battleship gray. Of what the gray painting covered there was a revelation one day when men appeared with ladders and removed the paint, waving hoarse torches that blew transparent flame along sections of wall until the old gray coating liquified and could be scraped off with tools like palette knives; then the timber showed through, unevenly toasted, black and brown. Next day the painters on their ladders, dipping brush in pail, drawing brush over pail's lip to measure the saturation, applied fresh gray fluid in long slapping strokes.

Three steps, oblong blocks of cement, went down from the front porch. One step bore the number 215 imprinted in the cement. Between the ground and the clapboarding of the house proper there was a wooden lattice perhaps thirty inches high along the front and under the porch, signifying that the basement did not extend that far. The porch was not in fact an addition built on to the house but was like an open front room, not very deep, to the left of the front door; that is, the porch ceiling made part of the floor of the bedroom above. Going in the front door you entered a square room, more than a hall, with an armchair to your left, two glass-enclosed bookcases against the wall behind it, a short flight of stairs going back to a landing with a window above it in the left wall, the stairs and banister then proceeding left to right to the ceiling.

On a table in the crook of the stairs rested telephone and lamp. There was a sofa beside the table. To the right you entered the parlor, whose bay windows overlooked the front yard. Also to the right, and to the rear of the parlor, was the dining room, and, behind swinging doors, the pantry. The plain kitchen table that stood in the pantry bore evidence of prolonged and assiduous whittling, as by someone with a lot to think over slowly—or by someone waiting for work: the initials A L, very deeply carved. My grandfather had bought this table at auction when the firm of Lincoln and Herndon was dissolved.

In the parlor against the near wall stood the upright piano, a Knabe, and piano bench, with a floor lamp beside it. The bay with three windows, duplicated upstairs in the bedroom where my father lay, was pretty well filled by a couch. A Persian rug, dark and thick, lay in the front room, another in the parlor. A fireplace with a small coal grate, quite superfluous, occupied one corner of the parlor; heat, in fact, came from a big radiator on the far wall. If you shuffled on the rug, your index finger, pointed at the radiator, would enjoy the thrill of a tiny spark before touching. On the parlor rug, on Sunday after Mass, you could spread out the colored funny papers, the Katzenjammer Kids and Slim Jim, and tire your elbows reading.

4

In this room my Uncle Ed always gave the hour after dinner to reading the *Illinois State Register*, the evening paper. Under the center fixture brightly lit he would sit, neatly folding and refolding the paper, giving attention to the local news, the business news, and the syndicated column that he chuckled over and called "Odd McIntyre." His fine profile was Barrymore-like and grave under the thinning hair to which he took military brushes several times a day. Before he came to make a household with his mother and my invalid father, he had managed theaters in Racine and Duluth for the Orpheum Circuit; now he kept up with show business by reading *Variety* every week. He was a valetudinarian who

went in for well-cooked vegetables, half rubbers, and long winter underwear woven of silk and wool. Sobriety and skepticism were his style.
When I acted up he would treat me to one of his silences, fixing me with
his bored blue eyes.

My grandmother favored the morning paper, the *Illinois State Journal*,
and always read it slowly after breakfast. She was devoted to a serial
story called "The Married Life of Helen and Warren." The thin gold
frame of her glasses left a bruised indentation on the soft bridge of her
nose. Her soft cheeks were finely wrinkled, sometimes made fragrant by
a touch from her powder puff. She remembered that when she was a
little girl in Galway her father one day took her on his knee and told her
that Mr. Lincoln had been shot. She had a shrewd gray eye and a reputa-
tion in the family for being a good businesswoman. On the second or
third of the month if Mrs. Brown, the florist, had forgotten her rent,
Grandmother would telephone her considerately and send me downtown to collect it among the glassed-in refrigerators and the humid
plants. She never ignored an appeal from a mission, so drifts of tawdry
holy cards piled up in her desk drawer, and prayers were being offered
for her intentions at many far and desolate places.

More than once I happened on what I remember as a kind of ritual
encounter in the parlor. My Uncle James has dropped in, between jobs,
as so often, and my grandmother is trying to resist an appeal for money.
He is pacing back and forth, running his hand through his pompadour;
she is seated with lips compressed and distressful breathing. To my
mind she is entirely too upset by the plea from her youngest, Jim, who
had played baseball at Fordham, who always joked about the Jebbies,
who when I was a very small boy had defined "ammunition" for me as
buttered toast. "Ma, give me two dollars," he repeats, and he, too, is
upset, his ruddy face looks ruddier than usual. It is only two dollars that
he always wants, the happy-go-lucky fellow. Is she stingy, is he humili-
ated? "God have mercy on us all, what will become of us?" she will say
in the end, putting two bills in his hand, and off he will go to buy
whatever two dollars can buy.

5

At one point or another in the room by the front door, depending on the
season and sunniness and time of day, a furry bar of orange and purple

light appeared, a treasure without a body, precarious, given to fading. One might not otherwise have noticed the small colored glass panel high in the front window. The bookcases in this room contained all volumes of *The Book of Knowledge*. They also contained novels by men with three names—Albert Payson Terhune, James Oliver Curwood, Edgar Rice Burroughs. Then there were *Rhymes of a Red Cross Man, Dere Mabel*, a book on the Lafayette Escadrille, and *Over the Top*, a book on the British in the trenches by a Yank named Arthur Guy Empey. *Treasure Island, The Adventures of Tom Sawyer*, and *Moby-Dick* were there in illustrated editions, and something I soon cared for even more: *Henry Esmond*, closely printed in a cheap yellow binding. The weightiest books were nineteenth-century volumes from my grandfather's library: *The Great Cryptogram*, for example, and *Battle Field and Bivouac*, a narrative of campaigns by the U.S. Cavalry in the 1870s against the Sioux. In this there were photographs of generals, Custer and Crook, and of Indian scouts, and fold-in maps of skirmish points in the Black Hills and on the Great Plains.

In winter, the radiator against the front wall could dry gloves, wet from making snowballs—knit gloves that dried to become themselves and leather gloves that shrank into parched stiff little paws.

The interior world and the outside world greatly differed. Although a matter of a few small rooms, the interior contained the far away and long ago: it contained the voyages of the Pequod and the Hispaniola. Accessible in the interior, to be borrowed for oneself, were Esmond's style and Jim Hawkins' and Ishmael's. Here people took refuge, slept, and dreamed; here they fortified themselves with food and put on their defensive dress, and felt themselves to be most safely what they were, beings with limited needful bodies and frail nagging souls and memories, who depended on one another. Swing a heavy door and step through, and you walked into the large and alien wind, blowing from who knows where over the wild-scented earth and its vegetation, or down paved ways amid strangers. Not to mention the steady wind of time. The house and practically everything in it and all those who lived in it except me have now vanished from the face of the earth, and so have the eight or nine other houses on that block. In their place is a new expensive State building, very glassy, set in broad lawns, and a parking lot on the railroad side.

6

A light-boned boy's metabolism must be nearly as wondrous as that of birds who have so much energy to burn. The excess could not be expended in playgrounds during school recesses but demanded exertion or exploring and roaming, in the great hours After School. During one whole autumn, my friend Dan O'Connell and I would head at four o'clock for a weedy junkyard on the far side of the railroad tracks between Capitol Avenue and Monroe Street, to take possession there of the wreck of a flivver. Dan wore for a time, as I did, a leather cap with ear flaps, shaped like an aviator's helmet. He was lusty and debonair. His favorite chant, which he could make mysteriously brazen or suggestive, was "Ja da, ja da, jada jada jing jing jing." At his father's shoe store on the Court House Square, Dan and I had been privileged one day to see and handle heroic accouterments of the Great War: sheathed in thick military khaki, the bayonet and gas mask that his older brother had brought home from France. The abandoned chassis in the vacant lot became our two-seater pursuit plane, flown on scouting or combat missions above the German lines. It had a machine gun synchronized to shoot through the propeller. When tired of battle in the air, we could go to a movie at one of the second-string movie houses beyond the Square: Bill Hart in a Western, or hairbreadth Harry Houdini sweating through a serial of escapes.

My likeliest companion on the Fourth of July, Halloween, and every day in summer was my near neighbor Henry Barber, a skinny boy, black-haired and brown-eyed, who wore glasses and tooth braces and lived in a big red brick house half a block away. In a darkened room on the south side of the first floor lived Henry's Grandpa, a very old man, white-bearded, with a black silk skull cap, who as Henry Rankin had been an office boy in the firm of Lincoln and Herndon in the 1850s and had written a life of Lincoln. When we were playing in the yard, if Henry went to Grandpa's window and rapped, the old face would appear smiling and the old fingers would push through an aperture in the window sash a card bearing four or five large gray pills. These apparently contained nothing but sugar, and were regarded as a treat both by Grandpa and Henry.

On summer days Henry's mother sometimes hired us to root out dandelions from the lawn. Supplied with paring knives and a bucket, squatting in the grass, we hitched around cross-legged from one dandelion colony to another while swapping the fantasies and conjectures of boyhood. Henry was double-jointed and could do amazing things with his thumbs. Sunny parts of the lawn on a hot day would redden our faces and bedew Henry's upper lip with sweat, but we could always knock off in favor of mumbly-peg in the shade, and there we would rest, jesting and gurgling, filled with tasty hosewater.

In my eighth-grade year, in the fall of 1923, when Henry was in the ninth grade or junior high school, he went to a college football game in Urbana. Sitting with me on his front steps next day, he told me of watching the game from a seat almost on a level with the players and close enough to see how gigantic they were. "Here was the calf of this guy's leg," he said, "like this"—and he made a hoop with his arms to show the girth, bigger around than he was. We were, just the same, getting big enough to foresee being really big, and for my birthday that fall I received my first regulation football.

Flat in its box lay the heavy pigskin with a hard pebbly surface, tan, unmarred, and clean, giving off a strong leather smell. Into it you were to fit the smooth stout rubber bladder, with its tube sticking out of the aperture. Then the rawhide lace would be passed in loose loops through the eyelets and the serrated tip of a football pump pushed and turned to the sticking point in the tube. As you pumped, the football filled and hardened until you could force no more air into it. Pinching the tube then, you withdrew the pump, folded the tube over and tied it with a doubled and redoubled rubber band before shoving it under the edge of distended leather and pulling the lace tight, its superfluous length tucked back under the crisscrossing.

With my heel I dented the ground beside the mulberry sapling on the left side of the front yard and placed the ball with one nose in the dent and the other in the air at a slight angle backward. Measuring a few steps behind the expectant ball, I loped forward to the place kick. If squarely booted in the right spot, the ball would soar away, on a trajectory rising twenty or thirty degrees, end over end in a backward tumble, crossing the street and dropping on the terrace or lawn opposite, a flight of perhaps forty yards. I practiced this time and again.

I also practiced the dropkick, a synchronized movement in which only two steps were taken as the ball, held well forward, was dropped and the kick executed just as it hit the ground. Had not Charley Brickley of Harvard dropkicked goals from midfield? Punting was another matter. For a punt you set the ball afloat high in front of you and kicked it in the air, on your whole instep, making a louder sound, a "boom" in the language of the sports writers. What you hoped for was a high, spiraling flight, giving your tacklers time to get downfield. I practiced punting in the middle of the street to keep away from the trees on either side. By practice I thought I would acquire prowess. At twelve, at thirteen, at fourteen, my tradition told me that what counted was not inborn ability but training and guts and a certain magic of equipment. I had a book on football by a man named Daly who had coached at West Point. "Football is war," he said, and roused me. "Go out there to fight and keep it up all afternoon."

The following year I was taken to see the Michigan-Illinois game, pitting a famous passing quarterback, Benny Friedman, against a famous broken-field runner, Red Grange. I saw two masses of giant heroes, regularly forming and breaking into melee on the gray November field. On end sweeps to the right three powerful blockers ran low ahead of Grange with his piston-driving stride, and all three most often hurled themselves one after another in vain against the Michigan left end, a towering Swede named Benny Oosterbahn, who, striving with great hands, would put them all aside and snag the runner.

On some Sunday afternoons when for one reason or another nothing athletic was afoot—no tennis, no biking, no sledding, no company—I might have liked to stick with my book, whatever it might be; but my father's program for me called for an hour outdoors, even in the dead of winter. I owned, and favored, a soft camel's hair cap that in zero weather could be pulled down over mouth and chin, leaving an opening for nose and eyes. In this, and in mackinaw and gloves and overshoes if needed, I stepped out on winter Sundays for exercise: if the front walk needed shoveling, for that. Once while I was banging away with a sharp spade at an ice crust, a very tall, very stately and stooped man in overshoes and a fur cap came by and smiled at me as I stood aside for his careful steps. He had long drooping mustaches, perfectly white. When I came in, my father, who from his bedroom window had seen the old man approach, said that he was De Witt Smith, and that as a boy he had been a muleteer on the Santa Fe Trail.

More often, my exercise consisted of a two-mile walk. I would turn south on Second Street and keep a steady pace past Edwards, Cook, Lawrence, Canady, Scarritt, toward South Grand Avenue. Few walkers or cars broke the stillness, only my own feet crunching or scuffing. If any wind blew, nose and cheeks would feel it and after a while, from numbness, would feel less. The low sun shone overhead on creaking elm and maple boughs. On South Grand Avenue I would walk eastward to Fifth or Sixth Street, then turn again left and northward on the return leg, down streets even quieter and more deserted, passing now several dark mansions of an older day, mansarded and turreted, deep on barren snow-sheeted lawns with fountain bowls and stained figures of nymphs or stags. You could see for a long way through the open winter vistas of bare trees.

In the course of this walk one afternoon I suffered, very suddenly, an entirely new sense of everything. I found myself unfamiliar. Nothing that I saw in this condition seemed familiar. Dimensions were felt to be arbitrary and precarious: the many trees, near and far, looked both like trees and like bunches of twigs fixed in the ground. It was as though the world had been made, or remade, in that instant: space, light, surfaces, bodies, all breathless with coming-to-be. Everything had become pure spectacle, subject to an unformulated but dazzling question: why all this, instead of nothing at all? The walker had become pure witness, disburdened of every interest and even every sensation but the overwhelming one of being there. And yet everything existed tenuously, as though it might as well not. I finished my walk; the strangeness faded; I said nothing; workaday facts remained unchanged. But once and for all they had been called in question.

Robert Fitzgerald's mother, Anne Stuart Fitzgerald, at the time of *The Sign of the Cross, c.* 1907.

Robert Fitzgerald's father, Robert Emmet Fitzgerald, lying abed with a tubercular hip in a summer tent, Springfield, Illinois, *c.* 1905.

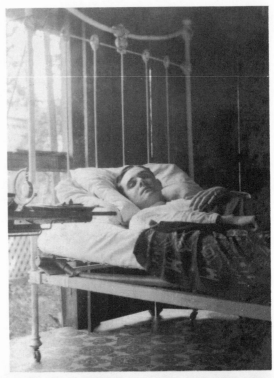

Robert Fitzgerald, in front of the house with bay windows, Springfield, Illinois, *c.* 1914.

Robert E. Fitzgerald with
Robert S. and Bernard M.
(Monty) Fitzgerald, in
Weekapaug, Rhode Island,
c. 1915.

Robert E. Fitzgerald, *c.*
1928.

Robert Fitzgerald in front of the Lincoln Statue, Springfield, Illinois, *c.* 1918.

Robert Fitzgerald, quarterback of the football team, wearing a Springfield High School sweater, *c.* 1927.

Robert Fitzgerald, yearbook photograph, Class of 1928, Springfield High School.

Robert Fitzgerald during a Harvard undergraduate summer, *c.* 1932.

215 East Jackson, Springfield, Illinois, in the 1960s. Bay windows are visible on the first and second floors.

The Third Kind of Knowledge

The Michaelmas term, as they called it, began in summery weather that went on day after day, changing only to a paler gold. The air barely stirred as a few crisp leaves fell through it on roof tiles and cobbles. At the hour when I fenced, few people were in the lanes, and walking toward the river, toward some distant cloud tucked above housetops, I could hear my heels on the stones. I held my foil by the blade and climbed a single flight to the *salle d'armes*, a bare room looking out through broad windows at gardens and trees. Through these ran the miniature river, dark green and reedy below a weir.

Foils rang and scraped. Three or four pairs of figures would be at play on the strips, and one of these figures might be the fencing master, a retired French Army captain. A shell fragment, fourteen or fifteen years before, had removed part of his back below the right shoulder and limited the play of his right arm. Even so, he handled young fencers like children. Tall, blond, and bland, M. Dap gave instruction with his mask pushed up like a visor. He wore a toothbrush mustache. His brows were permanently lifted in an expression of mild disbelief. A cigarette butt often clung to his lower lip. From my way of making myself compact he guessed that I had boxed, so he gave me a brief sermon on opening up and lengthening out. I was to consider that the little birds were like this, and he hunched, while the big birds—*les grands oiseaux*—were like this, erect, with wide, undulating wings. He made me practice parrying until my arm dropped. If the wrist is fully turned, the adversary's thrust will be deflected enough to pass your body. If the wrist is not fully turned—and here Dap's eyebrows went up even higher than usual—he will keel you.

As I went about my days, then and later, I sometimes pondered these instructions from Dap the comedian. It is better not to be a little bird, and better not to let yourself be run through, in one sense or another. Dap could talk; in his time he had seen men killed less tidily than by sword thrusts. But to think of such events was to put your finger on the diffi-

First published in *The Atlantic Monthly*, June 1980.

culty. Some weathers can make even a big bird take cover, and some threats are not to be parried.

At that time and in that place—I was twenty-one and at Trinity College, Cambridge—I enjoyed myself on the one hand to the point of enchantment, and on the other hand, in mind and ghost, contended with matters that seemed beyond my control or solution. The self that in some respects I enjoyed gave me great trouble in others. One was a state of mind that very rarely befell me, but, when it did, seemed at once a superior kind of knowledge and an unearthly visitation, mad or ill for all I knew. In the course of the year by luck I found at least a way of pinning this down.

In the foreground, coveys of young men and fewer young women on bicycles pedaled with gowns on their backs, this way and that, down the narrow streets on errands of learning. Ivy-grown Gothic and Tudor masonry led to recesses of paved and cobbled courts. Bells tolled and gownsmen paced to and fro. My college had a buttery. Little vistas and whiffs, in the slowly waning weather, conveyed the spell of past ages. Touches of antique discomfort could be felt as well. After sweating under Dap's eye and point, I might desire a bath. If so, a couple of inches of hot water could be made to flow, with sputtering, into the tub at Mrs. Fennemore's, where I lodged.

My two rooms were over a small grocery store at a corner. At full dusk a man on a bicycle came to light the gas lamp at the corner, managing with precision a long wand. At the right hour, putting on gown and cap, I made my way to dinner in the college hall, under lofty and elaborate painted beams, amid a blaze and hubbub of hundreds. Roast, sprouts, and Yorkshire pudding, a mug of ale, a sweet, and a savory. High on the wall beyond high table at the end of the room stood Henry VIII full-length by Holbein, his legs planted wide apart, exquisitely bearded and puffed and adorned and dangerous, presiding still over this establishment.

In my solitude during the fortnight or so before I really knew anyone, I began to identify myself, or pretend to, with Thomas Campion, a Cambridge man, a physician, a figure in a famous trial of 1613, and a matchless composer of lute songs. Vivian's beautiful edition of Campion was one of the few books I allowed myself to buy. There were nocturnal moments when I could tell myself that it had truly happened, I had called up that century, Campion and I were one musical spirit. I wrote in his person a song, his doing more than mine, a lute song for a Book of Ayres:

Night-tide, and my distress of love,
O speak, sweet numbers . . .

My solitude soon enough ended and the spell vanished, such as it was, but the song remained, like one of those tokens from a dream that are said to be left sometimes in the beds of dreamers.

It was October 1931. For breakfast Mrs. Fennemore served kippers, bacon and eggs, kidney stew, and porridge, in rough rotation. She would set it out on the study table while I shaved, using the tall, conical can of hot water she had left at my bedroom door.

Mrs. Fennemore's husband had a place in the background—Bert, slow, gray, and stolid, a diabetic, on a pension after a life in "building," a dim figure rarely seen, though his bike stood in the hall. Once she consulted me, a total loss, on how to measure the cc.'s of his insulin shot. The other thing in the hall beside Bert's bike was Mrs. Fennemore's big cage of canaries, a half-dozen of them, animating these lodgings with birdlife and birdsong. She took care of them daintily and tenderly, and as she went her rounds always paused for a twitting or an endearment.

To read classics meant to call once a week on your supervisor for conversation and for two well-printed sheets headed "Trinity College Lecture Hall." One contained a passage of unattributed English prose to be turned into Greek or Latin, the other passage of Greek or Latin to be put into English. That year, before events put it out of the question, I still thought that in the end I would command these languages as the dons did. Meanwhile I had hard going at my level. The page of Greek or Latin that I turned out each week, stewing until the small hours alongside my gas grate, would rarely pass with my supervisor.

Willing enough to labor for ancient literatures, I had not crossed the Atlantic for these alone, any more than I had for fencing. I thirsted for philosophy. What to make of an existence that I often found too much for me, or even how to think about it, I desired formally to know, if that were possible. A lucid book by A. S. Eddington, a Cambridge astronomer, had instructed me in the new physics, the conception of relativity, the quantum theory, and the Second Law of Thermodynamics. I had seen scientific procedures applied to literature by a Cambridge lecturer, I. A. Richards, at Harvard. I had heard the great Cambridge emeritus A. N. Whitehead lecture there on the Demiurge of Plato's *Timaeus*.

The work of Kant, consulted in Widener Library, had made me stare at the notion that time and space were only modes, our modes, of grasping the Real. Of what this Real might be in itself there seemed to be no unquestionable evidence. Through the senses, for example, what came? Touching had no resemblance to hearing, and neither in the least resembled seeing. You could not touch or smell a clang; you could not hear or smell a triangle. The curious, not to say upsetting, fact was that what the various senses delivered did not make up one world, since the sensations had nothing in common. They had nothing in common, that is, except oneself. Did sensations then constitute one's "self"? No, because that self, something apart, was aware of them, was aware of itself being aware of them, was aware of itself being aware of itself being aware . . . and the regression could continue. At times I could have jumped out of my skin.

These mysteries, and others of the kind, had been topics for talk in the course of walks on summer nights in Springfield. Old school friends sometimes came by after supper: Graham the logician, frowning, lifting his big frame, big adam's apple, ears, nose, brow, and cavernous carrying voice; Barber the mathematician, grinning like a bobcat, his glasses and black hair glinting. For hours we plodded together down dusty streets through strange neighborhoods, under thick leaves in the heat, past unlit porches where a cigar might glow out amid dim pallors of people at rest. In our hearts we would have denied that our exchanges and speculations were sophomoric.

Once, that August, after an evening with a girl, I had got home in the small hours when all the town was asleep. Coming from the garage where I had stilled and left the car, I stood on the front lawn for a while in the silence, in starlight, until with a sigh the mass of the universe opened for me above me, and I thought each of the innumerable leaves to be a year in time or a century or an interstellar year, dimly, silverly lit. Over the summer night of my childhood land presided the immense heaven of the past.

Now, in October, that cosmic America had sunk beyond the ocean, and in this place of history with its ancient human ways I felt, in loneliness, my own weightlessness and frailty; but I felt, too, great appetite and élan. I enrolled for C. D. Broad's lectures in the history of philosophy and for G. E. Moore's seminars in epistemology.

In gown and mortarboard, Dr. Broad entered the classroom on the hour, opened his notebook, and read aloud, slowly pacing between door and window. A dozen heads, including two in immaculate Sikh turbans, bent earnestly to take down what he said. Nut-brown and nearly bald, like a healthy monk, he read in an even tone at an even but slightly too rapid rate. In the course of the three terms he would take up in turn Descartes, Spinoza, Locke, Hume, Leibniz, Kant, and Hegel. He gave an account of each thinker's life and work, an exposition of his principal arguments, and an analysis of where, in logic, he had gone wrong. He was, in effect, dictating his own critical history of modern philosophy, and anyone who could keep up with him would possess it. I could almost do it but not quite.

Moore's seminars, by contrast, were entirely ad hoc. His text for an hour might be a single proposition from our book, Russell's *Problems of Philosophy*. He had no notes, but he relied on the blackboard and often darted at it, chalk in hand, his gown flying. We were invited to think and to articulate our thinking. He faced us eagerly, all attention, all quickness, with his sharp inquiring nose and bright eyes. Here that favorite Cambridge entity, the *sensum*, came into its own; we heard endlessly about *sensa*. But Moore's fine distinctions were distinctions in logic rather than in experience, and bore only at second hand on what I wanted to know. I wanted to know, for one thing, what respective values to give the examiner's attitude toward the Real and common attitudes toward the world of convention.

Common attitudes had the value of enabling a common life, in which so far as possible the insoluble and uncontrollable were disregarded. The world on the whole belonged to people who didn't press wicked questions. I could not say whether my lot lay with them or with those who did. Among those refractory to things as they are—and not usually in possession of many—a hidden community existed, a web of discernments and sympathies. I had long ago become aware of this, but on going to England I saw the strands of one such network distinctly touched. Vachel Lindsay had written notes about my being in Cambridge to a few literary people. One who responded was Ezra Pound, on a postcard to me from Rapallo saying there was no danger of his being in England; but that was not all. A few days later came a note inviting me as Ezra Pound's compatriot to tea at 4 Grantchester Road, signed "B. Scratton (It is 'Mrs.')."

It was a little low cottage of the English kind, in a row of places like it, with a scant living room where doilies might have been visible but were not, and a small coal grate. The stylist had here taken shelter; for that, it seemed, she could claim to be. With her dark gentle eyes and sidelong smile, she told me of Pound's liking for her prose, years before, and of his seeing to its publication in *The Transatlantic Review*. In speaking of

him she used his full name each time, never "Ezra" and never "Pound."
I was not informed and did not inquire whether Mr. Scratton was absent
or dead, but something about Bride Scratton made me feel that, for her,
neither condition registered very seriously.

She handed me on to a lady who had a drawing room and two daugh-
ters, each more handsome than the other, or so I thought when I called.
Translucent white curtains belled gently at French windows, and noting
my gaze the hostess remarked to me and the teapot, "It's the king's
wind." The two young women smiled back and forth and told me:
Chinese winds had rank according to the beauty of what they did to
drapery. These sisters might have been figures in an allegory suggested
by their names: Alethea fair and high-colored, in Edwardian white chif-
fon to her chin; brown Agatha in sweater and skirt, her nose uptilted,
her eyes irreverently shining. Alethea had returned to England after a
year in Paris on a weekly paper. Agatha was reading English at Newn-
ham. As I put my name in the guest book they showed me the small
signature of George Santayana, some pages back in another year.

Both girls became my friends, and I attended Agatha with emotion,
but I learned very little about this vivid family. As usual, it never occurred to me that I should. It was not so much that I felt curiosity to be
bad manners—though I did—as that the spectacle people made seemed
in itself all I could manage or desire. There they were, warm, visible,
audible, ponderable, telling about themselves with every breath and
syllable, and should the delighted spectator inquire like a drudge into
their history and biography? To Agatha one day I confided a new trick I
had learned, of remembering things at the same time I perceived them.
She had just remarked that all American jokes seemed to be about
Noah's ark, and I had said that that was an English joke, turning as I
walked to look her full in her impudent face, when I realized that the
trick was being performed.

Mrs. Scratton had me to tea again, and yet again, as the fall turned
somber. She gave me a Mary Butts novel to read, a novel Pound had
valued for some sorcery of style. And she told me of a summer twilight
in the Roman theater at Verona when, sitting between Pound and young
Eliot, she had been startled and had said to Eliot, "Why, you're rouged!"
at which he had drawn from his pocket a woman's compact and shown it
smiling. I felt that the musing lady understood this to have been neither
androgyny nor histrionics but something more exceptional and strange.
She trusted me with the story. About her, lines of remembering came
into my mind:

> Toward evening stained with leaves
> The lady presently to be unmourned
> Has lifted the clear silver for her friend
> And smiled at the faint play, fire mist in embers,
> The past year tranquil at the next year's end . . .

In Switzerland for the Christmas vacation, I visited one of the hardest-thinking of my Harvard friends: Ogle, who could sit across the room with his eyes closed and win at chess. At his family's house in Montreux I had a room looking across the sheet of lake at the sharp, snowy saw-teeth of the Dents du Midi. There was a Christmas party at a hotel, where I drank my first champagne just before waltzing with Ogle's pretty sister. To quench my thirst, as I thought, I took two glasses of this subtly effervescing pale golden chilly drink. Soon and suddenly, Ogle's sister had to help me through a revolving ballroom to a wall that at least had rigidity. For the next ten days, forsaking society, Ogle and I skied with Parry, another American friend of his, now studying at Vienna.

Going by sleigh from Gstaad to a small inn at the small town of Gsteig, the three of us got a room with bunks and a big porcelain stove. Parry's special interest was symbolic logic, a technique of thinking explored if not invented by Professor Lewis at Harvard, and Parry's use of it had won him his traveling fellowship. Lanky, fidgety, pale, unkempt, with domed forehead and weak eyes, he had in truth a noble philosopher's mind. He could not ski but never stopped trying, taking spill after spill with equanimity and hunting for his glasses in the snow. Ogle had grown up in Switzerland and gone to the Rosey; he skied without think-ing about it. Now he thought about it long enough to coach us, with pauses for laughter, up and down the big open slope to the west. In the afternoons we toiled and attempted runs, until dusk filled the valley and lights began going on in the village, even while the colossal stone face of the Oldenhorn, the peak to the east, still glowed with sunset.

Back at Mrs. Fennemore's, fewer and fewer baths seemed necessary as winter deepened. One bronchial cold succeeded another. Before the end of February, sure that I had tuberculosis of the lungs, I got myself x-rayed at a clinic in Camden Place. The report credited me with no disease and with "a very wonderful excussion downward," and I took a paralyzing clap on the back from the surgeon, a guardsman type, as he sent me forth into the drizzle with a gargantuan laugh.

As regularly as my wasting illness would allow, I went to Housman's lectures on the third book of Horace. These were of great purity, as even

I could appreciate: they concerned the choices between one reading or pointing and another, with no reference whatever to qualities of poetic composition. The old man spoke with dry emphasis through his mop of gray mustache, keeping his eyes on his text. The sleeves of his long winter underwear, a trifle dingy, protruded over his wrists. Hard wear and traces of splatter made rusty his ancient gown.

My visits to the *salle d'armes* picked up again when I had been assured of not being moribund. Briefly and wildly I took up the saber. Agatha and I went for muddy walks to Grantchester. But what mainly engaged me in this term was a paper that I set down with utmost concentration, to be given to Dr. Broad. My subject was The Third Kind of Knowledge in Spinoza.

Beginning in boyhood, on a Sunday walk in winter, I had had to distinguish between ordinary experience, including that of the senses, mind, and imagination—almost all, in short— and extraordinary experience, a kind that was rare, unwilled, *sui generis*, and superior. It came without any particular warning or preparation. It was as though everything waked up, as though everything drugged into somnolence by its own memory of being itself suddenly lost that memory and merely incredibly existed. In the following years this happened to me, in different settings, perhaps a dozen times at long intervals and worked precisely the same transformation each time. I could recall and invite the transformation, but by focusing intently I could only faintly induce it.

The experience had several consequences. Among states of cognition known to me I gave it without hesitation pride of place, and I supposed it religious though uncertainly related to faith or doctrine. I held it, too, as an aesthetic criterion. This, or something like it, must be the gift of the shuddersome poets, Crane in his way or Eliot in his: this set them apart, and the mysterious power of their greater work came of matching in poetry this ultimate strangeness. But the lightning of it seemed beyond nature and out of context with habitual ways and terms. It alienated me from these, and at times the sense of alienation, reaching a certain pitch, brought suffocating panic. I had, after all, friends, family, interests, appetites, humor, and a mind, all passable and usual, and I felt threatened by this visionary thing (if that was what it was) with inhumanity and madness. From the Cambridge thinkers I wanted light on how to comprehend and handle it, but I heard no news of it in Broad's peripatetic tone nor in Moore's flutterings to the blackboard. Apparently no one would know what I was talking about.

Now to this predicament a form of relief had come in late November when I began reading the *Ethics* and *De Intellectus Emendatione* of Benedict Spinoza. Beyond sense perception, the first, and reasoning, the second, Spinoza placed a third kind of knowledge, *scientia intuitiva*, which he credited with an adequate grasp of the Real and even (or therefore) of God in certain attributes. About all Broad in his lectures had had to say on this subject was that no doubt Spinoza had had "mystical experiences," rather a thorn in the side of philosophy, one gathered, and at any rate outside philosophy's province. The snub shocked me a little, as did the catchall category. I thought I might make Broad see what Spinoza possibly meant if I told him with exactitude the nature of the third kind of knowledge in my own experience. I wrote:

"The mind or consciousness or identity most familiar to me has on certain occasions been in a superior state which it is difficult to describe. But then it is difficult really to describe anything.

"A. The state I refer to is not the same as a dream. In dreams the waking powers of introspection and memory and the sense of space-time relations are not only disturbed but enfeebled. The kind of experience I am speaking of involves a transformation, but not an enfeeblement, of these faculties. It is quite definitely an extreme state of being awake.

"B. It is a concentration of self-consciousness and a release from thoughts irrelevant to the present reality. It is like the feeling of loneliness and reality which a child has when it is seized by a terror of actual death, only in this case the imagined death of the body is not in the mind's focus. What is there is the perceptual situation perceived, together with a sudden loss of the ordinary habit of assuming that such a situation is a consequence of something and that what happens in it is reasonable. The mind is acutely and even masterfully conscious of itself and of others and of our actual life of movement and thought in a space-time transparency. It regards things and events in isolation, since they are no longer parts of a progression or included in any obvious scheme, and isolated they appear more beautifully distinct from each other, they take on an individuality for which names and other general symbols are entirely inadequate, and they lose the relative values formerly attributed to them. For example, it would be of no consequence to a man whose mind was so clarified whether the waiter brought him his dinner or stabbed him in the back: either action would be valued for itself.

"C. A pleasant experience, but wholly without emotion of one kind or another. . . . Each thing and each occurrence being as valuable as any other, the expectance of pleasure or pain is simply obliterated from the consciousness and motives and emotions no longer exist.

"D. This is not because a certain Necessity is realized in everything apprehended. The point is perhaps important. If there were a Necessity in any ordinary sense of the term an apprehension of the necessity would include a resignation to it. There is no resignation; there is neither passivity nor activity; there is simply existence and the things that exist.

"E. Not Intellectual Detachment. It is possible for the ironic mind to withdraw indefinitely behind the scenes to which it is a witness, and behind itself. In the state I am describing there is no withdrawal from the object, but a sort of expansion and inclusion of it, the total consciousness participating.

"F. Not Heightened Consciousness. I am not speaking of a mere sharpening of the senses or a more sensitive awareness of tones in a situation, such as most good artists and many other people possess and improve by training. A "heightened consciousness" of this kind may exist without undergoing the transformation necessary to the condition of emotional vacuum I have described.

"G. Example in Literature. Dostoevsky must have experienced this state of consciousness to have been able to use it in the novel *The Possessed*. Having had the experience, he created a character whose state of consciousness should be constantly so clarified, and followed his life from the ordinary point of view. The hero of the novel was so keenly alive and in such complete unemotional control that he could experiment with the perceptual situation in ways which might be and were judged insane. It is this which makes the incident in which he pulls Garganov's nose so much more interesting than, for example, the incident in *Point Counter Point* in which Spandrell kills Webley to find out what it's like. Huxley's character is merely affected to an extreme with a conventional "disillusionment" and his motive in killing Webley is a vulgar one, despite the author's pains to surround it with ideas. . . .

"I have now said what I mean exactly insofar as I am able to say it, and what I mean is now understood exactly to that extent. . . . My suggestion is that Spinoza had this experience, or one essentially like it, that he found it superior, and that he went so far as to believe that it was, in fact, a perception of Reality. He consequently tried to induce it more often and to think up a method of inducing it in others, and his philosophy grew out of the necessity of explaining coherently in current philosophical terms the Reality so perceived. . . ."

In conclusion, I took up several points that had been questioned by the lecturer, suggesting ways of interpreting them. Broad had, for example, objected to Spinoza's attribution of a kind of pleasure, *beatitudo,* to the third kind of knowledge on the ground that this was to make an emotional experience out of a purely intellectual one. "Nowhere in Spinoza's system," I zealously pointed out, "is *beatitudo* classed as an emotion. . . ."

It ensued from this effort that one afternoon I climbed a Trinity staircase to Dr. Broad's rooms. Nobody had told me, or ever did tell me—I have only lately discovered it—that they had once been Isaac Newton's. Had I known this, I would have realized dimly that Broad occupied them by merit. They were dusky, bookish, low-ceilinged. My host received me gravely and kindly. His polished skull and brow shone faintly, his speculative gray eyes shone not at all. His questions and remarks were deliberative. At one point he said, "I rarely go abroad because I can't speak other languages." It was a thinker's decision, neither insular nor affected, and very much in character. If we ever got around to talking about Spinoza, I cannot remember what we said, but I do remember asking myself if it had been somehow bad form on my part to pursue the matter. A year later, back at Harvard, I had a letter from him on academic points in the course of which he asked, "Have you had any more mystical experiences?" As he again used the term to the use of which I had taken exception, I felt this, then, to be a little insistent, or a little absent-minded, or perhaps he even meant to pull my leg.

It is easy in retrospect to think this shyness and touchiness unreasonable. Certainly Broad was neither patronizing me nor making fun of me. The truth is that whatever value could be placed on my affliction or privilege—and I still wonder—it probably did not correspond to Spinoza's *scientia intuitiva,* which seems to have been a mathematician's rapture at grasping the logical order of the universe. I had, as it happened, addressed my submission to a man who was to become years later president of the Society for Psychical Research and to deliver at Trinity in the Lent terms of 1959 and 1960 two magisterial courses of lectures on that subject. Is this an example of the irony that dogs our lives? At any rate, in the spring of 1932 I went no further with my study of the saintly metaphysician and lens grinder of The Hague. I had tried to put my amazement into words and had received perhaps the only possible comment on it.

When the Cockroach Stood
by the Mickle Wood

1

One summer day in 1923 I was taken with two small cousins by trolley westward over the Queensborough Bridge. We were making an excursion to a matinee at Roxy's. To our left as we clanged across the great web of bridge I had my first full view of Manhattan, the buildings in their dreamy altitudes piling up down the island around the tallest of all, the Woolworth tower. A heat haze enriched light and shadow on the distant masses. Here and there small plumes of vapor appeared. As the vista slowly shifted, I felt the wonder expected of me as a visiting twelve-year-old from the Midwest. The city already belonged to myth, standing like Asgard beyond the East River water, more of the sky than of the earth. I felt, even so, some formless question stirring at the edge of my mind as to what sense of life that skyline honored or expressed. There was as yet nothing like it in the world.

Going downtown we had glimpses, from an open bus-top, of refined opulence behind plate glass. The very name of Tiffany's had an expensive sheen or nap: a name of chased silver. Not long before, I had been shown an article that my Uncle John had written for his newspaper on the centenary of Fifth Avenue. It concluded: "Amid the ages of the empires, Fifth Avenue is one hundred years young." The cadence thrilled me, and I thought of the words now as the bus bowled along between crowded sidewalks and shops. Uncle John was a first cousin of my mother and had married my father's only sister. My two small cousins were his children. The first fencing foils I had ever seen, as a very small boy, were his—crossed on the wall of the ivory-white apartment in Albany where he and my aunt first lived. An old photograph of a Georgetown crew showed him poised at bow oar with his curly head and high-hearted grin. Some defect of eyesight had kept him out of

First published in *The Yale Review*, Winter 1985.

Annapolis, to his lifelong regret, but in his late thirties, when at five or six I first knew him, he had the erect bearing and gaiety of a sea dog, with his oarsman's shoulders still. In those days, a moment after first meeting Uncle John, my younger brother and I would each in turn find himself high in the air, then handed around over shoulders and between legs and up again, breathless but secure. We wondered if he could lick Douglas Fairbanks, and rather thought he could.

Uncle John's father and mother, Uncle Charlie and Aunt Elizabeth, lived in comfort in their quiet up-and-down townhouse on Willett Street in Albany. Uncle Charlie had curly white hair and mustaches and attended without great effort to a business in coal and ice. Aunt Elizabeth, with her kind gray eyes magnified by her pince-nez, sat serenely over her knitting or needlework as she commented on daily matters in her cool, well-bred voice. She went in for beautiful grays—gray cashmeres and gray shetlands, gray shawls and throws. Her son had her vigilant eyes, but his were prepared to be merry. After the Albany Boys Academy and Georgetown, he had risen fast in newspaper work in Albany and then in New York, winning the confidence of Mr. Munsey, who had made him bureau chief for the New York *Herald* in London at the time of the Peace Conference. He and my Aunt Marie had lived for several years in places with literary names—Hampstead Heath, Kew Gardens, Golders Green—sending their Midwestern nephew at Christmastime Jaeger knitwear and gilded resplendent Christmas numbers of the *Tatler* and the *Illustrated London News*. Professional photographs in soft focus showed their small beautiful children in blond halos before tulip beds, and when they returned to America they brought with them an English nanny, Olive Winch. It was Nanny Winch who had charge of us on trolley and bus that day in 1923.

Closer to home, in Forest Hills, lay the daily and deep pleasures of the summer. My aunt and uncle had found and rented for a year a neat spacious house and garden, and in July and August they had a room for a nephew under the eaves. Half-timbering on the Long Island Railroad station and small shops nearby gave Forest Hills an English village air, and people spoke of going to shop "in the village." But even if there had been anything really snobbish about this it would have seemed all right to me, for among those well-off suburban homes and lawns a true aristocracy had its seat. For three or four weeks it showed its power on the curtained-off practice courts and in the small ivy-covered stucco stadium of the West Side Tennis Club, host to the best players on earth. I attended with passion the Davis Cup matches, the Wightman Cup matches, and the National Championships, often with my eight-year-old cousin, Jack. At ease on our cushions, waiting for a match in the sunlight, we looked down from our moderate height at the courts of shaven grass, where court attendants in olive green uniforms and little round-brimmed cotton hats perambulated the base lines and service and side lines at a brisk even pace, letting their marker carts gush ribbons of wet lime. Godlike young men or women in snowy whites came sauntering out with armloads of rackets—Olympian wealth, it seemed to me, since I had but one. Then there were the warm-ups, the pock . . . pock of superb ground shots, and the dauntless rallies. The striped marquee at the open end of the stadium held distinguished players with club members and guests, the elect in blazers enjoying the shade, but one day Helen Wills in pigtails, with her mother, climbed up the stadium tiers and sat near us to get a better view of a match. A day or two later she was going to beat Mrs. Mallory for the Championship. Now, not wearing her white eyeshade, the divinely strapping girl with her Greek profile munched away at an apple while my heart thumped and I tried not to stare.

Perhaps the best amenity of all was the appearance of a tea cart for the English Wightman Cup ladies in the long interval after the second set. There by the umpire's stand they sat, and still sit, all in white tunics and roomy white skirts, nodding to their warm cups or pouring another, while the spectator tastes the mustard in his stadium hot dog, the fresh stadium flags curl in the breeze, the stadium shadow steadily grows toward the center court. England and the English who invented lawn tennis were represented to me thus, after the soft Jaeger winter things of other years, and after the postwar English magazines with page after page of notices offering for sale country houses with billiard rooms and gun rooms—for sale, now that so many of the billiard players and huntsmen were no more.

And Miss Winch was their daily representative, fair and firm about good order and good manners, dressed properly by day in her nanny uniform and cap and presiding over tea with quartered jelly sandwiches in the nursery every afternoon. She had a visible overbite and a lovely blush and would be remembered for her long pale buttoning fingers with rather flat nails, well trimmed and scrubbed. One morning she gave me special cause to remember her. Immediately on waking I had to be sick, and was, leaning from the bedside as one leans from a ship's rail. At home in Illinois, after the death of my small brother four years before, I had been an only child whose least illnesses were always matters of great concern—thermometers, cool washcloths, calls to the doctor, worried faces. What was my astonishment, therefore, when Nurse Winch, entering to clean up the mess, gave me quite a scolding. In not trying to reach the bathroom I had behaved like a baby, and jolly thoughtless, too. Taken aback and rueful as I was, I recognized instruction when I heard it.

Though in fact very near the city, we seemed well out of it in that peaceful place of summer light, garden light, and games on grass. I taught my cousin baseball, as he taught me cricket. On rainy days I read *Puck of Pook's Hill*, or I lay on the floor in the library leafing through exhibition catalogues in which absorbing nudes were here and there to be found. In my bedroom eyrie I spent several nights of exhausting terror with Poe's tales in a macabre illustrated edition. Aunt Marie joked and hugged me and combed my hair, recalling that I had been her first baby, born to Anne my mother whom she had loved and who died long ago, and to my father her favorite brother, now for some years bedridden in Springfield where the electric fan hummed this way and that in sweltering August. She could sit down at her baby grand and play cascading *arpeggi* that reminded you of her girlhood studies in conservatories in Brussels and Berlin. I had seen a portrait photograph of the young beauty she had been, with her long throat and a wealth of white ostrich feather clasped to her head. She told me of her stock reply when anyone remarked on her surprising biceps: that she had got them washing diapers. I loved her humor, as I loved her powder puffs and scent bottles and ivory brush and comb on an ivory tray. Late one afternoon when we young ones were to dine apart because the elders were having a dinner party, she sent me to the village for a pint of cream. When I came back she had changed, seemed vague about the cream, seemed half-asleep, slow-spoken and redolent, and for the first time I knew that this quick-witted lovely woman, like her father and at least two of her brothers, could be so transformed. I scented, too, in my confusion, something secret and sweet and abandoned, a turn toward oblivion. But so far as I could see, though out of it, the evening party passed off well, and nothing so strange happened again that summer.

2

All is not well forever with prosperities and abilities and loving families, flowers and music and books. What the years do to almost everything they proceeded to do to that Long Island household, slowly but not very surreptitiously. While I was going to school and suffering my father's death and going on to college, good times became overblown and withered into hard times in the world. The change came home to me in a single shock when I returned to Illinois in the summer of 1932 and my Uncle Ed, whom I had never seen otherwise than dignified and spruce, came down the steps to embrace me, tieless and unshaven, his voice breaking. Before long I was to see distress in the East as well. Uncle John had taken a fearful beating in a crash on Queens Boulevard and spent a winter laid up with fractures and wounds that left him grayer and frailer and feeling, as he told me under his breath, like a hollow shell. He had moved his family to a house on the Sound where the winter damp, with cartons of Piedmont cigarettes, brought hard coughing on his injured chest. Then he was no longer a star reporter but a writer of press releases for devil-may-care aviation people, Mineola and Roosevelt Field people, with whom late nights in speakeasies were too often required. My aunt with her long yellow hair in braids would lie abed reading until all hours, waiting for the last train. The unpaid bills grew longer. The Depression and The Jitters grew worse.

Crossing the sunny courtyard of my college House one day in late May of 1933, I fell in with a swarthy Irish history tutor named Doolin who had no humor and always said quicky what he thought. "You should have had a *magna*," he announced abruptly. "What are you going to do? You should settle down to work." This last, at any rate, was true and would remain true throughout life. As to what I was going to do, I told Doolin truthfully that I didn't know, but I didn't tell him what I had in the back of my mind. In the course of the year, proof had been offered me that there would be no money for tuition at law school or for the study of philosophy in Paris, my earlier and later aspirations, and in short that I would have to make a living without undue delay. My Uncle John then suggested that I try working for a New York newspaper; one editor, a friend, he said with brave loyalty, would be sure to have a place for me. A few days after my exchange with Doolin, I confided this to a Mallarméan and professor of Greek whom I invited to lunch in my dining hall. This man, Milman Parry, had a thin bony face, a fine mustache and goatee, and black eyes, very bright. He studied me and my prospects for a moment over his coffee, then put the cup down and smiled vividly. "You go to your destruction," he said with relish and smiled on.

Parry liked the theater and had been a devotee in Paris of Sacha Guitry and Yvonne Printemps. He had coached me in a play of Sophocles performed by students in Greek. I took his remark as theatrical in a mock-tragic mode, but every now and again for years his voice would become audible to me, saying those words. They acquired great ironic pitch, because in two years he himself was gone from the earth, killed by a pistol jolted when the safety was off. Parry may have been right about my fate, but I would always prefer to believe that it was a near thing. In any case, my plans at the time were soon made: I who had never had a job of any kind and knew nothing but a little philosophy and Greek would jobhunt in the big city that had beglamored my boyhood. First I would look for work on my own in the summer and only as a last resort would I fall back on my uncle, who had indeed many friends in hard times or any. I revisited my remaining family in Illinois, then came East as I had often enough before, on the Pennsylvania Railroad in a lower berth on a Pullman sleeper.

The routine of railroading at that time broke this journey midway. Late at night at Altoona, between shuntings and couplings in the big yards, there would be long waiting and stillness in the dark. You might hear a muffled footstep or two as someone passed in the carpeted aisle. Finally the train would be under way again minus the diner and with a new locomotive, settling into a lulling rhythm, smooth and swift, clickety-click, clickety-click. That might be the last thing you remembered before you felt the porter's hand on your foot, mussing and shaking through sheet and blanket. The dense curtain on the aisle side of the berth rustled back in place, and he was gone. Pinching the center clamp of the window blind, you could push it up for early light on smoky New Jersey factory sidings or vistas of wastelands and reeds shaken by the wind. From the net hammock slung across the window you unfolded underwear and trousers and with contortions got into them. With luck you might reach the men's room in time to get a nickel-finished washbowl and join the other occupants, men in BVD shirts, lathering and shaving in silence, teetering a little when the train swayed.

When you came out in early morning into the main concourse, you looked up to crossbeams of sunlight, parallelograms great in span, under a vaulted loftiness of pale buff stone. No one thought or cared how lavish were these heights and volumes of air. The architects had never heard that form follows function, but they had designed this terminal on that principle: its function was to serve public convenience with majesty, not at all unlike the imperial Roman baths which had been its model. Across from the train side a flight of very broad shallow steps led toward Seventh Avenue by way of a shop-lined arcade, itself wide as an avenue, and just beyond the top landing on the left you could turn and enter the Savarin lunch room for breakfast. Here were fixed stools at long low counters and everything, again, luxuriously spacious and full of light. Black men in white jackets, as in a Pullman diner but here with all the elbow room in the world, moved about to bring the first customers orange juice, coffee, cereals, flapjacks, bacon and eggs, sausages, toast. The newcomer might be faint of heart and woozy with loss of sleep, but the city provided grandeur and refection on his arrival.

If the city was your destination, you would leave the main concourse at the taxi end, coming out in a cavernous ramp amid an ever-moving file of yellow cabs that concentrated in that chamber the engine roar and brake noise and blue exhaust fumes of the street. Arriving this time, I wanted no taxi but after breakfast went below to the Long Island station. My uncle and aunt were again to take me in. From my base, my bed in their house, I began making daily forays into Manhattan, wearing my old cotton seersucker, going through the newspaper want ads on the blowy, gritty Long Island train. Then I trudged the streets between dingy offices where I talked to discouraged men. Mr. Roosevelt's first administration had not yet relieved his countrymen of fear, nor were any that I interviewed reassured by me. A hundred times that summer I failed to get a job. When September came, I agreed that Uncle John might drop a word. What came of this was an appointment on a Monday to see Stanley Walker, city editor of the *Herald Tribune*.

From a plain entrance like a freight entrance on 40th Street, an elevator took me up to a bare vestibule kept by a one-eyed old lady beadily dressed, seated at a table with a few chairs nearby. She sent me through an open doorway into the city room, which took in most of one whole floor, furnished to my left and ahead with desks and typewriters in strong light, some of it daylight from tall windows on 41st Street. Typewriter noise came from here and there, not so loud as the perforating racket from a bank of teletype machines. Men in shirtsleeves and eyeshades drifted about. Office boys made haste. At the center of this scene at facing desks reigned the day city editor and his assistant, each having before him his phone, pencils, baskets, and spike.

Walker received me mumbling shyly, shirt collar unbuttoned, sleeves rolled up, for it was a warm day, and he used his handkerchief once or twice on his brow. After joking and sweating for a few minutes he asked me to come back same time, same day, next week. I did, and all went as before. Well into October he put me off from week to week, waiting for something to happen, I could never make out precisely what—waiting for me to vanish, the chances are. Then one day he introduced me to Wilcox, the managing editor, a leathery slow-moving presence in the background, and they hired me to do city reporting at eighteen a week. Walker took me over to meet a reporter who sat reading a paper at a desk nearby, a pale young man in a new light-gray suit who wore rimless glasses and looked like a bright student. He was lame, and limped a little when he rose to shake hands. Tom Sugrue. He had joined the paper after Fordham and had been reporting more than a year. My desk and typewriter would be next to his. He showed me how to handle a swatch of copy paper and how much, a third, to leave blank on the first one. After a while, using his cane, he took me down to dinner at Bleeck's, the local saloon on 40th Street. A dry martini, the first I had ever seen, appeared before him like a jewel.

3

Mr. Strunsky, who owned most of Washington Square South, brown-stones with top-floor studio skylights, wore an old brown overcoat a little ragged at the buttonholes, buttoned to the top, and a worn brown felt hat, beneath which his eyes were ingenious and kind. He told me I should read Pushkin and showed me the furnished room I could afford: a semiunderground room down a few steps at the corner of Sullivan and Third Streets. It had a bathroom to the left as you entered and a fireplace in the wall to the right. A barred window high in the left wall—the Sullivan Street side—and another on Third Street, both heavily curtained; a double bed covered in what had been a wine-colored spread; a table, a threadbare easy chair, a straight chair, and a standing lamp. Eight dollars a week. I moved in early in November. On the mantelpiece I placed a small silver fish, pliable with overlapping scales, that I had picked up in some Boston antique shop, and a bottle of Cointreau that someone had given me. Across the entryway was a similar apartment occupied by a young Japanese, to whom old Strunsky introduced me. I rarely saw him but owed to him the knowledge that tightly rolled newspapers would do, though briefly, as logs in the fireplace. Overhead in this place by day and night sounded the approaching racket of the Elevated, grating to round the Sixth Avenue corner some blocks away.

Now I had the city before me as a grid of bitter streets to be pillaged of sights and words daily in the name of news. Assignments were given out around two o'clock at the city editor's desk and entered on his assignment sheet. Off you would go by subway downtown or uptown or to another borough to ask questions and register scenes. You got the names, addresses, ages, and quotes by soft pencil on a wad of copy paper. Back at your desk you tried to read what you had written and to beat out before dinner the few paragraphs desired of your first or first two stories. If you needed background you got a packet of clippings out of the morgue. You might then with luck be assigned to a banquet. Organizations hoping for publicity for their speakers or themselves provided at banquets a press table with places for the morning dailies, the City News Service, and sometimes for specialized publications like *Variety* and *Women's Wear Daily*. The city desk passed these assignments out with careful equity to new and thin-bellied reporters to assure them each week of at least one good dinner with a cigar. A figure met fairly often on daily or evening rounds was the mayor. Small, round, genial, swarthy, with a black forelock and a piping voice, this perspiring bundle of force might turn up at any gathering anywhere in the city, ready to speak at the drop of a hat.

If La Guardia knew the town through the soles of his feet, the two Texans who ruled the city desk carried it all in their heads. On the day side Walker only at first seemed frail and boyish, his tousled head too big for his childlike stem of neck, his little chin tucked in. He mumbled around his cigar and never raised his voice, but before long you saw how on top of everything he was, quick and easy, hawk-eyed, yellow-eyed. Across from him sat the day assistant, John McLendon, burly and black-haired, the only editor who wore glasses, enlarging his indignant brown eyes. Around dinner time their successor came on. Engelking, Walker's counterpart, twice his height, pale, bald, big-boned, always in shirt-sleeves and the gunslinger's unbuttoned vest, always chewing a cigar, frowning under his green eyeshade, loomed and brooded over the desk. Nobody called him by his first names—or knew them: Lessing Lanham; older men called him Engel. His assistant was a lanky, alert young man named Joe Herzberg. To watch these men handle copy was to see an unconscious display of style. Engelking's L's marking indentation were inserted with small flourishes; with elegance he used the fork of two long fingers to deposit edited stories in the basket.

On the one hand the phantasmagoria of the great city, on the other this offhand professionalism at making a newspaper, gave me, six days a week and nine or ten hours a day, all I could cope with. Apart from the cigars, the atmosphere of that city room smacked not at all of *The Front Page*. There were no rowdy scenes. On the job, at least, nobody was ever drunk. A competitive spirit, never mentioned, in fact ran high. On each of my two or three daily assignments I would meet an opposition number from the *Times* for whom that single story would be the day's work. The *Times*, a block away, had twice the money and twice the staff, leaving agility to the *Herald Tribune*. One asset was a certain infusion of the New York wits. Walker counted as one and would soon publish a salty book on the nightclub era. Lucius Beebe did a column and could be seen at times in all his sang-froid and custom-made shirtsleeves. Very young men, Joe Alsop and St. Clair McKelway, to name two, were writing for the paper with fluency and élan. Out of his cubby and into the city room from time to time plodded Franklin P. Adams, homely and swarthy and savory, he too in shirtsleeves, eyeshade, and cigar, engaging in filling his column, The Conning Tower, with his own or contributed prose and verse. Agreeable reading, it almost always was, and soon after I went to work it contained to my blissful amusement the wildest of all Kipling parodies, by Don Marquis:

The cockroach stood by the mickle wood in the astral flush of dawn,
And he sniffed the air from the hidden lair where the Khyber swordfish
  spawn,
And the bulge and belch of the glutton Welsh as they smelted their warlock
  cheese
Surge to and fro where the grinding flo wrenched at the headland's knees.

Then there was a sonnet by Merrill Moore that memorably ended:

> Knowledge of nature gives exemption to
> No one, his father, and to no one's son.
> No one is probably the only one
> Who lives any longer than most mortals do.

At first I secretly felt that the term "copy" for all written compositions implied a slap at art. If so, the slap fell gently at the *Herald Tribune*. Practically everyone in the shop either wrote well or hoped to, up to a point. The older and seasoned hands, such as Allen Raymond, who covered the Scottsboro trial, and Joe Driscoll, who covered the trial of Bruno Hauptmann, rapidly turned out clear, accurate narrative and were praised for this. Bob Peck, dean of the rewrite desk, converted simple data into human-interest stories with a light hand that reporters admired. Nobody despised well-noted detail and well-turned paragraphs. One night, as I toiled over a piece on a Greek Orthodox ceremony, Herzberg came over to counsel cutting it short and startled me a little by using the term of art: "I think it's beautiful now and I don't want it overwritten."

If I had been smarter or more ambitious I might have studied the city, as I had a perfect chance to do, to get a grasp of it by sectors and departments and put my daily missions into some larger frame. As it was, I saw each for itself in its peculiar light, and if the light seemed pictorial to my imagination I would have gone on describing it all night if I could. "Let's see you charm *me*," said Engelking one evening from his great height over my desk, consenting to further paragraphs about something or other of no importance. I did not charm him, at any rate not enough to get that piece in the paper. The truth was that I had more taste in writing than skill at it. And it often took me too long, detaching one thing from another in my gummy mind and deciding what to put down in what order. They were patient with me, all the same, never sharp or caustic. No doubt they had Alsop in mind; he had rewarded patience after taking the better part of a year to get the knack. After I had been for some months on the 2 P.M. shift, they tried me for some months on the day rewrite desk alongside the city desk from ten to six. This job meant doing brief pieces for boxes and writing obituaries, for which one went to a booth and called the bereaved. It also meant taking news stories by phone from stringers outside the city, one of whom awed me by his impeccable dictation of an impeccable narrative about an Army pilot's bad time trying to fly the mail out of Newark in heavy weather.

When I knocked off on winter evenings or late at night, I took the shuttle from Times Square to Grand Central and the East Side subway downtown to Eighth Street, then I walked west to Washington Square. On freezing nights as I passed Wanamaker's I would see in the deep ground-floor window embrasures the shapes of many derelict men sleeping under newspapers. They must have had the benefit of some heat from inside the building. I could thank God for a warm room and a bath. I had many excellent meals, too, in the Automat on 42nd Street, where the beans baked with molasses came in small appetizing earthenware jars. I even bought two books, *The Gentleman from San Franscisco*, by Ivan Bunin, and *A Nest of Simple Folk*, by Sean O'Faolain. On the tenth of January I was able to attend the opening performance of the Ballet Russe de Monte Carlo, seeing Tamara Toumanova and David Lichine in *Petrouchka*, an access of life in movement and music that would lift up hearts to the end of time. Few hearts were more than middling high that winter.

Reported in the paper in those months were these events among many: Governor Wilbur Cross of Connecticut approved plans for the $15,000,000 Merritt Parkway, to run from Port Chester, New York, to Hartford, Connecticut; one hundred and seventeen professors were dismissed from the University of Berlin; Navy beat Notre Dame on Borries's touchdown in the third period; Governor Henry Horner of Illinois spoke at the dedication of a reconstructed New Salem; Henry Pennypacker, from whom in 1929 I had received a handwritten affirmative note, died after years as Harvard's Dean of Admissions; the Prix Goncourt went to *La Condition humaine;* the repeal of Prohibition went into effect, and the paper printed page after page of notices for licensed liquor stores; Judge John Munro Wolsey ruled in favor of *Ulysses,* and Morris Ernst called it another repeal—of squeamishness in literature.

In February, extreme cold, as low as fourteen below, came to the city. As it happened, I owned no overcoat but got along with a voluminous black Burberry, worn with a soft black hat and a Left Bank air. This garment now failed me. Nauseated and fevered on waking one morning, I went shuddering across the Square to the Fifth Avenue Chemists at the Eighth Street corner and called McLendon to say I had the flu and would not be in. All I could do then was to stay in bed, and I did so for three days, fully aware of not being missed on the newspaper or anywhere else. When the fever finally broke, I made it again, like thistledown, across the Square to the softly sparkling dining room of the Grosvenor Hotel, where a white-jacketed waiter served me hot milk and buttered toast, one on the other, sugared, steaming lightly, yellow and white, pure and delectable, alimentation's very soul.

4

Sam Brewer had been at the University of Paris the year before and had been taken on the paper at about the same time as I had, a tall, soft-spoken, cheerful boy whose instincts and destiny were those of a news-paperman. He was reading Jules Romains's *roman à fleuve* and lent me some of the volumes. We dined at Bleeck's a few times, watching Walker and the established reporters playing the famous match game, but the Automat better suited our position in life. On evenings when we got off early we would sometimes, for lack of anything better to do, spend an hour in Minsky's burlesque house on 42nd Street, listening to the bawdy buffoonery of comedians and watching the routines of the strippers, Gypsy Rose Lee pacing back and forth like a lady as she coquettishly plucked off her clothes, or pug-faced Georgia Southern, a striding strumpet, tossing her red hair in a tom-tom beat of bumps and grinds.

The only girl I had in the world, if indeed I had any, was holding down a job in St. Louis. No girls appeared in the city room, where there was only one woman reporter, steely-gray Emma Bugbee, who attended to society news. Too hard-pressed most of the time to think of that missing half of humanity, I could suddenly become aware of it after work and head for the Rosebud taxi-dance parlor on 42nd Street. Here a few dollars would buy tickets for brief dancing with the essentially naked though silk-sheathed figure of your choice, often a quite pretty and well-spoken girl. A number that winter were from Fall River, their jobs gone, no doubt, when the mills shut down. Dancing could be a preliminary with at least some of them, but I could afford no more and only made free now and then, as with one girl's memorable nipples that seemed the Rosebud incarnate. Olive-skinned and sturdy, she took no particular notice. Late in the winter I met through friends in the city two good-looking girls who were nicer, or at least not in need of employment. One, with honey hair, I took to a performance of *Tristan* at the Metropolitan and permanently miffed by dozing off beside her. The other I took to *Four Saints in Three Acts* and impulsively kissed at parting. She had left her compact in my pocket. The next day I was called to the telephone in the city room and had to arrange to return this, aroused but with sinking heart at what I divined to be my destiny.

"To Carthage then I came / Burning . . ." Apart from having fallen in love several times and communed with the girls in question in retired places—rather boldly, I thought in my ignorance—I had scarcely burned like the saint in the poem, before or after coming to Carthage. In Paris at eighteen I had made fun of my school roommate for wanting to try a cherished address someone had given him to a house in the Rue Blondel. What figures we would have cut! My companion had cursed me heartily and justly, but he had refrained. Now as the American city extended its snares I wouldn't have known how to fall into them if I had wanted to. But I had one startling experience of burning, not my own.

One night in mild weather at the end of winter I woke up at three or so in the morning to a scratching noise at my door. I thought it must be a dog, then heard in the dead silence of that hour a low voice that made my hair stand up, for it pled to be let in, not as one suffering from cold and exposure but as a wooer. It seemed a young man's educated voice but I had certainly never heard it before. "Oh, don't be afraid," it pled. "Oh, don't be afraid," it sobbed. Vain appeal. I was very much afraid,

afraid of the mystery of that extremity directed at myself, and afraid to do or say anything whatever. Homosexual advances had been made to me to my embarrassment in my teens: one by a feverish nudging youth in a movie theater, one by a graying small-town aesthete and satyr; but nothing had prepared me for this last-ditch supplication in the small hours. Whoever he was, in the end he gave up and went away.

Nightmares, then, were to be met in the city by night, and souls driven to verges. Of the traditional underworld of vice and crime I learned little on assignment beyond what a few police sergeants had to say to incidental questioning by phone. My desk in the city room was directly behind that of the police reporter, Lem Jones, who looked like a brawny plowboy, but what he had to say he usually said at length and loudly on his typewriter, and I saw nothing of him in other hours. Once, though, he loped in, flinging his jacket off, jerking at his tie, and as he sat down to bang away he expressed himself vocally for a change: "Jesus Christ I never saw anything like it in my life" followed by a few explosive details. What had broken was a story of perversion in the prison on Welfare Island, of prisoners with wigs and paint making themselves women for other prisoners. There was a nightmare, sure enough.

Other odd moments in the life of the city room would remain with me all my days: red-headed Jack Gould with his pale face and sardonic eyes grinning and murmuring out of the side of his mouth, "Look at Walker . . ." as the city editor paced balefully up and down behind a writer far behind in delivering necessary copy; Homer Bigart, stiffly busy, briefly amused, setting his honest face with its thin mustache against the badinage of reporters bent on wasting their time and his—his that would turn out as the years passed to be that of a first-rate professional; Ben Robertson, an ever cool and melodious Alabaman, speaking in his soft voice of the "Mr. Flood" stories that Joseph Mitchell of the *World Telegram* had begun to publish in *The New Yorker*, "Ah think Joe Mitchell's a genius . . ."

After my period of breaking in on the day rewrite desk, I went back on the 2 P.M. shift in the spring. Wilcox now gave me a raise to twenty-five a week. So enriched, I thought I could move up in the world, or at least out of Strunsky's basement. Half a block away on Sullivan Street two tenements had been remodeled into a small stucco apartment house with the amenity of a courtyard in which a puny fountain played. My room and bath on the top floor, up four flights, cost me thirty-five a month. Since an open kitchenette occupied one wall, I could save money by making my own breakfasts. I knew how to scramble eggs. At Macy's I bought on terms a studio couch, sheets, blankets, an unpainted chest of drawers, an unpainted table and chair, a desk lamp, a pot, a pan, a skillet, and a percolator, with a few cups and dishes and some tableware. My two windows gave on the courtyard, and under one I placed my table in the light from a lot of sky. Off to the right through many washing lines I could look down on a section of the Elevated. I bought two candlesticks and candles and set them on the table with my Oxford text of the *Odyssey* beneath, making a kind of lectern or altar in imitation of Aschenbach, toward whom in fact I felt irreverent. Ritually, when I could, I read a few lines of Homer by candlelight. I bought another book, Huxley's edition of Lawrence's letters. That would hold me.

It was not what the upper class is supposed to call a good neighborhood. In the tenements nearby were discontented women highly audible as windows were left open in the spring weather: viragos, who went in for prolonged bouts of screeching over their washing lines. Short of screeching back, nothing could be done about this. Then another threat to sleep in the morning hours came through the flimsy wall near which I lay—a far pleasanter but still rousing noise. At eight o'clock regularly someone began plucking at a stringed instrument, practicing, over and over, the tune of "Greensleeves." After a week of this, I got into bathrobe and slippers and knocked. A thin and dark young woman, saucer-eyed and voluble, sympathized at once and told me all about herself. Her father was Ernst Bloch, conductor of the Berlin Philharmonic. Her name was Suzanne. She had only one ovary. Her instrument was a lute. An upright piano stood against her wall. What a godsend! Assured of access to the piano by my new and admirable friend, I brought over my settings of Elizabethan lute songs.

As the weather turned warmer, a new and insidious distraction turned up. Across the courtyard lived a woman who wore nothing at all while she did her housework, briskly dusting her window sills. When her husband came home, she took him on in what seemed a naked fencing match. Aware that I had no business being aware of these people at all, I would try on my day off to sit and work at my table before the window, by turns denying and conceding my attention to the windows across the way. I told my friends that I had a couple of nudists for neighbors, a way of dismissing the matter lightly, but in truth I felt seduced and annoyed. Once more, something by my lights and previous learning unthinkable presented itself in the city.

That spring I covered among other things the model sailboat regatta in Central Park. I did a story on a foolhardy boy with an unpromising little sloop setting out on a round-the-world cruise. He sent me a letter from the Canal Zone, then disappeared forever. I wrote up a Civilian Conservation Corps camp across the Hudson under command of a regular Army major, a tall and extremely trim West Pointer, proud of the road his battalion of salvaged city boys had begun to build through the woods. There were days of great interest, like that one, and days on which I felt I did well as a reporter. I never shirked anything and I did a day's labor. There had also been, from the beginning, stale and weary days when the city room seemed alien and I had to call on fortitude to take me to work. Now in May came the assignment that brought things to a head for me on the paper: that of covering a demonstration at the National Academy of Sciences. Someone had had the bright idea of recording a symphony from various points in the orchestra so that strings, woodwinds, brasses, and percussion, for example, would each stand out as an entity. What I heard in the course of this experiment struck me as something other than music, and less. Back at the city desk I told Engleking it was worth three paragraphs, which I then produced. In the next day's *Times* Bill Lawrence, the science writer, made the front page with a signed two-column story on this event, correctly perceived as the beginning of all that it began.

No could miss this revelation of at least two traits that unfitted me for reporting as a profession. I was incurious about twentieth-century gadgets and almost pathologically unimpressed by them, and I had no real interest in the newspaperman's dream of a byline on the front page. The emulation that kept my friends on their toes, the longing for a scoop and the chance to bat it out, take after take, did not really move me at all. Although no one told me, I knew I had muffed that assignment and before long knew that conclusions had been drawn, when one day Walker confided to me that he heard there was a good job opening at J. Walter Thompson. Scorning J. Walter Thompson, I elected to stick at reporting, but the next thing I knew Walker amiably put me under the wing of the business editor, who needed an assistant, and I moved to a desk next to his in his corner.

This was not quite like being sent to Siberia. It was even a modest position of trust, because when the business editor took his two-week vacation in August I had the duty of filling his three columns daily and sweated faithfully over the job. But I had come to a standstill of a kind. The business editor, Harvey Runner, had been a newspaperman all his life, first on a number of small-town papers and then in the city; he knew no other life. Square-toed, narrow-shouldered, pale, Palooka-like, he always spoke a little as though his mouth were full, winning from Walker, so I had heard but I am sure he had not, the *commedia dell'arte* title, Flanneltongue. He lived alone in a flat somewhere and was a kind and decent man. "Business" meant the retail business. Norman Stabler, who edited the financial section and news of corporations and markets, never meddled with Runner's three columns, which appeared daily under their separate heading. His beat, which I now began to share, took him daily to the New York headquarters of various trade associations, notably the National Retail Dry Goods Association, for scuttlebutt from their press agents as well as news stories ready to release. Press releases, in any case, cut down and touched up, gave us a good proportion of our space. With him I got further instruction on the making of the newspaper, helping to write headlines to fit or going along to the press room, where corrections could be made directly on the linotype machines.

Two or three poems that I had done the year before appeared in *Poetry* that year. In the city room one day on the way to the water cooler I met Jack Gould and felt myself being looked over. "Say," he said, "did you have some stuff in *Poetry?* My sister says it's pretty good." As he did not disassociate himself from his sister, I took this as more friendly than not. It was one more reminder, though, of the distance between my daily occupation and the matters that I thought about when I could. Not that the business corner focused the mind on a negligible side of life. The uneasiness I had felt as a boy about the Manhattan skyline, for example, could now be formulated: while the steeples of America seen in country towns or inland cities invoked heaven and aspired to it, the skyscrapers did not; they chiefly aspired to multiply office floors upward so that a small plot of ground, of island rock, would hold a huge working force. So much for their ostentation and power. In the light of art and imagination my daily routine had become grubbier. At the same time the practice of art and imagination seemed more and more frequently recalled to mind. My friend Jim Agee over at *Fortune* with his transcending passion would not let them drop. Other friends turned up, gifted writing men who had weathered the year in poverty elsewhere: Bill Maxwell from the West Indies, Sherry Mangan from Mexico. I could and did sometimes visit Suzy in the flat next door and try things like "The Peaceful Western Wind" on her piano while she came in with her lute. When a professional friend, a gnomelike Dolmetsch, came over from England, Suzy did me the honor of having me in. A man I had known in college took me along to hear his friend Ralph Kirkpatrick beautifully play the Goldberg Variations on someone's grand piano. In September a sculptress, a moon-faced serious young woman, moved into the empty flat on my floor with her smock, her armatures, her wet clay under rags, so that now I had someone practicing an art on each side of me, hemming me in. Moreover I now fell in love, as I had thought I would, with the girl whom I had taken to *Four Saints in Three Acts*—a girl with a haunting flair for acting and dancing and writing as well.

Then there were the Stocktons. Herbert, big and gray and blind-looking but hearty, practiced law in a firm downtown, Miriam brought people who interested her together in their softly lit house on 76th Street. Over the mantel young Miriam with a ribbon round her lovely throat looked out with sibylline brown eyes as Sargent had seen her. He had not seen her in her rowboat with her Bostonian friend, Fanny, crossing the water to drop in on the monks at Mount Athos, a figure I preferred in fancy to Mr. Sargent's. The Stocktons had supported the Laboratory Theater in the '20s and were modest patrons of several arts. On every New Year's Eve they gave a party for classmates of their only son, Peter, whom they had lost to his own hand in Santa Fe. At this party, this year, I had met them. After that from time to time they invited me for an evening or, having a spare ticket, to a concert by the Dessof Choirs or the Philharmonic. They would have liked me to believe, as they did, in Rudolf Steiner.

In those days what I believed in and conceived, in spite of everything, to be my calling was the making of poems. And I had one underway, a movement that my ear had given me, perhaps under the spell of all the music—one that demanded a certain length. I had never composed anything remotely of that length. It was possibly the most important thing in the world. I had at most one day a week on which to envision it and hear it, to let it happen or make it happen. I wasn't getting anywhere, much, on this poem. And with one thing and another, as summer turned to fall, I began to feel pinned down. My Long Island uncle and aunt had taken their family to California, where Uncle John had a new and better job. "Hang on," he wrote to me. "Hang on a little longer." But I had on my hands, so to speak, the destruction prophesied by Milman Parry. Doubly defeated, I had failed as a reporter and I had failed my gift. And I could see no way out. Lying in bed that fall, in solitude at dead of night, I let myself go several times in a prisoner's paroxysm, resting on head and heels with my body buckled up rigidly as a bent bow. There in the darkness, contorted rather as in the old days in a Pullman berth but this time in anguish, I strove with my muscles against my fate.

OF TIME AND
THE GREAT DEAD

Death has engraved them
Lovely and lofty, and my metaphysic
Smiles to align them here, the shadowy ones
Tinted so faint, yet luminous as gems.

From "Colorado"

What measure shall I give these generations
That breathe on the void and are void
And exist and do not exist

Oedipus Rex

James Agee: A Memoir

1

The office building where we worked presented on the ground floor one of the first of those showrooms, enclosed in convex, nonreflecting plate glass, in which a new automobile revolved slowly on a turntable. On Sunday a vacant stillness overcame this exhibition. The building bore the same name as the automobile. It had been erected in the late '20s as a monument to the car, the engineer, and the company, and for a time it held the altitude record until the Empire State Building went higher. It terminated aloft in a glittering spearpoint of metal sheathing. From the fifty-second and fiftieth floors where Agee and I respectively had offices, you looked down on the narrow cleft of Lexington Avenue and across at the Grand Central Building, or you looked north or south over the city or across the East River toward Queens. As a boom-time skyscraper it had more generous stories than later structures of the kind, higher ceilings, an airier interior. Office doors were frosted in the old-fashioned way, prevalent when natural daylight still had value with designers. In a high wind at our altitude you could feel the sway of the building, a calculated yielding of structural steel. Thus contact of a sort was maintained with weather and the physical world. In our relationship to this building there were moments of great simplicity, moments when we felt like tearing it down with our bare hands. We would have had to work our way from interior partitions to plaster shell to exterior facing, ripping it away, girder after girder, until the whole thing made rubble and jackstraws in 43rd Street. Jim was vivid in this mood, being very powerful and long-boned, with long strong hands and fingers, and having in him likewise great powers of visualization and haptic imagination, so that you could almost hear the building cracking up under his grip.

He was visited on at least one occasion by a fantasy of shooting our employer. This was no less knowingly histrionic and hyperbolic than the

---

First published as an introduction to *The Collected Short Prose of James Agee* (Boston: Houghton Mifflin, 1968). Reprinted by permission of The James Agee Trust.

other. Our employer, the Founder, was a poker-faced strong man with a dented nose, well-modeled lips, and distant gray-blue eyes under bushy brows; from his boyhood in China he retained something, a trace of facial mannerism, that suggested the Oriental. His family name was a New England and rather a seafaring name; you can find it on slate headstones in the burial grounds of New Bedford and Nantucket and Martha's Vineyard. These headstones in the middle years of the last century were fitted with tintypes of the dead as living, reminders on the spot of what form they were to reassume on the Last Day, provided that the day should occur before the tintypes utterly faded, as now seems not altogether unlikely. The Founder had that seacoast somewhere in him behind his mask, and he had a Yankee voice rather abrupt and twangy, undeterred by an occasional stammer. A Bones man at Yale, a driving man and civilized as well, quick and quizzical, interested and shrewd, he had a fast sure script on memoranda and as much ability as anyone in the place. He had nothing to fear from the likes of us. Jim imagined himself laying the barrel of the pistol at chest level on the Founder's desk and making a great bang. I imagine he imagined himself assuming the memorable look of the avenger whom John Ford photographed behind a blazing pistol in *The Informer*. It is conceivable that the Founder on occasion, and after his own fashion, returned the compliment.

The period I am thinking of covers '36 and '37, but now let me narrow it to late spring or early summer of '36. Roosevelt was about to run for a second term against Alf Landon, and in Spain we were soon to understand that a legitimate Republic had been attacked by a military and Fascist uprising. One day Jim appeared in my office unusually tall and quiet and swallowing with excitement (did I have a moment?) to tell me something in confidence. It appeared very likely, though not yet dead sure, that they were going to let him go out on a story, a story of tenant farming in the deep South, and even that they would let him have as his photographer the only one in the world really fit for the job: Walker Evans. It was pretty well beyond anything he had hoped for from *Fortune*. He was stunned, exalted, scared clean through, and felt like impregnating every woman on the fifty-second floor. So we went over to a bar on Third Avenue. Here I heard, not really for the first time and certainly not for the last, a good deal of what might be called the theory of *Let Us Now Praise Famous Men*, a book that was conceived that day, occupied him for the next three years, and is the center piece in the life and writing of my friend. It may occur to you that if he had not been employed in our building and by our employer (though upon both at times he would gladly have attracted besides his own the wrath of God), he would never have had the opportunity of writing it. That is true; and it is also true that if he had not been so employed the challenge and the necessity of writing it might never have pressed upon him so gravely as for some years to displace other motives for writing, other ends to be achieved by writing, including those of which the present book is a reminder.

2

The native ground and landscape of his work, of his memory, was Knoxville and the Cumberland Plateau, but his professional or vocational school was one that for a couple of years I shared. You entered it from shabby Cambridge by brick portals on which were carven stone tablets showing an open book and the word VERITAS, a word—not that we paid it then the slightest attention—destined to haunt us like a Fury. The time I am thinking of now is February of 1930 in the Yard of that college where the stripped elms barely shadowed the colonial brickwork, and planks on the paths bore our feet amid clotted snow. On a Wednesday afternoon in the dust of a classroom I became sharply aware for the first time of Mr. Agee, pronounced quickly *Ay-gee*. We had been asked each to prepare a lyric for reading aloud. The figure in the front row on my right, looming and brooding and clutching his book his voice very low, almost inaudible but deliberate and distinct, as though ground fine by great interior pressure, went through that poem of Donne's that has the line *A bracelet of bright hair about the bone*. It was clear that the brainy and great versing moved him as he read. So here, in the front row, were shyness and power and imagination, and here moreover was an edge of assertion, very soft, in the choice and reading of this poem, because the instructor for whom he was reading did not belong to the new School of Donne.

After this, Agee and I would sometimes have a Lucky together and talk for a few minutes outside Seaver Hall in the bitter or sweet New England weather. Seniority was his, then and for that matter forever, since he was a year older and a class ahead. He lived in the Yard and we had no friends in common. Older, darker, larger than I, a rangy boy, alert and gentle, but sardonic, with something of the frontiersman or hillman about him—a hard guy in more than the fashion of the time—wearing always a man's clothes, a dark suit and vest, old and uncared for, but clothes. His manner, too, was undergraduate with discrimination. He was reading Virgil that year under a professor whose middle initial had drawn down upon him the name of Pea Green William; Agee grimly referred to him strictly as Green. In the Seaver classroom with a handful of others we gave our attention to English metrics as expounded by our instructor, the Boylston Professor, who had set his face against Eliot and Pound. Faintly graying, faintly blurred, boyish and cheerful, mannerly and mild, he turned back to us each week our weekly sets of verses with marginal scrawls both respectful and pertinent. He was also good at reading aloud. Our metrical sense was educated by such things as the hovering beat of "Hark All You Ladies," and we heard the heroic couplet doomed by Romantic orchestration in "Whether on Ida's Shady Brow."

Far away from college, in the realm where great things could happen, great things had in fact happened that year: works of imagination and art in newly printed books, and these we pored and rejoiced and smarted over: *A Farewell to Arms*, most cleanly written of elegies to love in war, in the Great War whose shallow helmets, goggled masks, and khaki puttees were familiar to our boyhood; *Look Homeward, Angel*, the only work by an American that could stand with *A Portrait of the Artist as a Young Man*; and *The Innocent Voyage*, from which we learned a new style of conceiving childhood. Agee and I were very fond of these books. We were also devoted to Ring Lardner and to all the Joyce that we knew. But "The Waste Land," which had made my foundations shift, had not affected him in the same way, nor did "Ash Wednesday" seem to him as uncanny and *cantabile* and beyond literature as it did to me. Here we diverged, and would remain divided in some degree, as he desired in poetry something both more and less than I did, who chiefly wanted it to be hair-raising.

In *The Harvard Advocate* that year there were poems by J. R. Agee, but to my intolerant eye they seemed turgid and technically flawed. I did not see until several years later the highly mannered and rather beautiful "Epithalamium" that he wrote in the spring. "Ann Garner" was a more complicated matter. This longish poem appeared in the quarterly, *Hound & Horn*, still known that year by the subtitle, *A Harvard Miscellany*, and edited by the princely Lincoln Kirstein, then in his last year as an undergraduate. Kirstein had known James Rufus Agee as a new boy at Exeter four or five years before, and there is a passage on Jim in his book, *Rhymes of a Pfc.*, finally published in 1964. "Ann Garner" had been written, in fact, while Jim was still at Exeter in 1928. Boys in prep school do not often write anything so sustained, and it is clear from one of Jim's letters what an effort it had been. In the first year of our friendship it impressed me more than any of his other verse for the ambition of the attempt at narrative with variations, not really like Jeffers but reaching like him toward myth, a vision of elemental life in the American earth.

What brought me fully awake to Agee as a writer was not this poem, callow even in its power, but a short story in the April *Advocate*. Two boys hunting with a BB gun in the outskirts of Knoxville got some infant robins out of a nest and decided they must be "put out of their misery," so while the mother bird flew shrill and helpless overhead they did the deed with stones. In puzzlement, in awe, in fascination, in boastful excitement—in shame, in revulsion. The younger boy threw up; the boys went home. That was about all, but the writer fully realized and commanded his little event. When I reread this story after thirty-three years I saw that he had put into it some of the skills and passions of his life: sympathy with innocent living nature, and love of it; understanding of congested stupidity and cruelty, and hatred of it; a stethoscopic ear for mutations of feeling; an ironic ear for idiom; a descriptive gift. No other contributor to the *Advocate* that year (in what other year?) wrote with ease, and repeatedly, prose like this:

> The birds were very young. A mildew fuzz covered their heads and backs, along their wings lay little white spikes, like hair-fine fishbones. Through the membrane globing their monstrous bellies the children could see a mass of oystery colours, throbbing faintly. The birds kicked, and gaped, and clenched their wings.

Significantly, too, the story intimated a pained interest in the relation between the actuality of birds and boys—licking and gaping—and the American institution of "Church" or weekly Christian observance. The two hunters, parting uneasily after their crime, agreed to meet at Sunday school.

3

By simply descending a flight of steps and pushing through a turnstile for a nickel you could leave the university behind and set off for the big-city mystery of Boston, where wine in coffee cups could be drunk at the Olympia or *arak* at the Ararat on Atlantic Avenue; then other adventures would follow. If the Yard was our dooryard, Boston and neighborhood were the backyard we explored, and Jim later wrote a short catalogue of attractions that he liked:

> Window table in Tremont St. Childs, brilliant Sunday midmorning; the New England Boxing Tournament, for steady unsparing (if unskillful) ferocity; Boston Common with an actor and hangover and peanuts and pigeons, midafternoon; the Common on a rainy afternoon or night; on a snowy night; on a Sailor's night; the Fenway at about dusk, fair weather; for good movie stuff: the Arlington Theatre and lampposts from just beyond the level bridge; the debouchement of the Forest Hills subway . . . Revere Beach in midwinter, for sea sounds and pure ghoulishness; East Boston for swell houses, stunted trees struck through with mordant street lamps, and general dilapidation; the Arnold Arboretum in October or May; up the Charles at midnight, down at dawn; the fishboats unloading before dawn. . . .

We lacked neither opportunity nor time for excursions like these and for a good deal of what we had to concede was Young Love. As for the university, it could be contented with a few classes a week and a few sleepless nights before exams. Considering human bondage in general and the demands of any other mode of life, it is remarkable that Agee and I both talked of breaking for freedom from this one, but we did, and he even had a plan of bumming to the Coast that spring on the chance of getting a movie job. If he had, the American Cinema might have felt his impact twenty years before it took place. I reconcile myself to things having turned out as they did. He waited until summer and went west to work as a harvest hand and day laborer in Oklahoma, Kansas, and Nebraska.

Jim had been briefly in England and France in the summer of his sixteenth year, on a bicycle trip with his boyhood and lifelong friend, Father James Flye. Although he never returned to Europe, he had absorbed enough to sharpen his eye and ear for his own country. It can be said of him that he was American to the marrow, in every obvious way and in some not so obvious, not at all inconsistent with the kind of interest that some years later kept us both up until three in the morning looking through drawings by Cocteau, or some years later still enabled him to correct for me a mistranslation of Rimbaud. He took Patrick Henry's alternatives very seriously. Deep in him there was a streak of Whitman, including a fondness for the barbaric yawp, and a streak of Twain, the riverman and Romantic democrat. What being an American meant for an imaginative writer was very much on his mind. His summer wandering fell in, so to speak, with his plans.

Two short stories written out of his working summers appeared in the next year's *Advocate* and are reprinted in this book. They are the last fiction Jim published as a young man, the last he would publish until *The Morning Watch* in 1950. In both stories you may feel the satisfaction of the narrator in being disencumbered of his baggage, intellectual or cultural, urban and familiar and social, and enabled to focus on the naked adventure at hand. The adventure in each case partly happened and was partly made up; the stories are pure fiction in the usual way of pure fiction, as much so as stories by Hemingway, their godfather. My point is that to conceive and feel them on his skin he had deprived himself of all the distraction that he liked—company, music, movies, and books—and had lived in lean poverty like a lens. To write them, and almost everything else that he had to work on for any length of time, he took on destitution by removing himself from class-bells, Thayer Hall, and his roommates and holing up in the *Advocate* office for days and nights until the job was done. Advocate House at that time was a small frame building up an alley, containing a few tables and chairs and an old leather-covered couch, all pleasantly filthy; and there were of course places round about where you could get coffee and hamburgers or western sandwiches at any hour of the night. A boardinghouse bedroom or an empty boxcar might have been still better.

Did he ever draw any conclusions from all this? He certainly did. He never forgot what it meant to him to be on the bum, and he managed it or something like it when he could. His talent for accumulating baggage of all the kinds I have mentioned was very great, as it was very endearing, and he spent much of his life trying to clear elbowroom for himself amid the clutter. But on the question as to whether he had any business coming back to college that year, his third and my second, the answer is Yes, and the best reason was Ivor Armstrong Richards.

In the second semester, on his way back to Magdalene, Cambridge, from a lectureship at Tsing Hua University in Peking, Richards paused at Harvard and gave two courses, one on modern English literature and the other carrying on those experiments in the actual effects of poetry that he had begun at Cambridge and had written up in his book, *Practical Criticism* (1929). Jim and I attended both courses and found ourselves at full stretch. Though he appeared shy and donnish, Richards was in fact intrepid and visionary beyond anyone then teaching literature at Harvard; when he talked about our papers he sometimes gave me the impression that he had spent the night thinking out what he would say in the morning. By pure analysis he used to create an effect like that produced by turning up an old-fashioned kerosene lamp, and he himself would be so warmed and illuminated that he would turn into a spellbinder, gently holding sway, fixing with his glinting gray eyes first one quarter and then another of the lecture room. When he spoke of the splendors of Henry James's style or of Conrad facing the storm of the universe, we felt that he was their companion and ours in the enterprise of art.

Richards' exacting lucidity and Jim's interest in the "Metaphysicals" are reflected in a poem in octosyllabics called "The Truce," printed in the *Advocate* for May 1931, the first poem of Jim Agee's that seemed to me as fully disciplined and professional as his prose. I not only admired but envied it and tried to do as well. The image of the facing mirrors fascinated him and made its last appearance in his work twenty years later, in *The Morning Watch* and in his commentary for the film, *The Quiet One*. There is an echo in "The Truce," as there is also in one of the sonnets, of a great choral passage ("Behold All Flesh Is as the Grass") in the Brahms *Requiem*, which he sang that spring in the Harvard Glee Club; the surging and falling theme stayed in our heads for years.

Along with his stories, "The Truce" would be evidence enough— though there is explicit evidence in one of his letters—that in the spring of 1931 Jim held the English Poetic Tradition and the American Scene in a kind of equilibrium under the spell of Richards, and lived at a higher pitch, but at the same time more at ease with his own powers, than in any other college year. He was elected President of the *Advocate* and thus became the remote Harvard equivalent of a big man on campus. We still saw one another rarely aside from class meetings, but had now one or two friends in common, including Kirstein and a superb girl at Radcliffe, a dark-eyed delicately scornful being who troubled him before she troubled me; I can still see his grin of commiseration and tribute.

4

In the world at large where the beautiful books had happened, something else had begun to happen that in the next few years fixed the channel of Jim Agee's life. I was in England in '31–'32 and saw nothing of him that year, when he got his degree, nor in the next year when I was back at Harvard to get mine. What gradually swam over everyone in the meantime was an ominous and astringent shadow already named by one cold intellect as the economic consequences of the peace. Worse evils and terrors were coming, but at the time this one seemed bad enough, simple as it was. People had less and less money and less and less choice of how to earn it, if they could earn any at all. Under a reasonable dispensation a man who had proved himself a born writer before he left the university could go ahead in that profession, but this did not seem to be the case in the United States in 1932. Neither in Boston nor New York nor elsewhere did there appear any livelihood appropriate for a brilliant President of *The Harvard Advocate*, nor any mode of life resembling that freedom of research that I have sketched as ours at Harvard. In the shrunken market the services of an original artist were not in demand. Hart Crane and Vachel Lindsay took their lives that spring. Great gifts always set their possessors apart, but not necessarily apart from any chance to exercise them; this gift at that time pretty well did. If a freshman in '29 could feel confined by the university, in '32 it seemed a confinement all too desirable by contrast with what lay ahead—either work of the limited kinds that worried people would pay for, or bumming in earnest, winter-bumming, so to say. Agee thankfully took the first job he could get and joined the staff of *Fortune* a month after graduation.

During the next winter, back in Cambridge, where my Senior English tutor was studying *Das Kapital* and referred to capitalist society as a sick cat, we heard of Jim working at night in a skyscraper with a phonograph going full blast. Thus a writer of fiction and verse became a shop-member on a magazine dedicated by the Founder to American business, considered as the heart of the American Scene. It is odd and, I think, suspicious that even at that point in the great Depression Jim did not live for a while on his family and take the summer to look around. Dwight MacDonald, then on the staff of *Fortune*, had been in correspondence with Jim for a year or two and had bespoken a job for him on the strength of his writing—which incidentally included a parody of *Time*, done as one entire issue of the *Advocate*. The man who was then managing editor of *Fortune* was clever enough to recognize in Agee abilities that *Fortune* would be lucky to employ, and he would have had it in him to make Jim think he might lose the job if he did not take it at once. I do not know, however, that this occurred. What else Jim could have done I don't know either; but again at this time there was the alternative of Hollywood, and there might have been other jobs, like that of forest ranger, which would have given him a healthy life and a living and left his writing alone. Now and again during the next few years he would wonder about things like that.

At all events, he hadn't been on *Fortune* three months before he applied for a Guggenheim Fellowship, in October 1932. Nothing came of this application, as nothing came of another one five years later. In the '32 application (of which he kept a carbon copy among his papers) he proposed as his chief labor the continuation of a long satirical poem, *John Carter*, which he had begun at Harvard, and said he would also perhaps finish a long short story containing a "verse passacaglia." The title of the story was to be "Let Us Now Praise Famous Men"; I never saw and have not recovered his draft of it. For opinions of his previous writing he referred the judging committee to Myron Williams, an English teacher at Exeter, Conrad Aiken, and I. A. Richards. For opinions of *John Carter* he referred them to Archibald MacLeish, Stephen Vincent Benét, Robert Hillyer, Theodore Spencer, and Bernard DeVoto. Phelps Putnam, he said, would also be willing to give an opinion. If awarded a fellowship he would work mainly on the poem, "which shall attempt a diversified and comprehensive reflection and appraisal of contemporary American civilization and which ultimately, it is hoped, will hold water as an 'Anatomy of Evil.'" He would work on it "as long as the money held out," and he thought he could make it last at least two years. "I don't think I would spend much time about any university," he said; "I expect I would live in France, in some town both cheap and within reach of Paris." It is a fair inference from this that in October '32, he did not yet know that he would marry Olivia Saunders in the following January. Both in October and January he must have considered that he had a good chance of a Guggenheim. On his record he was justified in thinking so. Yet in the last sentence of his "project" for *John Carter* his offhand honesty about the prospect of never finishing it may have handed the Guggenheim committee a reason for turning him down.

The two long sections that he got written, with some unplaced fragments, have been printed in *The Collected Poems of James Agee*. His hero, never developed beyond conception in the poem as it stands, would have owed something not only to Byron's Don Juan but, I think, to the Nihilist superman Stavrogin in *The Possessed* of Dostoevsky, a novel we were studying with Richards in the spring of '31—greatly to the increase of hyperconsciousness in us both. Jim's fairly savage examination of certain Episcopalian attitudes and décor—and even more, the sheer amount of this—indicates quite adequately how "Church" and "organized religion" in relation to awe and vision bothered his mind. Another value, almost another faith, emerges in the profound respect (as well as disrespect) accorded to the happy completion of love. When

Jim spoke of "joy" he most often meant this, or meant this as his criterion.

5

Moderate ambitions may be the thing for some people at some ages, but they were not for James Agee, and certainly not at twenty-three. To make "a complete appraisal of contemporary civilization," no less, was what he hoped to do with his long poem. Now the Founder, Henry Luce, with his magazines, actually held a quite similar ambition, and this accounts for the mixture of attraction and repulsion in Agee's feeling for his job. Attraction because *Fortune* took the world for its province, and because the standard of workmanship on the magazine was high. Also because economic reality, the magazine's primary field, appeared grim and large in everyone's life at that time, and because by courtesy of *Fortune* the world lay open to its editors and they were made free of anything that in fact or art or thought had bearing on their work. Repulsion because that freedom in truth was so qualified, because the ponderous and technically classy magazine identified itself from the start, and so compromised itself (not dishonestly, but by the nature of things), with one face of the civilization it meant to appraise; whatever it might incidentally value, it was concerned with power and practical intelligence, not with the adventurous, the beautiful, and the profound—words we avoided in those days but for which referents none the less existed. At heart Agee knew his vocation to be in mortal competition, if I may put it so, with the Founder's enterprise. For *Fortune* to enlist Agee was like Germany enlisting France.

Nevertheless he had now three uninterrupted years of it. One blessing was the presence on *Fortune* of Archibald MacLeish, a Yaleman like the Founder and one of the original editors, but also a fine artist who knew Jim for another, respected him, and helped him. MacLeish in 1932 was forty and had published his big poem, *Conquistador*. Being experienced and distinguished, he could pick the subjects that appealed to him, and being a clearheaded lawyer-turned-poet, he wrote both well and efficiently. His efficiency was a byword on *Fortune*. Requiring all research material on cards in orderly sequence, he merely flipped through his cards and wrote in longhand until five o'clock, when he left the office. Often enough other people, including Jim, would be there most of the night.

I had a brief glimpse of the scene when I got to New York in the summer of '33. The city lay weary and frowsy in a stench of Depression through which I walked for many days, many miles up and down town, answering ads, seeing doubtful men in dusty offices, looking for a job. MacLeish got me an interview with a rather knifelike *Fortune* editor who read what writing I had to show and clearly sized me up as a second but possibly even more difficult Agee, where one was already enough. Staring out of the window reflectively at Long Island he told me in fact that the Founder had taken a good deal from Agee, allowing for Agee's talent, but that there were limits. Back in MacLeish's office I waited while he, the old backfield man, warm and charming as ever, called up Jim. So Jim came in and we poets talked. One subject was the current plight of Kenneth Patchen, a poet dogged by misfortune. Archie also mentioned Hart Crane, whom he had once persuaded *Fortune* to take on for a trial. Hart had been completely unable to do it. It did not cross my mind that this had any relevance to me. I felt elated over my visit, and Jim took me home to dinner.

The basement apartment on Perry Street had a backyard where grew an ailanthus tree, and there under the slim leaves we sat until dark, he and Via and I, drinking I don't remember what but I imagine Manhattans, a fashion of the period. After dinner we went to the piano and sang some of the Brahms *Requiem*. Then he got out his manuscripts, read from *John Carter*, and read a new poem, a beauty, "Theme with Variations" (later he called it "Night Piece"). *Fortune*, I suppose at MacLeish's suggestion, had assigned him an article on the Tennessee Valley Authority, and in the course of preparing it he had gone back that summer to the countryside of his boyhood: hence, I think, this poem. In that evening's dusk and lamplight neither of us had any doubt that we shared a vocation and would pursue it, come what might. We were to have a good many evenings like it during the next three years while that particular *modus vivendi* lasted for Jim Agee as office worker and husband.

Jim must have thought *Fortune* would have me (*Time*, instead, had me, but not until February of '36), because at the end of August when I was temporarily out of town I had a letter from him that concluded: "I'm wondering what you'll think of a job on *Fortune*, if you take it. It varies with me from a sort of hard, masochistic liking without enthusiasm or trust, to direct nausea at the sight of this symbol $ and this % and this *biggest* and this some blank billion. At times I'd as soon work on *Babies Just Babies*. But in the long run I suspect the fault, dear *Fortune*, is in me:

that I hate any job on earth, as a job and hindrance and semisuicide."
His TVA article appeared in *Fortune* for October. It opened:

> The Tennessee River system begins on the worn magnificent crests of the
> southern Appalachians, among the earth's older mountains, and the Ten-
> nessee River shapes its valley into the form of a boomerang, bowing to its
> sweep through seven states. Near Knoxville the streams still fresh from
> the mountains are linked and thence the master stream spreads the valley
> most richly southward, swims past Chattanooga and bends down into
> Alabama to roar like blown smoke through the flood-gates of Wilson Dam,
> to slide becalmed along the crop-cleansed fields of Shiloh, to march due
> north across the high diminished plains of Tennessee and through Ken-
> tucky spreading marshes toward the valley's end where, finally, at the
> toes of Paducah, in one wide glassy golden swarm the water stoops for-
> ward and continuously dies into the Ohio . . .

Soon after this Luce called him in and told him that he had written one of
the best things ever printed in *Fortune*. It was characteristic of the Founder to acknowledge this; it was also characteristic of him to indicate, as
Agee's reward, the opportunity to write a number of straight "business
stories" whereby to strengthen his supposed weak side. The first of
these concerned The Steel Rail, and according to Dwight MacDonald,
the Founder himself buckled down to coach Agee in how to write good
hard sense about the steel business.* Eventually he gave up and the job
went to someone else, but the article as it appeared in December retained
traces of Jim's hand:

> Caught across the green breadth of America like snail paths on a mon-
> strous plantain leaf are 400,000 . . . steel miles. If, under the maleficent
> influence of that disorderly phosphorus which all steel contains, every
> inch of this bright mileage were suddenly to thaw into thin air . . .

6

During that fall and winter and the following year we pretty often had
lunch or dinner together. I would call for him in his lofty office, or I
would look up over my typewriter in the newspaper city room where by

---

*A story later got around that the Founder for a time considered sending Agee to the
Harvard Business School. "That story," Luce wrote to me in 1964, "is quite plausible—
though I do not actually recall it. A problem in journalism that interested me then—and still
does—is to combine good writing and 'human understanding' with familiarity with business."

that time I worked and see him coming down the aisle from the elevator. He would come at his fast loose long-legged walk, springy on the balls of his feet, with his open overcoat flapping. We would go to a saloon for beer and roast beef sandwiches. I wish very badly that I could recall the conversations of those times, because in them we found our particular kind of brotherhood. Both of us had been deeply enchanted and instructed, and were both skilled, in an art remote from news writing, an art that we were not getting time or breath to practice much. You would underestimate us if you supposed that we met to exchange grievances, for of these in the ordinary sense we had none. We met to exchange perceptions, and I had then and later the sense that neither of us felt himself more fully engaged than in talk with the other. My own childhood enabled me to understand his, in particular his schooling at the monastery school of St. Andrew's in Tennessee. We were both in the habit of looking into the shadow of Death. Although we came of different stock and from different regions, we were both Catholic (he, to be precise, Anglo-Catholic) by bringing-up and metaphysical formation; both dubious not to say distressed about "Church"; both inclined to the "religion of art," meaning that no other purpose, as we would have put it, seemed worth a damn in comparison with making good poems. Movies, of course, we talked about a good deal. My experience was not as wide as his, my passion less, but we admired certain things in common: ZaSu Pitts in *Greed* and the beautiful sordidness of that film; the classic flight down the flights of steps in *Potemkin*; Keaton; Chaplin. We saw, sometimes together, and "hashed over," as Jim would say, the offerings of that period: the René Clairs, the Ernst Lubitsches; *The Informer; Man of Aran; Grand Illusion; Mayerling; The Blue Angel; Maedchen in Uniform; Zwei Herzen* . . .

The various attitudes covered by "taking care of yourself" interested Jim Agee, but rarely to the point of making him experiment with any. Rubbers, for example, he probably thought shameful and never wore in his adult life; on the contrary, in that period, his shoes both winter and summer were often worn through, with cracked uppers. But he had some conventional habits and impulses. He wore a hat, a small one that rode high on his shock of dark hair. For several entire weeks in '34 he gave up cigarettes for a pipe. The episode of the pipe was the last effort of that kind that he would make until many years later, when he cut down smoking after his first heart attack.

Another thing he did with Via was to keep a catboat at City Island and go out there to sail and swim on Sundays in summer. I think he had been

on the swimming team at Exeter; at any rate he had an enviable back-
stroke. On one of these Sunday excursions when I went along I remember that we amused ourselves during the long black blowy subway ride
by playing the metaphor game: by turns each describing an inanimate
object in such a way as to portray without naming a public figure. Jim
developed a secondhand silver flute into Leslie Howard, and a Grand
Rapids easy chair into Carl Sandburg. Later that evening we had a memorable and I suppose comic conversation about whether or not the Artist
should Keep in Shape. In the course of this I quoted Rémy de Gourmont
to the effect that a writer writes with his whole body, bringing immediate
and delighted assent from Jim, but not to the inference I myself would
draw. His own body seemed so rugged and his stamina so great that I
thought he could overlook his health and get away with it. The truth is
that he was not as rugged as he looked. He had an inclination to hemo-
philia that had nearly cost him his life when he had his tonsils out in
1928, and at Exeter, too, he had first hurt his heart trying to run the mile.
He never mentioned any of this.

Many-tiered and mysterious, the life of the great city submerged us
now, me rather more, since I had no eyrie like his but all day long
spanieled back and forth in it and at night battered at my deadlines; and I
think Jim envied me the unpretentious but hard craft I had got into.
Whatever other interests we had, one became fairly constant and in time
inveterate: the precise relation between any given real situation or event
and the versions of it presented in print, that is, after a number of
accidents, processes, and conventions had come into play. The quite
complicated question of "how it really was" came before us all the time,
along with our resources and abilities for making any part of that actuality known in the frames our employers gave us. Of those frames we
were acutely aware, being acutely aware of others more adequate.
Against believing most of what I read I am armored to this day with
defenses worked out in those years and the years to follow. Styles, of
course, endlessly interested us, and one of Jim's notions was that of
writing an entire false issue of the *World Telegram* deadpan, with every
news item and ad heightened in its own style to the point of parody. He
could easily have done it. Neither of us felt snide about eye-witness
writing in itself or as practiced by Lardner or Hemingway; how could
we? We simply mistrusted the journalistic apparatus as a mirror of the
world, and we didn't like being consumed by it. Neither of us ever
acquired a professional and equable willingness to work in that harness.
For him to do so would have been more difficult than for me, since he

had a great talent for prose fiction and I had not. After being turned down for the Guggenheim, in fact, he thought of trying to publish a book of his stories, and went so far as to write a preface for it.

"I shall do my best to stick to people in this book," he wrote. "That may seem to you the least I could do; but the fact is, I'm so tied up with symbols and half-abstractions and many issues about poetry which we'd better steer clear of now, that it is very hard for me to see people clearly as people . . . someday, if my life is worth anything, I shall hope to give people clearly in clear poetry, and to make them not real in the usual senses of real, but more than that: full of vitality and of the ardor of their own truth . . ."

But he dropped the idea of publishing any stories at that point. Instead, with MacLeish's encouragement, he gathered the best of his old poems together with some new ones to make a book, and in October 1934, in the Yale Younger Poets series, in which MacLeish and Stephen Vincent Benét were then interested, the Yale Press published *Permit Me Voyage*.

7

Of how I felt about Jim's book then, it is perhaps enough to say that at bad times in the next year or two I found some comfort in being named in it. So far as I can discover, none of the contemporary comments on it, including the foreword by MacLeish, took much notice of what principally distinguished it at the time: the religious terms and passion of several pieces, rising at times to the grand manner. In two of his three pages MacLeish did not refer to the book at all, being engaged in arguing that neither of the current literary "programs," America Rediscovered and Capitalism Be Damned, mattered in comparison with *work* done. As to Agee, "Obviously he has a deep love of the land. Equally obviously he had a considerable contempt for the dying civilization in which he has spent twenty-four years." But he said nothing of the fact that Agee's book appeared to be the work of a desperate Christian; in fact, he rather insisted on saying nothing, for he concluded that by virtue of the poet's gift, especially his ear, and his labor at his art, "the work achieves an integral and inward importance altogether independent of the opinions and purposes of its author."

This was true enough, but some of the poems were so unusual in what they suggested as to call, you might think, for a word of recognition.

One gusty day years later, as we were crossing 49th Street, Jim and I halted in the Radio City wind and sunlight to agree with solemnity on a point of mutual and long-standing wonderment, not to say consternation: how rarely people seem to believe that a serious writer means it; he means what he says or what he discloses. Love for the land certainly entered into *Permit Me Voyage;* contempt for a dying civilization much less, and contempt here was not quite the word. It could even be said, on the contrary, that a sequence of twenty-five regular and in some cases truly metaphysical sonnets rather honored that civilization, insofar as a traditional verse form could represent it. The most impressive things in the book were the "Dedication" and the "Chorale," and what were these but strenuous prayers? They could have no importance, because no existence, independent of the opinions and purposes of the author.

A sense of the breathing community immersed in mystery, exposed to a range of experience from what can only be called the divine to what can only be called the diabolical, most intelligent in awe and most needful of mercy—a religious sense of life, in short—moved James Agee in his best work. If in introducing that work the sensitive and well-disposed MacLeish could treat this motive as unmentionable, that may give some idea of where Agee stood amid the interests and pressures of the time. It must be added that those interests were also Agee's, and that those pressures he not only profoundly felt but himself could bring to bear.

Four years at Harvard had complicated out of recognition his youthful Episcopalianism (he preferred to say Catholicism), but he hated polite academic agnosticism to the bone. In one *Advocate* editorial as a senior he had even proposed Catholicism as desirable for undergraduates. The poem, *John Carter,* that he had begun there, and would have carried on if he could, was to be an "anatomy of evil" wrought, he said, by an agent of evil in the "orthodox Roman Catholic" sense. At twenty-five, after two years in New York, he published an openly religious book of poems. MacLeish was not alone in ignoring what it said; the reviewers also ignored it. It was as if the interests and pressures of the time made it inaudible.

Inaudible? Since I still find it difficult to read the "Dedication" and the "Chorale" without feeling a lump in my throat, I do not understand this even now. If he had been heard, surely a twinge of compunction would have crossed the hearts of thousands. But the book itself, Jim's poems in general, remained very little known or remarked during his lifetime, and for that matter are little known even now. One reason for this, I am well aware, is that in the present century the rhymed lyric and the sonnet for

a time seemed disqualified as "modern poetry." Jim was aware of it, too;
so aware that his sequence ended with a farewell to his masters, the
English poets:

> My sovereign souls, God grant my sometime brothers,
> I must desert your ways now if I can . . .

The concluding poem in the book, the title poem, was indeed a conclusion, but it enfolded a purpose.

> My heart and mind discharted lie—

with reference, that is, to the compass points, religious, literary, and
other, within which at St. Andrew's, at Exeter, at Harvard, and in New
York he had by and large lived and worked. This was more than the
usual boredom of the artist with work that is over and done with. He
turned away now from Christian thought and observance, and began to
turn away from the art of verse. Yet his purpose was to rechart, to
reorient himself, by reference to the compass needle itself, his own independent power of perception, his own soul . . .

8

> Therein such strong increase to find
> In truth as is my fate to know.

Everyone who knew Jim Agee will remember that in these years there
grew upon him what became habitual almost to idiosyncrasy: a way of
tilting any subject every which way in talk, with prolonged and exquisite
elaboration and scruple. He was after the truth, the truth about specific
events or things, and the truth about his own impressions and feelings.
By truth I mean what he would chiefly mean: correspondence between
what is said and what is the case—but what is the case at the utmost
reach of consciousness. Now this intent has been delicately and justly
distinguished from the intent of art, which is to make, not to state,
things; and a self-dedication to truth on the part of Shakespeare or
Mozart (Ageean examples) would indeed strike us as peculiar. On the
other hand, with philosophy dethroned and the rise of great Realists,
truth-telling has often seemed to devolve almost by default upon the
responsible writer, enabling everyone else to have it both ways: his truth
as truth if they want it, or as something else if they prefer, since after all
he is merely an artist. Jim Agee, by nature an artist and responsive to all

the arts, took up this challenge to perceive in full and to present immaculately what was the case.

Think of all that conspired to make him do so. The place of Truth in that awareness of the living God that he had known as a child and young man and could not forget. The place of truth at the university, *Veritas*, perennial object of the scholar's pains. New techniques for finding out what was the case: among them, in particular, sociological study, works like *Middletown* in the United States and *Mass Observation* in England, answering to the perplexity of that age, and the "documentary" by which the craft of the cameraman could show forth unsuspected lineaments of the actual. (An early and what would appear a commonplace example of this craft, *The River*, by Pare Lorentz, excited Agee and myself.) Then, to sicken and enrage him, there was the immense new mudfall of falsehood over the world, not ordinary human lying and dissimulation but a calculated barrage, laid down by professional advertisers and propagandists, to corrupt people by the continent-load. Finally, day by day, he had the given occupation of journalism, ostensibly and usually in good faith concerned with what was the case. In the editing of *Fortune* all the other factors played a part: the somewhat missionary zeal of the Founder, a certain respect for standards of scholarship, a sociological interest in looking into the economic conditions and mode of life of classes and crafts in America, an acquiescence in advertising and in self-advertisement, and, of course, photography.

The difficulties of the period were, however, deepened by an intellectual dismay, not entirely well-founded but insidious under many forms: *What was the case* in some degree proceeded from the observer. Theoretical in abstract thought for centuries, this cat seemed now to have come out of the bag to bewitch all knowledge in practice: knowledge of microcosmic entities, of personal experience, of human society. Literary art had had to reckon with it. To take an elementary example, Richards would put three x's on a blackboard disposed thus . ˙ . to represent poem, referent and reader, suggesting that a complete account of the poem could no more exclude one x than another, nor the relationship between them. Nor were the x's stable, but variable. *Veritas* had become tragically complicated. The naïve practices of journalism might continue, as they had to, but their motives and achievements, like all others, appeared now suspect to Freudian and Marxian and semanticist alike; and of what these men believed they understood James Agee was (or proposed to make himself) also aware. Hence his self-examinations, his ambivalences ("split" feelings) on so many things. As he realized well enough, they could become tedious, but they were crucial to him and had the effect that what he knew, in the end, he knew with practiced definition. It must be added that the more irritated and all-embracing and scrupulous his aspiration to full truth, "objective" and "subjective" at once, the more sharply he would know his own sinful vainglory or Pride in that ambition, in those scruples; and he did. Few men were more sensitive to public and private events than he was, and he would now explore and discriminate among them with his great appetite, his energy, his sometimes paralyzing conscience, and the intellect that Richards had alerted. I am of course reducing a long and tentative and often interrupted effort into a few words.

I named three books arbitrarily as stars principal in our first years at Harvard; I will name three more, arbitrarily again, to recall the planetary influences after graduation. In the spring of '34, after Judge Wolsey's decision, Random House published *Ulysses* for the first time legally in America, and even if we had read it before, as Jim and I had, in the big Shakespeare & Co. edition, we could and did now read it again, in a handier form suitable for carrying on the subway. Or for the Agee bathroom, where I remember it. Joyce engrossed him and got into his blood so thoroughly that in 1935 he felt obliged, as he told a friend of mine, to master and get over that influence if he were ever to do anything of his own.

Céline's *Voyage au Bout de la Nuit* was our first taste of the end-of-the-rope writing that became familiar later in Miller and later still in Beckett. Malraux's *Man's Fate* had another special position. This story, with Auden's early poems, counted as much as the Russian movies of Eisenstein and Dovzhenko in swaying Jim toward Communism. The attraction in any case was strong. The peaceful Roosevelt revolution had only begun; there was a real clash of classes in America. I had myself, in a single day of reporting, seen the pomp of high capitalism to be faded and phoney at a National Association of Manufacturers convention in the Waldorf, and the energies of laboring men to be robust and open at a union meeting. On one side of his nature Jim was a frontiersman and a populist to whom blind wealth and pretentious gentility were offensive. Besides this he had the romantic artist's contempt, "considerable contempt," for the Philistine and for what were then known to us as bourgeois attitudes—though he distinguished between the human souls that inherited them. For poverty and misery in general he had a sharp-eyed pity. The idea of a dedicated brotherhood working underground in the ghastly world held his imagination for several years—spies amid the enemy, as Auden had imagined them; at the same time he had no great difficulty in seeing through most of the actual candidates for such a brotherhood, including himself. The Party fished in vain for Agee, who by liking only what was noble in the Revolution liked too little of it.

9

Embedded in *Fortune* for those years are several of Jim's best efforts at telling how things really were. As in the description of the Tennessee River, these are most often concerned with American landscapes and American living. In September 1934, for example, there was this opening to an article on the Great American Roadside:

> . . . This continent, an open palm frank before the sky against the bulk of the world. This curious people. The automobile you know as well as you know the slouch of the accustomed body at the wheel and the small stench of gas and hot metal. You know the sweat and the steady throes of the motor and the copious and thoughtless silence and the almost lack of hunger and the spreaded swell and swim of the hard highway toward and beneath and behind and gone and the parted roadside swarming past. This great road, too; you know that well. How it is scraggled and twisted along the coast of Maine, high-crowned and weak-shouldered in honor of long winter. How in Florida the detours are bright with the sea-lime of rolled shells. How the stiff wide stream of hard unbroken roadstead spends the mileage between Mexicali and Vancouver. How the road degrades into a rigorous lattice of country dirt athwart Kansas through the smell of hot wheat and this summer a blindness and a strangulation of lifted dust). How like a blacksnake in the sun it takes the ridges, the green and dim ravines which are the Cumberlands, and lolls loose into the hot Alabama valleys. How in the spectral heat of the Southwest, and the wide sweeps of sage toward the Northwest, it means spare fuel strapped to the running board. . . . Oh yes, you know this road; and you know this roadside. You know this roadside as well as you know the formulas of talk at the gas station, the welcome taste of a Bar-B-Q sandwich in midafternoon, the oddly excellent feel of a weak-springed bed in a clapboard transient shack, and the early start in the cold bright lonesome air, the dustless and dewy road . . .

In October of the same year, on "The Drought":

> That this has been by all odds the most ruinous drought in U. S. history is old stuff to you by now. So are the details, as the press reported them, week by broiling week, through the summer. But all the same, the chances

are strong that you have no idea what the whole thing meant: what, simply and gruesomely, it was. Really to know, you should have stood with a Dakota farmer and watched a promissory rack of cloud take the height of the sky, weltering in its lightnings . . . and the piteous meager sweat on the air, and the earth baked stiff and steaming. You should have been a lot more people in a lot more places, really to know. Barring that impossibility, however, there is the clear dispassionate eye of the camera, which under honest guidance has beheld these bitter and these transient matters, and has recorded this brutal season for the memory of easier time to come . . .

These quotations must suffice, and they are not carelessly chosen. In 1935 he did a thorough re-examination of the TVA, published in May, and a study of Saratoga, New York, published in August. These and other examples of sheer ability won him a taste of the freedom he craved. Beginning in November, *Fortune* gave him a six months' leave of absence, most of which he and Via spent in Florida on a small coastal island, Anna Maria, south of St. Petersburg and Tampa.

In a notebook of his, half-filled with jottings of that winter, I find the first entry amusing at this distance: it was a name and an address—*The New Masses*—later canceled out by a scribble. He was now steadily devouring Freud and recording his dreams. "Read Freud until midnight" is an entry several times repeated. There are pages like Stephen's or Bloom's waking thoughts in Ulysses. There are notes and self-injunctions about writing. For instance:

My need for tone, tension & effect in writing limits me very badly. Yet cd. be good. But in many ways needless effort. And in many ways false. Its attempt in long run: to give, at once, frame and fluescence to pic. of universe. Seem to feel I have no right to give the looseness till is established the tightness wherein it moves . . . Must throw brain into detail. And into fearlessness, shamelessness & naturalness abt writing . . . Poem or prose in line between The Barge She Sat In and a social report of a wedding. What was worn. Who was there. etc. / Bks not of one thing—stories, poetry, essays, etc. / but of all, down to most casual . . .

In December he wrote some ottava rima, a few stanzas mocking something Sir Samuel Hoare, then British Foreign Minister, had said in the course of diplomacy that winter over the Italian war against Ethiopia. It was the last spasm of *John Carter*. He read *Crime and Punishment*, Caroline Spurgeon on *Shakespeare's Imagery* and *The Counterfeiters*. Gide, he wrote,

. . . makes me realize more clearly than I have for a long time what a damned soft and uncertain customer I am. Had again, still have, though now my head and purposes are woolly, feeling of necessity to go plain to the bone and stay there. The 40-day fasts and that kind of thing. Misnamed virtues: they clear you: which is a state of grace or virtue. / Virtual / feel in many words, suddenly like little puffs of light, nowadays, the shine and silver quality wh. is equivalent (EQUIVALENT is such a word) to a whole certain tone in Bach. Does Bach and don't many composers reduce to 2 or 3 dominant tones? & I don't mean idioms either. Same with writers. Mozart's very skillful chromatic developments & returns that an ear holds a lot less surely than much trickier 20th Century stuff. Analyze (can you) quality of excitement in minuet of Jupiter. Sense of a full ochestra in a Beethovenish way of being full, even in 1st measure when woodwinds have it. Mozart's queer "darker" music, something like Hopkins' love of the dappled, the counter, original, spare, strange. In some rather homely themes of scherzi—and, likelier to turn up in them than in slo mvts & finales? 1st movt of G-minor has some of it, too. Also vide great values of the prosy & verbose line in poetry, & of bromide almost. Note some of Mozart's more strenuous & some of his more tossed off slow mvts; lyrics in Songs of Innocence; many passages in Schubert; quite a few in Beethoven . . .

Among many entries on music, there is one noting "the great beauty of West End Blues" and another, written firmly with a fresh pencil as if he wanted badly to get it down:

Swing music is different from any contemporary Art Mouthpiece. Barring straight folk stuff and vaude & burlesk adlibbing, runs roughly this way. Writing last had this freedom in Elizabeth's time, with something half like it but crippled in Byron. Sculpture of Africans has it. Music lost it (roughly) with Mozart. Beethoven had but did not use and finally buried it. The 19th and 20th centuries are solidly self-conscious and inhibited. Only swing today is perfectly free and has in its kind a complete scope. Some directors have it. Eisenstein does or did. Disney does or did. Chaplin did. There may be bits of it in some surrealist art. With words, does Perelman have some? and Groucho some? and Durante some? But all pretty much of a kind: not at all capable of wonderful lyric scope of swing. Can words spoken or written possibly break through it again, break through and get free . . .

He worked on some of the poems that were published over the next three years or so, on some that were never published or worth publishing, on others that have not survived. He drafted autobiographical material that would serve him years later in the novel published after his death, as the following entry indicated:

Have been working (c. 12–15,000 words) on the footloose in Knoxville idea. Don't know.

One entry of great importance, because it stated an obsession that had its relevance to everything and especially to "Church" and Christianity, was this:

> Truth goes much less far than falsehood: at every transition, more misunderstanding comes aboard: gradually becomes handleable by those too corrupted by falsehood to handle bare truth. Radium into lead.

I have been quoting these notes generously in the hope that you will hear at least remotely a voice in them and get at least an inkling of what his talk was like. But one final entry I will quote as a thing in itself, comparable to one of Hopkins' beautifully delineated studies of nature in the *Notebooks*. This was during a walk on a misty night under an almost full moon down the beach on Anna Maria.

> Surf as rounded point, coming in at acute angle, running along its edges on shallow sand with tearing glistening sound, like drawn zipper opening. Then around pt., meet surf broadside. In darkness you see it, well out on the dark, explode like opening parachute, and come in. Another kind: where in 2–3 parts on single line it whitens and the white widens—again the glistening zipper action—till all white meets and in it comes. Also: smallish tendons of it, private to themselves, bearing up (no white) and smacking themselves straight down on hard sand beneath a few inches of water with great passion and impact, PFFUHHH. Also, lovely and violent, competent folding-under of seam, pursing as of lips, when wave crest falls so prematurely as to undermine its own back: so you get a competent, systematic turning under in long lines. Also sink and drying of water in sand as shallow wave draws down.

10

In May 1936, some time before the great day of the assignment in Alabama, Jim and I journeyed together to Bennington to read our verses to the college. In that budding grove he was almost inaudible, as usual when reading his own or other poems, but then as a kind of encore he did a parody of a southern preacher in a hellfire sermon, and this was more than audible: it brought down the house. I have not found it in manuscript, but I have included in this book a prose parody of the same period, to show the sort of thing he occasionally did. You do not hear much of his parodies. You do not hear much, either, of his mimetic powers, great as they were, though years later he had a bit part as a "vagrant" in one of his movies. At the time I am thinking of, one of his best acts was a recital of "When the lamp is shattered" in the accent and pitch of rural Tennessee.

We saw a good deal of one another all that spring—by this time I was married and working for *Time*—but by midsummer he was gone into the Deep South with Walker Evans on the tenant farmer job. Walker has written very well about that in his short foreword to the 1960 reissue of *Let Us Now Praise Famous Men*.

Jim's passionate eye for the lighted world made him from boyhood a connoisseur of photography, and among all photographers I think the one who had moved him most was Mathew Brady. The portraits and Civil War photographs of Brady were a kind of absolute for him, calling him and sounding in him very deeply. Another near-absolute was the photography in von Stroheim's *Greed*; he especially loved the burning-white powdery kind of sunlight produced by the "orthochromatic" film of that period. These kinds of studied finality and fiery delicacy in images of contemporary existence he found above all in the photographs of Walker Evans. Their work together that summer made them collaborators and close friends for life. It is strange that Jim never wrote much about Evans' photographs. Perhaps this was because only a couple of years later the Museum of Modern Art held a big Evans exhibition for which Lincoln Kirstein wrote a full and handsome introduction. Jim did write, in 1942, an introduction for a proposed book of photographs by another artist he admired, Helen Levitt. For a full and pondered statement of what photography meant to him you will do well to consult this book, *A Way of Seeing*, finally published in 1965 by the Viking Press. The heart of what he wrote is this:

> The artist's task [in photography] is not to alter the world as the eye sees it into a world of esthetic reality, but to perceive the esthetic reality within the actual world, and to make an undisturbed and faithful record of the instant in which this movement of creativeness achieves its most expressive crystallization. Through his eye and through his instrument the artist has, thus, a leverage upon the materials of existence which is unique . . .

After the summer in Alabama I should guess that he got his *Fortune* piece done in September or October, and I remember it hanging fire in the autumn, but I can't be sure of these dates. Why did the magazine in the end reject the article that the editor, knowing Agee and therefore presumably knowing more or less what to expect, had assigned him to write? Well, one reason was very simple: the editor was no longer the same man. He was no longer the same man because *Fortune*'s repute in the Duquesne Club and the Sky Club and the Bohemian Club—in those places, in short, where subscribers met—had been damaged by what appeared to the subscribers as a leftward drift in the contents of the magazine. In 1935 Jim's piece might have been printed, but in 1936, by the excellent disposition of Providence, the new editor, not much liking his duty, did his duty and turned it down.

Now all hands at last had more than a glimmer of a fact I have alluded to earlier—that Agee's vocation, at least at that point and as up to that point meditated by himself and inflamed by his recent experience, was in competition with *Fortune*. It appeared that the magazine, committed of course to knowing what was the case, had had the offhand humanity and imagination and impertinence to send an ex-President of the Harvard *Advocate* into the helpless and hopeless lives of cotton tenant farmers, but that it did not have the courage to face in full the case he presented, since the case involved discomfort not only for the tenants but for *Fortune*. Anything but that. Well and good, this gave him his chance to show *Fortune* and everyone else how to treat the case: he would make the assignment his own and make a book of his own on the tenant farmers. His friend Edward Aswell at Harper & Bros. induced that firm to offer Agee and Evans a contract and an advance, but for the time being Jim did not accept it, fearing that it might affect the writing. He remained loosely attached to *Fortune*. I believe no high words passed.

In 1937 he was in and out of the office on three jobs. The most interesting took him to Havana on an excruciating Caribbean "vacation cruise," of which his narrative, appearing in September as "Six Days at Sea," was a masterpiece of ferocity, or would have been if it had been printed uncut. He had become grimmer about American middle-class ways and destinies, and would become grimmer still. His inclination to simple cleanliness, for example, turned to anger for a while as he discerned meanness and status and sterility even in that.

In the good poems of this period, the one to his father in *Transition*, the one called "Sunday: Outskirts of Knoxville," and some of the lyrics in *The Partisan Review*, he did things unachieved in *Permit Me Voyage*. But most of the topical poems in quatrains, published or unpublished, are not so good. He never did as well in this vein as in the epigrammatic "Songs on the Economy of Abundance" that he had sent to Louis Untermeyer for the 1936 edition of *Modern American Poetry*. His skill with traditional meters declined; it remained, now, mistrusted and for long periods unused, or used only casually and briefly. The Auden-MacNeice

Letters from Iceland came out that year with a section of brilliant Byronics, and if Jim had had any intention of going on with *John Carter*—as I believe that by now he did not—those pages might have dissuaded him. Auden's unapproachable virtuosity may, in fact, have had something— not much, but inevitably something—to do with Jim's writing verse more seldom. "Seen this?" he came in saying one day, with a new book in his hand, and read aloud the Auden poem that opens with such beauty:

> Out on the lawn I lie in bed,
> Vega conspicuous overhead,
> In the windless nights of June . . .

In the Bickford's Cafeteria at Lexington and 43rd, over coffee at some small hour of the morning, we read together and recognized perfection in a set of new lyrics by Robert Frost in *The Atlantic;* one was the short one beginning:

> I stole forth dimly in the dripping pause
> Between two downpours to see what there was . . .

Perfection of this order Jim now scarcely any longer tried for in verse.

Under one strain and another his marriage was now breaking up; I remember the summer day in '37 when at his suggestion we met in Central Park for lunch and the new young woman in her summer dress appeared. It seems to me that there were months of indecisions and revisions and colloquies over the parting with Via, which was yet not to be a parting, etc., which at length would be accomplished as cruelly required by the laws of New York. Laceration could not have been more prolonged. In the torments of liberty all Jim's friends took part. At Old Field Point on the north shore of Long Island, where the Wilder Hobsons had somehow rented a bishop's boathouse that summer, a number of us attained liberation from the *pudor* of mixed bathing without bathing suits: a mixed pleasure, to tell the truth.

One occasion in this period that I remember well was a public meeting held in June 1937, in Carnegie Hall, by a "Congress of American Writers," a Popular Front organization, for the Spanish Loyalist cause. Jim and I went to this together, and as we took our seats he turned to me and said, "Know one writer you can be sure isn't here? Cummings." Mac-Leish spoke, very grave. His speech was a prophetic one in which he might very well have quoted "Ask not for whom the bell tolls: it tolls for thee." Then he introduced Hemingway. It must have been the only time in his life that Hemingway consented to couple with a lectern, and as a matter of fact he only stood beside it and leaned on it with one elbow. Bearish in a dark blue suit, one foot cocked over the other, he gave a running commentary to a movie documentary by Joris Ivens on a Spanish town under the Republic. Jim Agee hoped for the Republic, but I don't think he ever saluted anyone with a raised fist or took up Spanish (my own gesture—belated at that). He had joined battle on another ground.

In October he put in his second vain application for a Guggenheim Fellowship. His "Plans for Work" (of which he kept a carbon) are printed in this book [*The Collected Short Prose of James Agee*, not the present volume] and will give you an idea of his mood at the time, maverick and omnivorous as a prairie fire, ranging in every direction for What Was the Case and techniques for telling it. As in '32 he did not fail to indulge in those gratuitous honesties (now about Communism, for instance) that would make it tough for the Guggenheim committee. I do not know how he lived that winter, or lived through it.

Not, however, till the spring of '38 did he take the Harper's contract and settle down with Alma Mailman, in a small frame house at 27 2nd Street, Frenchtown, New Jersey, to write or rewrite and construct his book. Jim wrote for the ear, wanted criticism from auditors, and read to me, either in Frenchtown or in New York, most of the drafts as he got them written. There isn't a word in *Let Us Now Praise Famous Men* that he—and I and others—did not ponder many times. Frenchtown was then quiet and deep in the dense countryside, traversable whenever and as far as necessary in an ancient open flivver; they had a goat, God knows how acquired, in the backyard; there was a tennis court in the town. Jim played an obstinate and mighty game, but wild, against my obstinate and smoother one.

He labored all summer and fall, through the Sudeten crisis and the international conferences and the Nazi mass meetings at Nuremberg and elsewhere that sent the strangled shouting of *Der Führer* and *Sieg Heil, Sieg Heil* in an ominous rhythmic roar over the radios of the country. He labored into the winter. I have found among his things a journal in which he noted on December 1st that when the rent was paid he would have $12.52 in the world and in the same breath went on with plans for his wedding to Alma later that month. In January or February *Fortune* came to the rescue with an assignment: the section on Brooklyn in an issue to be devoted to New York City. For the rest of the winter and spring they moved to a flat in St. James Place, taking the goat with them.

When Wilder Hobson went to see them once he found that the neighborhood kids had chalked on the front steps: "The Man Who Lives Here is a
Loony."

11

In the living room or backyard of that place I heard several drafts of his
prose on Brooklyn, and by some accident kept two drafts in a file.
Twenty-four years later these turned out to be the only vestiges of this
work in existence. In this case, too, *Fortune* found Jim's article too strong
to print, and it did not appear in the New York issue (June 1939). *Fortune's* editor, however, appreciated his labor. As epigraph to the tamer
article (by someone else) that finally got into print, the editor lifted one
lyric sentence from Jim's piece and quoted it, with attribution. The version printed in this book is Jim's preliminary draft: "Southeast of the
Island: Travel Notes." The later version prepared for *Fortune* editing on
May 15, 1939 (by the "ditto" process, which produced a number of
legible copies), was shorter by nearly half and lacked the particularity of
the earlier piece. Compression and generality served him well in one
passage only, funny and biting if you remember that *Fortune* was rather
given to Ripley-like statistical play:

> Courtship and marriage are difficult matters to speak of, and it will be
> the better part of valor not to speak of them, beyond remarking that no
> park has ever been more eloquently designed beneath the moon for its
> civic purpose than Prospect; that more homes are owned in Brooklyn than
> elsewhere in New York City; that there are more children per capita; that
> the divorce rate is only . . . per cent per head that of Manhattan; that
> there are 48,000 electric refrigerators in Flatbush alone; and that if all the
> perambulators in Brooklyn were pushed end to end, at the pace of a
> walking mother, they would soon reach three times around the origin of
> species, the history of religion, the cause of imperialistic war, sexual ethics
> and social fear, and the basis of private property and universal prenatal
> spiritual suffocation . . .

After the Brooklyn interlude, the Agees returned to Frenchtown for
the summer. Some weeks before we heard Mr. Chamberlain's weary
voice declaring that a state of war existed between His Majesty's Govern-
ment and Nazi Germany, Jim Agee's manuscript of a book entitled *Three
Tenant Families* was in the hands of the publishers. The war began, and
the German armored divisions shot up Poland. In the Harper offices

Jim's manuscript must have appeared a doubtful prospect as a rousing topical publishing event. The publishers wanted him to make a few domesticating changes. He would not make the changes. Harper's then deferred publication; they could live without it. He was broke and in debt, and in the early fall he learned that fatherhood impended for him in the spring. I had just fallen heir to the job of "Books" editor at *Time*, so we arranged that he should join me and the other reviewer, Calvin Fixx, at writing the weekly book section, and he and Alma found a flat far over on the West Side somewhere below 14th Street.

Now for eight or nine months we worked in the same office several days and/or nights a week. Early that year or maybe late the year before, I can't remember precisely when, the Luce magazines had moved to a new building called the Time & Life Building in Rockefeller Center between 48th and 49th Streets (now superseded by a later and of course bigger and better T & L Building farther west). We had a three-desk office on the twenty-eighth floor with a secretary's cubbyhole. Our secretary, or "checker," was a girl I had known in 1934 when she was Lewis Gannett's secretary on the *Herald Tribune*—a crap-shooting hoydenish girl who used to get weekly twenty-page letters from a lonely and whimsical young man in a San Francisco YMCA, by the name, then unknown, of William Saroyan. In the years between '34 and '39 Mary had been in South Africa and had come back statelier but still *au fond* not giving a damn; her father was an Episcopal canon. She kept track of the review books and publication dates and spotted errors in what we wrote. The other reviewer, Fixx, was a Mormon, a decent, luminously inarticulate man engaged in living down some obscure involvement in the Far Left. He knew a great deal about that particular politics and history, now a great subject for "re-evaluation" after the Ribbentrop-Molotov embrace. Each of us read half-a-dozen books a week and wrote reviews or notes— or nothing—according to our estimates of each.

Jim Agee of course added immeasurably to the pleasure of this way of life. If for any reason a book interested him (intentionally or unintentionally on the author's part) he might write for many hours about it, turning in many thousands of words. Some of these long and fascinating reviews would rebound from the managing editor in the form of a paragraph. We managed nevertheless to hack through that barrier a fairly wide vista on literature in general, including even verse, the despised quarterlies, and scholarship. With light hearts and advice of counsel we reviewed a new edition of the classic *Wigmore on Evidence*. One week we jammed through a joint review of Henry Miller, for which Jim did *Tropic of Cancer* and I *Tropic of Capricorn*, both unpublishable in the United States until twenty years later. Our argument that time was that if *Time* ought to be written for the Man-in-the-Street (a favorite thought of the Founder), here were books that would hit him where he lived, if he could get them. In all our efforts we were helped by T. S. Matthews, then a senior editor and later for six years managing editor and a friend to Jim Agee.

Not because I idolize Jim or admire every word he ever wrote but again to show his mind at work, this time in that place under those conditions, I will quote the first paragraph of his review of Herbert Gorman's *James Joyce* and the final paragraphs from his review of *The Hamlet* by William Faulkner.

> The utmost type of heroism, which alone is worthy of the name, must be described, merely, as complete self-faithfulness: as integrity. On this level the life of James Joyce has its place, along with Blake's and Beethoven's, among the supreme examples. It is almost a Bible of what a great artist, an ultimately honest man, is up against . . .

> Whatever their disparities, William Faulkner and William Shakespeare share these characteristics: 1) Their abundance of invention and their courage for rhetoric are bottomless. 2) Enough goes on in their heads to furnish a whole shoal of more temperate writers. 3) By fair means or foul, both manage to play not for a specialized but for a broad audience.

> In passages incandescent with undeniable genius, there is [in *The Hamlet*] nevertheless not one sentence without its share of amateurishness, its stain of inexcusable cheapness.

12

Of the physical make and being of James Agee and his aspect at that time, you must imagine: a tall frame, long-boned but not massive; lean flesh, muscular with some awkwardness; pelt on his chest; a long stride with loose knee-joints, head up, with toes angled a bit outward. A complexion rather dark or sallow in pigment, easily tanned. The head rough-hewn, with a rugged brow and cheekbones, a strong nose irregular in profile, a large mouth firmly closing in folds, working a little around the gaps of lost teeth. The shape of the face tapered to a sensitive chin, cleft. Hair thick and very dark, a shock uncared for, and best uncared for. Eyes deep-set and rather closely set, a dull-gray-blue or feral blue-gray or radiantly lit with amusement. Strong stained teeth. On the right middle finger a callous as big as a boil: one of his stigmata as a writer. The hands and fingers long and light and blunt and expressive, shaping his thought in the air, conveying stresses direct or splay, drawing razor-edged lines with thumb and forefinger: termini, perspectives, tones.

His capacity for whisky, as for everything else, was very great. I saw him once or twice violent with drink, but I never saw him disabled by it and don't know anyone else who ever did. As a rule, with every drink he only became more interested in any subject or line of action—any except going home and going to bed. A little conviviality was enough to get his comic genius off the ground and into such flights as his one-man rendition of the Bach Toccata and Fugue as arranged by Stokowski—a magistral act in which varieties of fruity instrumentation were somehow conveyed by voice and gesture, e.g. the string section by a flapping left hand and "fiddle-faddle, fiddle-faddle, fiddle-faddle." At the invention of American place names, or personal names, Jim had no peer; one of his best compositions, brought off while wandering late at night with Wilder Hobson, was the man's name, "George F. Macgentsroom." Very rarely, he might follow through with an inspiration from one of those evenings. In his war against middle-class folkways he struck a happily premeditated blow at the Christmas card custom by sending out, one Christmas, a card bearing as its olde winter scene a photograph of a pair of polar bears in innocent copulation, with season's greetings.

At the piano he sat well back and more than erect, head withdrawn and watchful, eyes downcast over the length of arms and fingers in hard exertion at the keyboard. It was the old upright that his grandmother had given him; I think he had it for twenty years. When he played he would have the whole form of the sonata or whatever it was before him in his mind. Bettered conclamant notes, quite a few near misses, very little sweet shading or pianissimo. At his writing he looked the same: his left hand pinning down at arm's length a stack of yellow second sheets, leaning far back from it frowning (by this time he was getting far-sighted; he tried, but discarded, some steel-rimmed glasses), power flowing through the sharp pencil into the tiny closely organized script. Wholly focused on it, as I remember him in warm weather once, oblivious of the closed office window behind him, stifling in a fog of cigarette smoke, with a small pure space cleared before him amid mountains of litter.

He wore blue or khaki work shirts and under the armpits there would be stains, salt-edged, from sweat; likewise under the arms of his suit jacket, double-breasted dark blue, wrinkled and shiny. He was too poor to afford a lot of laundering, and he didn't believe in it, anyway. After the baby arrived in March '40, I remember one big scene in which Jim was engaged in spooning Pablum into Joel. The father sat, all elbows and knees, in an arm chair upholstered in some ragged and ancient fabric that had grown black absorbing through the years the grime of New York. The infant in his lap mouthed with a will at the Pablum but inevitably gobs of it splattered down even on the richly unsanitary arms of the chair, whence Jim would scoop it in long dives lest it drip—irretrievably, you could hope—on the floor.

The time was about over for all fragile arrangements and lightness of heart. In those days the German airborne troops were taking Norway. There was nothing we could do about it. One fine day in late spring, playing tennis with Jim on some courts south of Washington Square, I broke a bone in my instep. *Life* with a wealth of illustration assured us that General Gamelin was the flower of military science and the French Army the finest in Europe. Within a week or so it looked as though *Life* had exaggerated. While I was still getting around on a plaster clubfoot the British were evacuating Dunkirk and the panzers were going through the Ardennes. The dress parade of the German Army down the Champs-Elysées was reported by the *World-Telegram* with a photograph of the Arc de Triomphe and the headline ICI REPOSE UN SOLDAT FRANÇAIS MORT POUR LA PATRIE. I looked at this and realized that so far as I was concerned a decade had come to an end, and so had a mode of life, to flatter it by that term, that included working for *Time*. To see what could be done about my *modus vivendi* in general, I turned over "Books" to Agee, Fixx and Whittaker Chambers and departed, taking my first wife away to the West and eventually to Santa Fe for the winter. There I settled down on my savings to do unnecessary and unpaid work for the first time in five years. I had resigned. Taking no offense, and with great accuracy of foresight, the people at *Time* made it a leave of absence until a year from that October. I intrude these details because I am about to quote a few passages from Jim's letters to me during the year. At some point in the spring or summer Houghton Mifflin, to their eternal credit, accepted the manuscript that Harper's had released to him. Well, from a letter in December:

> . . . Excepting Wilder, whose getting-a-job has done him a favor as leaving-it has you, everyone I see, myself included, is at a low grinding ebb of quiet desperation: nothing, in most cases, out of the ordinary, just the general average Thoreau was telling about, plus the dead-ends of one of the most evil years in history, plus each individual's little specialty act. I don't think I'll go into much if any detail—for though I could detail it blandly and painlessly and some of it is of 'clinical' interest, it could possi-

bly have an intrusive and entangling effect. So I can most easily and honestly say that it isn't as bad as I've perhaps suggested, except by contrast with health and free action—is, in fact, just the average experience of people living as people shouldn't, where people shouldn't, doing what people shouldn't and little or nothing of what people should. Journalists, hacks, husbands, wives, sisters, neurotics, self-harmed artists, and such. Average New York Fall.

The book is supposed to be published January or February—no proofs yet, though. I now thoroughly regret using the subtitle (Let Us Now Praise Famous Men) as I should never have forgotten I would. I am rather anxious to look at it, finished and in print—possibly, also, to read it in that form—but I have an idea I'll be unable to stand to. If so, it might be a healthy self-scorching to force myself to: but that's probably my New England chapel-crank blood. Mainly, though, I want to be through with it, as I used to feel about absolution, and to get to work again as soon as I can. I am thirty-one now, and I can conceivably forgive myself my last ten years only by a devotion to work in the next ten which I suspect I'll be incapable of. I am much too vulnerable to human relationships, particularly sexual or in any case heterosexual, and much too deeply wrought-upon by them, and in turn much too dependent in my work on 'feeling' as against 'intellect.' In short I'm easily upset and, when upset, incapable of decent work; incapable of it also when I'm not upset enough. I must learn my ways in an exceedingly quiet marriage (which can be wonderful I've found but is basically not at all my style or apparent 'nature') or break from marriage and all close liaisons altogether and learn how to love alone & keep love at a bearable distance. Those are oddly juvenile things to be beginning to learn at my age: what really baffles me is that, knowing them quite well since I was 15, I've done such thorough jobs in the opposite direction. Well, nothing would be solved or even begun tonight by any thing I wrote or thought, or at any time soon: my business now and evidently for quite a while to come is merely to sit as tight and careful as I can, taking care above all to do no further harm to others or myself or my now virtually destroyed needs or hopes, and doing a timorous or drastic piece of mending when or wherever there seems any moment's chance to. I haven't been very intelligent—to say nothing of 'good'—and now it's scarcely a chance for intelligence or goodness—only for the most dumb and scrupulous tenacity. On the whole, though, it's time I had a good hard dose of bad going, and if I find I'm capable of it the winter will be less wasted than it otherwise might be. Meanwhile, though, I find I'm so dull I bore myself sick. A broken spirit and a contrite heart have their drawbacks: worst of all if at the same time the spirit is unbroken and ferocious and the heart contrite only in the sense of deep grief over pain and loss, not at all in true contrition . . .

I thought *The Long Voyage Home* quite awful . . .

I feel very glad you like the reviews. I wish I did. As a matter of fact I have hardly judgment or feeling, for or against, and on the whole, not a bad time with the job, except a general, rather shamed feeling, week by week, that with real intelligence & effort I could do much better, whatever the limitations of space and place. Then a book as important as Kafka's *Amerika* can't even get reviewed, and I shrug it off again . . .

The magazine you write of [an imaginary one.—R. F.] makes my mouth water. I spend a lot of time thinking of such things and of equivalent publishers. They really existed in France and Germany and even in England. The fact that they don't here and I suppose won't ever, by any chance, makes me know just a little better what a fat-assed, frumpish hell-on-earth this country is. Last stronghold of just what . . . But I do love to think about magazines like that. And the writing *can* be done—the only really important thing—whenever and wherever qualified people can cheat their inferiors out of the time it takes. Thank God you're getting it . . .

That is the longest excerpt. A shorter one, from a letter of February or March (he never dated his letters):

. . . I'm in a bad period: incertitude and disintegration on almost every count. Somehow fed up and paralytic with the job; horribly bad sleeping rhythm; desperate need to live regularly & still more to do new work of my own; desperate knowledge that with all the time on earth I could as I spiritually feel now be capable of neither . . . Alma is in Mexico—so is Joel—nominally, presumably, perhaps very probably, that is broken forever. And so far, I am not doing the one thing left me to do if it is ever possibly to reintegrate: entirely leave knowing Mia. It is constantly in the bottom of my gut—petrifying everything else—that I must, and will; and I still do nothing. A kind of bottomless sadness, impotence and misery in which one can neither move a hand nor keep it still without some further infliction on one or another . . . For some doubtless discreditable reason it is of some good to speak of it, but I hope I don't do so at your expense, in sympathy or concern (I've known such things to derail me)—There is truly no need; as I say, I'm only too detached and anesthetized.

I delayed 2 months in all this trouble, in correcting proofs, but all is done now so I presume the machinery is turning. Don't yet know the publication date though.

Another one from about June, 1941:

Your last letters have sounded so thoroughly well in the head and health and so exciting in potentiality, that the thought of its shutting-off in a few more months, with your return to work, has made me probably almost as sick as it makes you.

I think this could be rather easily solved as follows:

What with one expense and another I shall nowhere near have paid off my debts by October and so will nowhere near be free to quit work and get to my own. So why don't I continue at this work and you continue at yours, for 6 months or 8 or a year (we can arrange that) during which I could send you and Eleanor $100 a month.

That would be very scrawny to live on most parts of this country; but apparently in Mexico would be: in Mexico City an adequate poverty; elsewhere an amplitude. This would, then, involve living where perhaps you might rather not; but a living, and free time, would be assured. And when I am able to quit work, if you are ready or need to come back, you could do likewise for me on some general equalization—

I think that by this or some such arrangement we & others might really get clear time when we are ripe for it, and it seems a better chance than any other—What do you think? . . .

Another a bit later:

. . . Nothing on earth could make me feel worse than that you should for any reason whatever have to come back now that you are ripe for so much.

As for the money, I feel as you do, that it belongs to him who most needs it at a given time—your need for it for the next year or so is far out of proportion to any I could have short of a year or so of freedom first, and greater too than you would be likely to have again, without a long stretch of preparatory freedom. I think neither of us should think twice about you later paying me back—that is a wrong conception of the whole thing. I'll be able to take care of myself, one way or another, when my time comes for it—meanwhile I'll be best taking care for things I care for most, if I can make freedom and work possible for you when you can make best use of it.

I'm talking badly out of turn in all this walking-in and urging—I hope you can forgive it. It seems terribly crucial to me that you stay free at this particular time, and criminal if you don't . . .

Chambers is still moving Books at *Time*—Stockley does Letters, and an occasional review. If you should come back—which God forbid—I imagine I could get switched to movies & you could replace me here . . .

13

I hope an occasional reader will understand that the foregoing private things are quoted after long hesitation and at the expense of my heart's blood. I think I am aware of every way in which they—and he, and I—can be taken advantage of. Jim Agee's agonies and his nobleness are equally the affair of no one who cannot keep still, or as good as still, about them, and there is no chance that all of you can. But some of you can, and some of you are thirty or thirty-one and hard beset and bound to someone in brotherhood, perhaps in art, and you may see that the brotherhood you know is of a kind really wider than you may have thought, binding others among the living and the dead. It is best, at any rate, that you should have the living movement of his own mind about his New York life and the dissolution of his second marriage, and it is essential that you should see proof of selflessness in a man who often appeared self-centered, and often was.

Before the publication of *Let Us Now Praise Famous Men*, just before I returned to New York, I received the book in September '41, for review in *Time*. When Jim got word of this he wrote at once, airmail special, to make sure whether I had been consulted, whether I had time to spare for it, and whether if, consulted or not, I did have time and would write the review, we shouldn't agree that he would not read it. I wrote a review but the editor who had invited it thought it was too stiff and reverent (he was right) and sent it back. He reviewed the book himself, recognized great writing in it, but classified it as "a distinguished failure." By this he, as an old *Fortune* editor, did not really mean that if *Fortune* had done it it would have been a success, but that was true: it would have been objective and clearly organized and readable and virtuously restrained, and would have sounded well and been of small importance beyond the month it appeared. A failure on the contrary it consciously was, a "young man's book," and a sinful book to boot (as Jim called it in a letter to Father Flye) and was thereby true to the magnitude and difficulty of the case including the observer. It is a classic, and perhaps the only classic, of the whole period, of the whole attempted *genre*. Photographs and text alike are bitten out by the very juices of the men who made them, and at the same time they have the piteous monumentality of the things and souls represented. Between them Agee and Evans made sure that George and Annie Mae Gudger are as immortal as Priam and Hecuba, and a lot closer to home.

I refused to take about a quarter of Jim's already mortgaged income, as he proposed, and returned to work for *Time* from October '41 to May '43, when to my relief I joined the Navy. That October of my return he got "switched to movies," all right, and the last and perhaps the best phase of his life began. He and Mia Fritsch, who was to be his third wife, moved into the top-floor flat on Bleecker Street where they lived for the next ten years. Before I went to Fort Schuyler I managed to revise my manuscript of poems and put them together in a book, but not until Jim had commented on each in the most minute and delicate written criticism I ever had.

How more than appropriate, how momentous, it was that after 1941 James Agee had "Cinema" for all occupation could scarcely have been realized to the full by anyone, but a few of us at least felt uncommonly at peace about Jim's employment. He loved movies more than anyone I ever knew; he also lived them and thought them. To see and hear him describe a movie that he liked—shot by shot, almost frame by frame— was unquestionably better in many cases than to see the movie itself. Once when I was driving him across the Brooklyn Bridge in an open Model-A, he put on beside me such a rendering of Jimmy Cagney in a gangster film that I had to take my eyes off the road and give him my close attention. There must have been moments on that ride when we were both absolutely uninsurable.

He had wanted for years to do a scenario for Chaplin; whether he ever did more than imagine it, I have been unable to find out. By the late '30s he had, however, not only written but published two scenarios, both stunning exercises in what must be called screenwriting as literature. Both are published in this book.

The first, entitled "Notes for a Moving Picture: The House," was printed by Horace Gregory in a collection called *New Letters in America*, in 1937. Detailing every shot and every sound, second by counted second, with his huge sensuous precision and scope, he constructed a screen fantasy for the camera, his angelic brain, before whose magnifying gaze or swimming movement a tall old house disclosed its ghastly opulent moribundity until blown and flooded apart in an apocalyptic storm. Compare this with the efforts of more recently "rebellious" young men if you want to see how close to artistic nonexistence most of these are.

His second scenario was published in the first number of a review, *Films*, edited by Jay Leyda in 1939. In this one he merely (if you could use that word of anything Jim did) transposed into screen terms the famous scene in *Man's Fate* in which the hero, Kyo, waits with other Chinese Communists to be thrown by the Nationalists into the boiler of a locomotive. I am told that Malraux, who thought he had got everything out of this scene, thought again when he read the Agee script.

Concerning his movie reviewing for *Time*, T. S. Matthews has told me of one incident. Matthews as managing editor late one Sunday evening received and read a cover story Jim had written, on Laurence Olivier's *Hamlet*, and in Jim's presence indicated that he found it good enough, a little disappointing but good enough and in any case too late to revise; he initialed it for transmission to the printer (*Time* went to press on Monday) and in due course left for home presuming that Jim had also done so. At nine the next morning Jim presented him with a complete new handwritten version. Fully to appreciate this you would perhaps have to have felt the peculiar exhaustion of Sunday night at *Time*.

Jim Agee, however, had now found a kind of journalism answering to his passion. Beginning in December '42, he began the signed movie column for *The Nation*, every other week, that Margaret Marshall, the literary editor, invited and backed, and that in the next several years made him famous. He began to be called on at *Time* for general news stories to which no one else could do justice. Whatever he wrote for the magazine was so conspicuous that it might as well have been signed. In the Western Pacific I recognized at once his hand in *Time*'s page-one piece on the meaning of Hiroshima and Nagasaki:

. . . In what they said and did, men were still, as in the aftershock of a great wound, bemused and only semi-articulate, whether they were soldiers or scientists, or great statesmen, or the simplest of men. But in the dark depths of their minds and hearts, huge forms moved and silently arrayed themselves: Titans, arranging out of the chaos an age in which victory was already only the shout of a child in the street . . .

. . . All thoughts and things were split. The sudden achievement of victory was a mercy, to the Japanese no less than to the United Nations; but mercy born of a ruthlessness beyond anything in human chronicle. The race had been won, the weapon had been used by those on whom civilization could best hope to depend; but the demonstration of power against living creatures instead of dead matter created a bottomless wound in the living conscience of the race. The rational mind had won the most Promethean of its conquests over nature, and had put into the hands of common man the fire and force of the sun itself . . .

. . . The promise of good and of evil bordered alike on the infinite—with this further, terrible split in the fact: that upon a people already so nearly drowned in materialism even in peacetime, the good uses of this power might easily bring disaster as prodigious as the evil. The bomb rendered all decisions made so far, at Yalta and at Potsdam, mere trivial dams across tributary rivulets. When the bomb split open the universe and revealed the prospect of the infinitely extraordinary, it also revealed the oldest, simplest, commonest, most neglected and most important of facts: that each man is eternally and above all else responsible for his own soul, and, in the terrible words of the Psalmist, that no man may deliver his brother, nor make agreement unto God for him.

Man's fate has forever been shaped between the hands of reason and spirit, now in collaboration, again in conflict. Now reason and spirit meet on final ground. If either or anything is to survive, they must find a way to create an indissoluble partnership.

Enough, and perhaps more than enough, has been said by various people about the waste of Jim's talents in journalism. It is a consolation and a credit to his employers that on this occasion, as on some others, he was invited and was able to dignify the reporting of events.

14

When I got back to New York in 1946 I found Jim in a corduroy jacket, a subtle novelty, and in a mood far more independent than before of Left or "Liberal" attitudes. He had become a trace more worldly and better off (I'm sure Matthews saw to it that he was decently paid) and more sure of himself; and high time, too. His years of hard living and testing and questioning had given him in his *Nation* articles a great charge of perceptions to express. His lifetime pleasure in cinema had made him a master of film craft and repertory. He had had some of the public recognition that he deserved. Most important of all, I think, this critical job had turned his mind a few compass points from the bearing Truth to the bearing Art. He was ready to take a hand, as he was soon to do, in the actual and practical making of films.

We were never estranged, but we were never so close again, either, as we had been before the war. The course of things for me (here I must intrude a little again) had not only broken up my own previous marriage and way of life but had brought me back in astonishment, with a terrific bump, into Catholic faith and practice; and though Jim intensely sympathized with me in the breakup, he regarded my conversion with careful reserve. He saw an old friend ravaged and transported by the hair into precisely the same system of coordinates that he had wrestled out of in the '30s. Or rather, not precisely the same. For in my turn I had reservations, now, about the quality of his old vision. It struck me that for him it must have been a matter of imagination and empathy, a profound and sacramental sense of the natural world, but only a notion of the incommensurable overhead, the change of light and being that leaves a man no fulcrum by which to dislodge himself from his new place. With my all-too-negative capability and other flaws, I could easily have been self-deceived, as he must have imagined. I was not, however. At any rate, I now wanted to lead a kind of life that Jim had rejected and, in his own and general opinion, outgrown; and there was (at most) one art that I might practice, the art of verse that he had likewise left behind.

All the same, the memory of what he had aspired literally to be, in college and for the first years thereafter, could return now and again to trouble him. One day in 1947 when he and Mia brought their first baby, Teresa, to spend an afternoon with my wife and myself, he handed me the two very sad and strange sonnets on the buried steed, published three years later in *Botteghe Oscure* and now included in the collection of Agee's poems recently edited by myself. His hand at verse had barely retained but not refined its skill, and there is a coarseness along with the complexity of these and other late sonnets. Two or three of the final poems are very beautiful, though. "Sleep, Child" certainly is, and so is the peerless Christmas ballad in Tennessee dialect (but I am not sure how late that one is, and have no clue as to when it was written).

The last verses that he wrote were some rather casually attempted drafts, by invitation, for a musical that in the late winter and spring of 1955 Lillian Hellman and Leonard Bernstein were trying to make of *Candide*. Both playwright and composer felt that these drafts wouldn't do, but Miss Hellman is not sure that Jim, who was more desperately ill than he knew, understood this before his fatal heart attack on May 16th. "He was not a lyric writer," Miss Hellman says. "Good poets often aren't." At my distance I find the episode fairly astringent. In their most nearly completed state, the drafts appear in Agee's *Collected Poems* at the end of Part IV. They may be compared with the lighter lyrics by various hands, mainly Richard Wilbur's, for the show as produced in December 1956.

Helen Levitt has told me that only a year or so before his death in 1955 Jim seriously said to her that poetry had been his true vocation, the thing he was born to do, but that it was too difficult; on the other hand, work in films was pure pleasure for him. I think he had in mind the difficulty for everyone—not only for himself—of making true poetry in that time; I think, too, that what he was born to do, he did.

Jim's leaning to self-accusation does not seem to me very deplorable, however. It was, rather, part of what gave him his largeness among his contemporaries, most of whom were engaged in pretending that they were wonderful and their mishaps or shortcomings all ascribable to Society or History or Mother or other powers in the mythology of the period.

I gather that he got cooler and tougher about everything in his last years, in particular about love. Before he went to the Coast, in the late '40s, he wrote a draft scenario, never worked up for production or publication, in which with disabused and cruel objectivity he turned a camera eye on himself in his relations with women.

After my wife and I moved away from New York in the summer of 1949, we saw him only once again, for an evening, in the following spring. His last letter to me was from Malibu Beach in 1952: I had written to say how much I liked *The African Queen*. Of his final years I can have little to say. (I had been in Italy for two years when the shocking cable came to tell me of his death.) I am told that young men in New York began heroizing him and hanging on his words, but late one night at a *Partisan Review* sort of party a younger writer in impatience saw him as "a whisky-listless and excessive saint." I myself felt my heart sink when I began to read *The Morning Watch*; the writing seemed to me a little showy, though certainly with much to show; and I wondered if he were losing his irony and edge. It is pretty clear to me now that he had to go to those lengths of artifice and musical elaboration simply to make the break with journalism decisive. He never lost his edge, as *A Death in the Family* was to demonstrate—that narrative held so steadily and clearly in the middle distance and at the same time so full of Jim's power of realization, a contained power, fully comparable to that in the early work of Joyce. Let the easy remark die on your lips. Jim arrived at his austere style fifty years and a torn world away from Edwardian Dublin and Trieste; if it took him twenty years longer than it took Joyce, who else arrived at all?

The comparison with Joyce is worth pausing over a moment more. Each with his versatile and musical gift, each proud and a world-plunderer, each choosing the savage beauty of things as they are over the impossible pieties of adolescence, each concerned with the "conscience of his race." Agee had less ice-cold intellect; he could not have derived what Joyce did from Aquinas. He had, of course, nothing like Joyce's linguistic range. His affections were more widely distributed and perhaps dissipated. He inherited the violence that Americans inherit: a violence, too (it will not have escaped you), no more directed against office buildings, employers, and bourgeois horrors than against himself. The cinema that interested Joyce in its infancy had by Agee's time become a splendid art form, a successor perhaps to the art of fiction, and who else understood it better than he? The record is there in two volumes. Joyce had more irony, but Joyce, too, sentimentalized or angelicized the role of the artist. In all Agee's work the worst example of this is in the scenario of *Noa Noa,* and anyone can see that script becoming at times a maudlin caricature of the artist-as-saint.

Jim's weakness and strength were not so easy to tell apart. Consider, if you will, his early story, "They That Sow in Sorrow Shall Reap." Through weakness, through not being able to do otherwise, the boy narrator brings the laborer to the boardinghouse and so precipitates the catastrophe that leaves the scene and people in ruins. Or is it entirely through weakness? Is it not also through a dispassionate willingness to see his microcosm convulsed for the pure revelation of it, for an epiphany that he may record? Was it weakness later that kept James Agee at *Fortune,* or was it strategy and will, for the sake of the great use he would make of it? Ruins were left behind then, too, but in New York journalism of the '30s no one created anything like the Alabama book. Likewise, no weekly reviewer of the '40s created anything like the body of new insights contained in his *Nation* film pieces. Again, no writer of film pieces prepared himself to write for cinema with such clean and lovely inventiveness (barring the instance I have noted). Finally, no scriptwriter except possibly Faulkner exercised, or learned, in film writing the control over fiction that went into *A Death in the Family.* When you reflect on his life in this way, weakness and strategy, instinct and destiny seem all one thing.

In one of the best novels of the '60s, a charmer by a Southerner, I find a sentence running like this, of cemeteries that at first look like cities from a train passing at a slight elevation: ". . . tiny streets and corners and curbs and even plots of lawn, all of such a proportion that in the very instant of being mistaken and from the eye's own necessity, they set themselves off into the distance like a city seen from far away."* It is an Agee sentence, so I conclude that his writing has entered into the mainstream of English. But I share with him a disinclination for Literary History and its idiom. Jim may be a Figure for somebody else, he cannot be one for me.

> This breathing joy, heavy on us all

—it is his no longer; nevertheless, I have written this in his presence and therefore as truly as I could. Quite contrary to what has been said about him he amply fulfilled his promise. In one of his first sonnets he said, of his kin, his people:

*From *The Moviegoer,* by Walker Percy.

'Tis mine to touch with deathlessness their clay,
And I shall fail, and join those I betray.

In respect to that commission, who thinks that there was any failure or
betrayal?

Time writers from the 25th anniversary issue of March 8, 1948. Among those pictured are: *front row*, Duncan Norton-Taylor and T. S. Matthews (third and fourth from left); *second row*, Henry Anatole Grunwald (second from right); *fourth row*, Irving Howe (fourth from right); *fifth row*, Robert Fitzgerald (bearded) and Robert Cantwell (second and fourth from right); *back row*, Douglas Auchincloss, James Agee, and Ben Williamson (first, second, and third from left). Photo credit: Herb Gehr, *Life Magazine* © Time Warner Inc.; used by permission.

James Agee in 1945. Photograph © Helen Levitt; used by permission.

Flannery O'Connor, *c.* 1946.

Robert Fitzgerald, *c.* 1948. Photograph by Walker Evans.

James Laughlin and Robert Fitzgerald in Italy, *c.* 1954.

Robert Fitzgerald and five of his and Sally Fitzgerald's six children in Italy, *c.* 1960.

Flannery O'Connor: A Memoir

1

She was a girl who started with a gift for cartooning and satire, and found in herself a far greater gift, unique in her time and place, a marvel. She kept going deeper (this is a phrase she used) until making up stories became, for her, a way of testing and defining and conveying that superior knowledge that must be called religious. It must be called religious but with no false note in our voices, because her writing will make any false note that is applied to it very clear indeed. Bearing hard upon motives and manners, her stories as moralities cut in every direction and sometimes go to the bone of regional and social truth. But we are not likely to state what they show as well as they show it. We can stay on the safe side by affirming, what is true and usefully borne in mind, that making up stories was her craft, her pleasure, and her vocation, that her work from first to last is imaginative writing, often comic writing, superbly achieved and always to be enjoyed as that. We had better let our awareness of the knowledge in her stories grow quietly without forcing it, for nothing could be worse than to treat them straight off as problems for exegesis or texts to preach on.

2

The new severely cut slab of marble bearing her name and the dates March 25, 1925–August 3, 1964 lies in the family plot on a bare elevated place in the Milledgeville cemetery, beside another slab of identical shape marking the grave of her father, but his has also a soldier's headstone for Edward F. O'Connor, Jr., Lt. 325th Infantry, 82nd Division, who died February 1st, 1941. I have been out there with her mother to note it all and to say my heart's prayer as I should, though generally I feel as I gather Flannery felt about cemeteries, that they and all they contain

First published as an introduction to Flannery O'Connor's *Everything That Rises Must Converge* (New York: The Noonday Press–Farrar, Straus & Giroux, 1966). Reprinted by permission of Farrar, Straus & Giroux.

are just as well left in God's keeping and that one had better commune with persons, living or dead, than with gravestones and the silent earth. Milledgeville on a mild winter day without leafiness or bloom suggests no less remarkably than in the dogwood season (when I came before) the strict amenity of the older South, or at least this is what I make of there being so many pillared white houses. It was, after all, the capital of Georgia until after the War Between the States.

At the Cline house in town I have been out on the front porch, hatless and coatless in the sun, between the solid handcarved columns, fluted and two stories high, that were hoisted in place when the house was built in 1820 and the slaves, they say, were making by hand the bricks for the house and the openwork walls around the garden. Peter Cline acquired this place in 1886. He was a prominent man, in our American phrase, for many years mayor of the town, and he married successively two sisters, Kate L. and Margaret Ida Treanor. By the former he had seven children and by the latter nine, of whom Regina, Flannery's mother, was the seventh. All of these people were old Georgia Catholics. The first Mass in Milledgeville had been celebrated in the apartment of Hugh Treanor, father of Kate and Ida, in the Newell Hotel in 1847. Mrs. Hugh Treanor gave the plot of ground for the little church that was built in 1874.

From the house in town to the farm called Andalusia is about five miles on the Eatonton-Atlanta highway. A quarter of a mile off the road on rising ground, the white farmhouse looks narrow and steeply roofed with a screen porch across the front of it and a white watertank on very tall stilts behind. The driveway cuts through a red clay bank and curves gently uphill until it swerves around back of the house where there is a roof running out from over the kitchen door to make a broad shelter, and beyond this there are three cedar trees, one with a strong straight bough about eight feet off the grass. The grass is sleeted white by droppings from the peacocks that roost at night on the bough. In the background off to the left is the low darkly weathered clapboard house with a low open porch where the Negroes live and beyond it the barn with farm machinery in the yard. From the carport you see geese going by in single file and there are swans preening in the middle distance; you also see the peacocks proceeding sedate and dainty through the shrubbery to denude it of berries and through the flowerbeds to denude them of buds. There are maybe a dozen or twenty peacocks in sight, fabulous in throat and crest, to say nothing of the billowy tensile train behind. Between the fowls of this farmyard and the writings of Flannery O'Connor, who bought and cared for them and loved to look at them, I do not at all mind drawing a certain parallel, to wit, that if you miss the beauty of plain geese the peacocks will knock your eye out.

I have been in the dining room looking at old photographs with Regina. There is a big one of Flannery at about two, in profile, sitting crosslegged on a bed and frowning at a large book with an elegantly curled page lit within by reflected light. There is another of her father, a robust amused young man, looking very much the Legion Commander that he was, sitting like the hub of a wheel with his five gay younger brothers beside and behind him. They were a Savannah family, the O'Connors, and Ed, as Flannery always called him, had been in the real estate business there, and Flannery was born and lived her childhood there in a tall narrow brownstone house, going to St. Vincent's parochial school and later to the Sacred Heart. There is a studio photograph of the child at five or six, standing on a bench beside her mother, who is an absolute beauty with a heart-shaped face and large gray eyes and dark hair smoothly drawn down from the part. That would be about 1930 or '31 in Savannah. They moved to the Cline house in Milledgeville toward the end of the decade when Mr. O'Connor was ill with a fatal disease called lupus for which no effective treatment was then known. Flannery in her turn would suffer it and die of it or its consequences.

I have also been in the front room on the other side of the house, Flannery's bedroom, where she worked. Her aluminum crutches, acquired in 1955, are standing against the mantel. The bed is narrow and covered by a plain spread. It has a tall severe wooden headboard. At the foot is one of those moveable tray stands used in hospitals. On the low table to the right of the bed there is a small pile of books covered in black leather, three books in all, on top a Sunday missal, below that a breviary, below that a Holy Bible. To the left of the bed is her work desk, facing away from the front windows, facing the back of a wardrobe that is shoved up against it, no doubt to give her as nearly as possible nothing to look at while she worked. Behind it on a table under the window is a new electric typewriter still unused, still in the corklight plastic box it came in. There are a lot of books in plain bookcases of various sizes around the interior walls. Her painting of a rooster's angry head, on a circular wooden plaque, glares from the top of the tallest bookcase.

In the hall, in the dining room, and in the comfortable small living room of the "addition" they built in 1959, the paintings on the walls are all Flannery's, all done during the last thirteen years when she lived, in more or less infirmity, at the farm. They are simple but beautiful paintings of flowers in bowls, of cows under trees, of the Negro house under the bare trees of winter. I use this word "beautiful" with all possible premeditation. Once when I was working at a university I was asked with a couple of my friends who taught there to take part in a symposium on Flannery's work, a symposium which I expected would be favorable if critical, but it turned out that one of my friends didn't like her work at all because he thought it lacked a sense of natural beauty and human beauty. Troubled by this, I looked in the stories again and took a sentence from "The Artificial Nigger" to say what I felt she perceived not only in natural things but in her characters: "The trees were full of silver-white sunlight, and even the meanest of them sparkled." Surely even the meanest of them do. I observed that in the violent tale called "A Good Man Is Hard to Find" the least heroic of the characters was able, on his way to be shot, to shout a reassurance to his mother (though supporting himself against a tree) and that his wife, asked if she would like to follow him, murmured "Yes, thank you," as she got up with her baby and her broken shoulder. These were beautiful actions, I argued, though as brief as beautiful actions usually are.

To come back to the paintings, they are not only skilled in the application of paint but soundly composed and bold and sensitive in color and revelatory of their subjects, casual as the whole business was for her. She went deeper in this art as well. I know because I have looked through a sheaf of drawings she made before she was twenty when she was going to the Georgia Woman's College in Milledgeville and doing linoleum cut cartoons for the college paper, *Colonnade*. In one of the sketches one fish is saying to another, "You can go jump out of the lake," an idea in which I can hear, already, the authentic O'Connor humor. In the linoleum cuts the line was always strong and decisive with an energy and angularity that recall the pen drawings of George Price, drawings that in fact she admired. For the yearbook, *Spectrum*, for 1945, when she graduated, she tried a rounder kind of comic drawing, not so good. She was editor of the literary magazine, *The Corinthian*, that year and so clearly on her way to being a writer that one of her teachers took the initiative in getting her a fellowship to the Writers' Workshop at the University of Iowa. She began to publish before she got her M.A. there in 1947. After one more year at Iowa, she worked on her writing at Yaddo and in New York.

3

My wife and I met her early in 1949 when she was not yet twenty-four. A friend of ours brought her to our apartment in New York to bear him out in something he had to tell, and she did this with some difficulty, frowning and struggling softly in her drawl to put whatever it was exactly the way it was. She sat facing the windows and the March light over the East River. We saw a shy Georgia girl, her face heart-shaped and pale and glum, with fine eyes that could stop frowning and open brilliantly upon everything. We had not then read her first stories, but we knew that Mr. Ransom had said of them that they were *written*. Before she left that day we had a glimpse of her penetration and her scornful humor, and during the spring we saw her again and saw the furnished room where she lived and worked in a drab apartment hotel on the upper West Side. Among the writing people who were our friends Flannery, as a devout Catholic, was something of a curiosity (they were curiosities to her, too). She could make things fiercely plain, as in her comment, now legendary, on an interesting discussion of the Eucharistic Symbol: "If it were only a symbol, I'd say to hell with it."

The manner in which Flannery came to live with us that year was this. Having two small children and the promise of more, we were looking for a home in the country, and in July we found and bought one, a stone and timber house that lay back in a wilderness of laurel and second-growth oak on a hilltop in Connecticut. Over the garage part of the house was a separate bedroom and bathroom with a stairway of its own, suitable for a boarder. We badly needed a boarder, and Flannery volunteered. Our new house had character but no good joinery or other luxury, and the O'Connor study-bedroom was austere. The only piece of furniture I can distinctly remember was a Sears Roebuck dresser that my wife and I had painted a bright sky blue. The walls were of beaverboard on which we had rolled a coat or two of paint, vainly hoping to make them smooth. Between beaverboard and timbering the fieldmice pattered as the nights turned frosty, and our boarder's device against them was to push in pins on which they might hurt their feet, as she said. She reassured us a few years later that she had not had to put layers of New York *Times* between her blankets that winter. I know for a fact that she had to stuff newspaper in the window cracks; we did, too. We all stayed healthy, nevertheless.

The working day as we set it up that fall began with early Mass in Georgetown, four miles away. My wife and I took turns making this drive with our boarder while one of us remained to amuse the infants and get breakfast. After her egg the boarder would disappear up the back stairs. She would reappear about noon in her sweater, blue jeans, and loafers, looking slender and almost tall, and would take her daily walk, a half mile or so down the hill to the mailbox and back. No one lingered over lunch, but in the evening when the children had been fed and quieted for the night we would put a small pitcher of martinis to soak and call the boarder. Our talks then and at the dinner table were long and lighthearted, and they were our movies, our concerts, and our theater.

Flannery was out to be a writer on her own and had no plans to go back to live in Georgia. Her reminiscences, however, were almost all of her home town and countryside, and they were told with gusto. We heard a great deal even then about the farm outside Milledgeville which her mother had inherited from a brother, Flannery's Uncle Bernard, and was already managing with hired help, though she lived in town. The Negroes included, and still do, Jack and Louise and their boarder, Shot. Flannery would shake with laughter over some of their remarks and those of other country characters. We heard comparatively little about Iowa City, though one of the friends she had made there, Robie Macauley, won our pleased attention that year by bringing out a new edition of the Tietjens novels of Ford. Our boarder corresponded with a number of other young writers, wandering souls, from whose letters she would sometimes read us a passage of bravado.

I owe to Flannery my first reading of *Miss Lonelyhearts* that winter, as I owe her also my reading of *As I Lay Dying*. These are the only two works of fiction that I can remember her urging on me, and it is pretty clear from her work that they were close to her heart as a writer. So was Lardner. Literary criticism in general was not, but one essay that we all read and liked was Andrew Lytle's classic piece on Caroline Gordon, whom we knew and who later gave Flannery a lot of close and valuable counsel. We read and passed on to one another Newman and Acton and Father Hughes' history of the Church. At the college where I was working, an hour's drive away, I took up the *Divine Comedy* with some students, and I am almost sure I lent Flannery the Binyon version. Though she deprecated her French, now and again she would read some, and once carried off one of those appetizing volumes of Faguet from which I had learned about all I knew of old French literature. The interior life interested her, but less at that time than later as material for fiction. She maintained, for example, that Harry in *The Family Reunion* actually had pushed his wife overboard, against a theory that he had done so only in his mind. "If nothing happened, there's no story."

Meanwhile the typescript of yellow second sheets piled up in the room over the garage. Her first hero, Hazel Motes, had been imagined for a story that she published in the *Sewanee*, and this story, thinned out and toned down, was the opening of the novel she worked on now. The central episodes with Enoch Emery and Hoover Shoates (a name we all celebrated) were written in the winter and spring. In the summer of 1950, when she had reached an impasse with Haze and didn't know how to finish him off, she read for the first time the Oedipus plays. She went on then to end her story with the self-blinding of Motes, and she had to rework the body of the novel to prepare for it.

So that year passed in our wilderness. The leaves turned, the rains came, the woods were bared, the snows fell and glittered, fenders were belted by broken chains, the winter stars shone out. In the early mornings we had the liturgies of All Hallows, All Souls, Advent, Christmas, Epiphany. The diaper truck and the milk truck slogged in and slogged out. We worked on at our jobs through thaws and buds, through the May flies, and into summer, when we could take our evening ease in deckchairs on the grass. In May we had a third child to be baptized, this one held by Flannery O'Connor as godmother. Standing with her was Robert Giroux, who had become her editor (he too had met her in 1949) and later was to become her publisher. She was now one of the family, and no doubt the coolest and funniest one. She often entertained a child in her room or took one for a walk, and she introduced me to the idea and the Southern expression of *cutting a switch* to meet infant provocation—a useful recourse then and later. She was sure that we grownups were known to the children in private as "he," "she" and "the other one."

In the second autumn I had reason to be especially glad of our boarder's company at home, because I had to be away on a job half the week. But in December, just after the long labor of typing out her first draft, Flannery told us with amusement of a heaviness in her typing arms. When this got worse, we took her to the doctor at Wilton Corners. Rheumatoid arthritis, he was afraid it was, but he advised her to have a hospital checkup in Georgia when she went home for Christmas. On the train going South she became desperately ill. She did not have arthritis but a related disease, lupus, the disease that had killed her father.

4

For the rest of that winter and spring she was mostly in Emory Hospital in Atlanta, and very sick indeed. Disseminated lupus, as it is technically called, is an autoimmune disease in the same general group as arthritis and rheumatic fever. The trouble is that the body forms antibodies to its own tissues. It is primarily a blood vessel disease and can affect any organ; it can affect the bones. I have these details from Dr. Arthur J. Merrill in Atlanta, who pulled Flannery through that first onset with blood transfusions and was able then to arrest the disease with injections of a cortisone derivative, ACTH, in those days still in the experimental stage. Her hair all fell out after the high fevers, her face became terribly swollen, and he had to dehydrate her and put her on a salt-free diet. It is a fair indication of how sick she was that, until summer, we had no letter from her at all but corresponded through her mother. When at last Dr. Merrill let her go home she was too weak to climb stairs, and Regina O'Connor, deciding to take her to the farm, made a home there which was to be hers and Flannery's for thirteen years.

It must have been in late spring or early summer that Giroux accepted the first complete draft of the manuscript of *Wise Blood* for publication at Harcourt, Brace, for I find an undated letter from Regina referring to this, and to attempts at revision that Flannery had been making before a recurrence of high fever sent her back to Emory. When this particular bout was over she slowly improved for the rest of the year and began to write to us regularly. In September she reported being down to two moderate shots a day from four large ones. "The large doses of ACTH send you off in a rocket and are scarcely less disagreeable than the disease, so I am happy to be shut of them. I am working on the end of the book while a lady around here types the first part of it . . . I have twenty-one brown ducks with blue wing bars."

She sent the retyped manuscript to us and we forwarded it, at her request, to Caroline Gordon, who had read Flannery's few stories with intense interest. "She sent it back to me," Flannery wrote later, "with some nine pages of comments and she certainly increased my education thereby. So I am doing some more things to it and then I mean to send it off for the LAST time . . . I have got me five geese." A little later: "Enclosed is Opus Nauseous No. 1. I had to read it over after it came from the typist's and that was like spending the day eating a horse blanket . . . Do you think Mrs. Tate would [read it again]? All the changes

are efforts after what she suggested in that letter and I am much obliged
to her."

One of Caroline's main points was that the style of the narrator should
be more consistently distinct from the style of the characters, and I
believe that Flannery saw the rightness of this and learned quickly when
and when not to use a kind of indirect discourse in the country idiom she
loved. Before the first of the year the publishers had the manuscript in its
final form, and it was published in May 1952. The reviewers, by and
large, didn't know what to make of it. I don't think anyone even spotted
the bond with Nathanael West. Isaac Rosenfeld in *The New Republic*
objected that since the hero was plain crazy it was difficult to take his
religious predicament seriously. But Rosenfeld and everyone else knew
that a strong new writer was at large.

. Flannery had announced in December that she aimed to visit us some-
time in 1952. "I am only a little stiff in the heels so far this winter and am
taking a new kind of ACTH, put up in glue . . ." This worked so well
that in the course of the spring she decided to come in June. Reactions to
her grisly book around Milledgeville were of course all that could have
been expected. One of the kin delighted her with a telling and memorable remark: "I wish you could have found some other way to portray
your talents." In May she wrote: "My current literary assignment (from
Regina) is to write an introduction for Cousin Katie 'so she won't be
shocked,' to be *pasted* on the inside of her book. This piece has to be in
the tone of the Sacred Heart Messenger and carry the burden of contemporary critical thought. I keep putting it off."

She came, looking ravaged but pretty, with short soft new curls. She
was still on the salt-free diet, so my wife gave her cress and herbs. It
proved to be a difficult summer. We now had four small children and
were taking a small Negro slum child for a two-week country holiday. I
had to go off on a six-week job in the Middle West. Our domestic
particular, an old shepherdess from Gorizia, after being helpful for a
year, had learned from Croatian acquaintances of the comparative delights of life in Jersey City, and had begun to turn nasty. Before I got
back, my wife was ill and Flannery, herself on the verge of a relapse, had
to return to Milledgeville. She took the Negro child, Loretta, with her as
far as New York. I'm afraid she had no high opinion of our quixotic
hospitality to Loretta, who, she wrote to me, "might have been control-
lable if there had been a U.S. marshal in the house." My wife says this
was pure Georgia rhetoric on Flannery's part, Loretta having been too

shy during her visit to do anything but stand around caressing the blond heads of our young. Flannery had picked up a virus infection, which aroused her lupus, and Dr. Merrill had to put her dose of ACTH up temporarily from .25 cc. to 1 cc. a day. As to this, she wrote, "I have gotten a kind of Guggenheim. The ACTH has been reduced from $19.50 per bottle to $7.50." Soon she was better, up, and working, "and have just ordered myself a pair of peafowl and four peachicks from Florida . . ."

That year, in spite of illness, she did a lot of writing, some of it as good in its way as she would ever do. The story entitled "The Life You Save May Be Your Own," an inimitably funny one that is also a triumph over Erskine Caldwell and a thing of great beauty, I remember reading in manuscript on the road to Indiana. She showed us, too, the opening of a second novel, so powerful that we felt, one and all, that since it would be very hard to sustain it might have to be toned down. It was later, a little, and became part of *The Violent Bear It Away*. She wrote "The River." In the fall John Crowe Ransom invited her to apply for a Kenyon Review Fellowship, and she applied, she said, "before the envelope was opened good." By Christmas she knew that she had it. "I reckon most of this money will go to blood and ACTH and books, with a few sideline researches into the ways of the vulgar. I would like to go to California for about two minutes to further these researches, though at times I feel that a feeling for the vulgar is my natural talent and don't need any particular encouragement. Did you see the picture of Roy Rogers' horse attending a church service in Pasadena?"

News and other items in the press of our favored land were always a solace to her. She turned eagerly for years to the testimonial ads for a patent medicine called HADACOL, and these she would often pass on, especially after we moved to Europe late in '53 and were cut off from the savor of American life. Early that year, when she began to receive her fellowship money, she reported a mild change in the interest shown her work by the countryside. "My kinfolks think I am a commercial writer now and really they are very proud of me. My uncle Louis is always bringing a message from somebody at the King Hdw. Co. who has read *Wise Blood*. The last was: ask her why she don't write about some nice people. Louis says, I told them you wrote what *paid* . . . I am doing fairly well these days, though I am practically baldheaded on top and have a watermelon face . . ."

In another letter of about the same time I find: "The Maple Oats really send me. I mean they are a heap of improvement over saltless oatmeal, horse biscuit, stewed kleenex, and the other delicacies that I have been eating . . . The novel seems to be doing very well, I have a nice gangster in it named Rufus Florida Johnson . . ." Disappearing from the novel, he turned up a long time later in one of the stories in this volume. Dr. Merrill, whom she liked and called "the scientist," told her in the summer that she was "doing better than anybody else has that has what I got," and she flew up to see us in August. It was our last meeting as a family for five years.

The correspondence for 1954 begins: "I got word the other day that I had been reappointed a Kenyon Fellow, so that means the Rockerfellers [the Foundation supplied funds for the fellowships] will see to my blood and ACTH for another year and I will have to keep on praying for the repose of John D.'s soul . . . Today I got a letter from one Jimmie Crum of Los Angeles, California, who has just read *Wise Blood* and wants to know what happened to the guy in the ape suit . . . I am also corresponding with the secretary of the Chef's National Magazine, the Culinary Review . . ." She was acquiring what she called a "gret" reading public. She would soon have enough short stories for a collection. And her disease had apparently been checked. Late in the year, however, we heard of a new ailment in a letter to my wife: "I am walking with a cane these days which gives me a great air of distinction . . . I now feel that it makes very little difference what you call it. As the niggers say, I have the misery." In the same letter: "I have finally got off the ms. for my collection and it is scheduled to appear in May. Without your kind permission I have taken the liberty of dedicating (grand verb) it to you and Robert. This is because you all are my adopted kin . . . Nine stories about original sin, with my compliments . . ."

The misery referred to in this letter turned out to be disheartening enough. Either her disease or the drug that controlled it, or both, caused a softening or deterioration of the bones, her jaw bones and also her leg bones at the hip. Finally, a year later, the doctor put her on crutches. At more or less the same time, though, she was able—thank God—to switch from ACTH to a new wonder drug, taken in tablets, in tiny doses, and "for the first time in four years don't have to give myself shots or conserve on salt." Meanwhile her book of stories, *A Good Man Is Hard To Find*, went into a third printing. Early in '56 she learned that Gallimard was publishing *Wise Blood* in Paris in an expert translation by Maurice Coindreau. She found herself now and henceforward a woman-of-letters. And in fact she and her devoted and keenwitted mother, who learned thoroughly to understand what Flannery was up to, became an effective team. Regina ran the farm and guarded Flannery's limited strength and saw to it that she had her mornings free for writing. At noon they would drive in to town for the mail and most often have lunch at the Sanford House, where behind the white pillars there is excellent cooking, and over the mantel there is a photograph of General Lee. In the afternoon Flannery could take the air on her crutches and feed her various fowl. She wrote that she had sixteen peachickens and her sense of well-being was at its height.

The new drug and the crutches increased Flannery's mobility so much that she began to accept invitations to give talks and readings at relatively distant points. After the isolated life in Connecticut and the confinement of her illness, these trips—and in the next six or seven years she made a score of them—brought her into the world again and gave her a whole new range of acquaintances. In her talks she had wonderful things to say. I didn't quite realize this—I just wanted to see her—when I got her to come to Notre Dame in the spring of '57 (I was working there on temporary leave, self-accorded, from the job I had in hand in Italy). I met her in Chicago and flew down with her to South Bend. She seemed frail but steady, no longer disfigured by any swelling, and her hair had grown long again. She managed her light crutches with distaste but some dexterity. Her audience that evening was already instructed in a number of topics of concern to her, but it was better instructed when she finished. I have this paper before me now, and can remember my pleasure as she read it out, intent upon it, hanging on her crutches at the lectern, courteous and earnest and dissolvent of nonsense.

"I doubt if the texture of Southern life is any more grotesque than that of the rest of the nation, but it does seem evident that the Southern writer is particularly adept at recognizing the grotesque; and to recognize the grotesque, you have to have some notion of what is not grotesque and why . . ."

"Southern culture has fostered a type of imagination that has been influenced by Christianity of a not too unorthodox kind and by a strong devotion to the Bible, which has kept our minds attached to the concrete and the living symbol . . ."

"The Catholic sacramental view of life is one that maintains and supports at every turn the vision that the story teller must have if he is going to write fiction of any depth . . ."

"The Church, far from restricting the Catholic writer, generally provides him with more advantages than he is able or willing to turn to account; and usually, his sorry productions are a result, not of restrictions that the Church has imposed, but of restrictions that he has failed to impose on himself. Freedom is of no use without taste and without the ordinary competence to follow the particular laws of what we have been given to do . . ."

Toward the end of the year she wrote to us (we were living in Liguria) that Cousin Katie in Savannah wished to give her and her mother a trip to Lourdes with a company of pilgrims from Savannah. Dr. Merrill permitted this on condition that she depart from the "tour" to rest with us for a week. So in April I brought her and Mrs. O'Connor down to our place from Milan, and after the visit my wife went along to Lourdes to help with the languages and details of travel. Flannery dreaded the possibility of a miracle at Lourdes, and she forced herself to the piety of the bath for her mother's sake and Cousin Katie's; she also accompanied the pilgrims to Rome for an audience with Pope Pius XII, who received her with interest and gave her a special blessing. On May 11, home again, she wrote: "I enjoyed most seeing you all and the Pope . . ." There was no miracle but what seemed a small favor: her bone trouble got no worse.

For the rest of that year she worked on the new novel. Early in '59 she had finished a draft at about the time the Ford Foundation gave her (as also to me, a bolt from the blue) one of eleven grants for creative writing. Her hip and her general condition now allowed her to drive around Milledgeville "all over the place in the automobile just like a bloody adult." We had some correspondence about the novel, in particular about reworking the character of Rayber who had been, she said, "the trouble all along." She made the middle section more dramatic by adding the episode of the girl revivalist. By mid-October it was done, and it was brought out by her present publisher in May 1960.

I saw Flannery twice again, once on a visit to the farm when the dogwood was flowering in April 1961, and then at the Smith College commencement in 1963 when she received an honorary degree. The serenity of the natural scene on these occasions now frames for me the serenity of our old boarder, who had fought a good fight and been illluminated by it. In '63 as in '56 she won the first prize in the annual O. Henry short story collection, and she was working on a third novel. But early in '64 her great respite came to an end. She had to have an abdominal operation. In the aftermath of this her lupus returned, in April, and proved uncontrollable. In May, as I learned later, Caroline Gordon found her looking wan and wasted. She was in the Piedmont Hospital in Atlanta for a month in May and June. I heard nothing of this and had no notion that she was seriously ill until a note came from her with a new anecdote of farm life and the single sentence: "Ask Sally to pray that the lupus don't finish me off too quick." Late in July she was taken to the Milledgeville hospital with a severe kidney failure, and she died there in a coma on the morning of August 3.

5

The black sky was underpinned with long silver streaks that looked like scaffolding and depth on depth behind it were thousands of stars that all seemed to be moving very slowly as if they were about some vast construction work that involved the whole order of the universe and would take all time to complete. No one was paying any attention to the sky. The stores in Taulkinham stayed open on Thursday nights so that people could have an extra opportunity to see what was for sale.

(*Wise Blood*)

A catchword when Flannery O'Connor began to write was the German *angst*, and it seemed that Auden had hit it off in one of his titles as the "Age of Anxiety." The last word in attitudes was the Existentialist one, resting on the perception that beyond any immediate situation there is possibly nothing—nothing beyond, nothing behind, nada. Now, our country family in 1949 and 1950 believed on excellent grounds that beyond the immediate there was practically everything, like the stars over Taulkinham—the past, the future, and the Creator thereof. But the horror of recent human predicaments had not been lost on us. Flannery felt that an artist who was a Catholic should face all the truth down to the worst of it. If she worried about the side effects of the ungenteel imagination, she took heart that year from Mauriac's dictum about "purifying the source"—the creative spirit—rather than damming or diverting the stream.

In *Wise Blood* she did parody the Existentialist point of view, as Brainard Cheney has said (in the *Sewanee Review* for Autumn 1964), but the parody was very serious. In this and in most of her later writing she gave to the godless a force proportionate to the force it actually has: in episode after episode, as in the world, as in ourselves, it wins. We can all hear our disbelief, picked out of the air we breathe, when Hazel Motes says, "I'm going to preach there was no Fall because there was nothing to fall from and no Redemption because there was no Fall and no Judgment because there wasn't the first two. Nothing matters but that Jesus was a liar." And in whom is *angst* so dead that he never feels, as Haze puts it:

"Where you came from is gone, where you thought you were going to never was there, and where you are is no good unless you can get away from it."

Note the velocity and rightness of these sentences. Many pages and a number of stories by this writer have the same perfection, and the novels have it in sections though they narrowly miss it as wholes. I am speaking now of merits achieved in the reader's interest: no unliving words, the realization of character by exquisitely chosen speech and interior speech and behavior, the action moving at the right speed so that no part of the situation is left out or blurred and the violent thing, though surprising, happens after due preparation, because it has to. Along with her gifts, patient toil and discipline brought about these merits, and a further question can be asked about that: Why? What was the standard to which the writer felt herself answerable? Well, in 1957 she said:

"The serious fiction writer will think that any story that can be entirely explained by the adequate motivation of the characters or by a believable imitation of a way of life or by a proper theology, will not be a large enough story for him to occupy himself with. This is not to say that he doesn't have to be concerned with adequate motivation or accurate reference or a right theology; he does; but he has to be concerned with them only because the meaning of his story does not begin except at a depth where these things have been exhausted. The fiction writer presents mystery through manners, grace through nature, but when he finishes, there always has to be left over that sense of Mystery which cannot be accounted for by any human formula."

This is an open and moving statement of a certain end for literary art. The end, and some of the terms used here, seem to me similar to those of another Christian writer who died recently, T. S. Eliot. I do not propose any confusion between a London man of letters who wrote verse and criticism and a Southern woman who wrote fiction, for indeed they lived a world apart. Only at the horizon, one might say, do the lines each pursued come together; but the horizon is an important level. It is also important that they were similarly moved toward serious art, being early and much possessed by death as a reality, a strong spiritual sensation, giving odd clarity to the appearances they saw through or saw beyond. In her case as in his, if anyone at first found the writing startling he could pertinently remind himself how startling it was going to be to lose his own body, that Ancient Classic. Sensibility in both produced a wariness of beautiful letters and, in the writing, a concision of effect.

When it comes to seeing the skull beneath the skin, we may remark that the heroes of both O'Connor novels are so perceived within the first few pages, and her published work begins and ends with coffin dreams. Her *memento mori* is no less authentic for being often hilarious, devastating to a secular world and all it cherishes. The O'Connor equivalent for Eliot's drowned Phoenician sailor ("Consider Phlebas, who was once handsome and tall as you") is a museum piece, the shrunken corpse that the idiot Enoch Emery in *Wise Blood* proposes as the new humanist jesus.

> "See theter notice," Enoch said in a church whisper, pointing to a type-written card at the man's foot, "it says he was once as tall as you or me. Some A-rabs did it to him in six months . . ."

And there is a classic exchange in "The Life You Save May Be Your Own":

> "Why listen, lady," said Mr. Shiftlet with a grin of delight, "the monks of old slept in their coffins."
> "They wasn't as advanced as we are," the old woman said.

The state of being as advanced as we are had been, of course, blasted to glory in "The Waste Land" before Flannery made her version, a translation, as it were, into American ("The Vacant Lot"). To take what used to be called low life and picture it as farcically empty, raging with energy, and at the same time, *sub specie aeternitatis*, full of meaning: this was the point of "Sweeney Agonistes" and the point of many pages of O'Connor. As for our monuments, those of a decent godless people, surely the asphalt road and the thousand lost golf balls are not a patch on images like that of the hillside covered with used car bodies, in *The Violent Bear It Away:*

> In the indistinct darkness, they seemed to be drowning into the ground, to be about half-submerged already. The city hung in front of them on the side of the mountain as if it were a larger part of the same pile, not yet buried so deep. The fire had gone out of it and it appeared settled into its unbreakable parts.

Death is not the only one of the Last Things present in the O'Connor stories; Judgment is there, too. On the pride of contemporary man, in particular on flying as his greatest achievement, Tarwater in *The Violent* has a prophet's opinion:

> "I wouldn't give you nothing for no airplane. A buzzard can fly."

Christ the tiger, a phrase in Eliot, is a force felt in O'Connor. So is the impulse to renounce the blessèd face, and to renounce the voice. In her work we are shown that vices are fathered by our heroism, virtues forced upon us by our impudent crimes, and that neither fear nor courage saves us (we are saved by grace, if at all, though courage may dispose us toward grace). Her best stories do the work that Eliot wished his plays to do, raising anagogical meaning over literal action. He may have felt this himself, for though he rarely read fiction I am told that a few years before he died he read her stories and exclaimed in admiration at them.

6

The title of the present book comes from Teilhard de Chardin, whose works Flannery O'Conor had been reading at least since early 1961 when she recommended them to me. It is a title taken in full respect and with profound and necessary irony. For Teilhard's vision of the "omega point" virtually at the end of time, or at any rate of a time-span rightly conceivable by paleontologist or geologist alone, has appealed to people to whom it may seem to offer one more path past the Crucifixion. That could be corrected by no sense of life better than by O'Connor's. Quite as austere in its way as his, her vision will hold us down to earth where the clashes of blind wills and the low dodges of the heart permit any rising or convergence only at the cost of agony. At that cost, yes, a little.

The better a poem or piece of fiction the more corrective or indeed destructive it is likely to be of any fatuous happiness in abstractions. "Rising" and "convergence" in these stories, as the title story at once makes clear, are shown in classes, generations, and colors. What each story has to say is what it shows. If we are aware that the meaning of the stories is to be sought in the stories and well apprehended in the stories alone, we may try a few rough and cautious statements about them. Thus the title story shows, amid much else in a particular action of particular persons, young and old and black and white to be practically sealed off against one another, struggling but hardly upward or together in a welter of petty feelings and cross purposes, resolved only slightly even by the tragic blow. "Slightly," however, may mean a great deal in the economy of this writer. The story is one of those, like "The Artificial Nigger" in her first collection and "Revelation" in this, in which the low-keyed and calibrated style is allowed a moment of elevation.

What is wrong in this story we feel to be diffused throughout the persons and in the predicament itself, but in at least two of the stories, and those among the latest and most elaborate, the malign is more concentrated in one personage. I do not mean *il maligno*, as the Italians call the devil. There are few better representations of the devil in fiction than Tarwater's friend, as overheard and finally embodied in *The Violent;* but in these two stories, "The Comforts of Home" and "The Lame Shall Enter First," the personage in question is not quite that. He need not be, since the souls to be attacked are comparatively feeble. Brainless and brainy depravity are enough, respectively, to bring down in ruin an irritable academic and a self-regarding do-gooder. The latter story is clearly a second effort with the three figures of the novel, Tarwater, Rayber, and Bishop, who are here reworked, more neatly in some respects, as Johnson, Shepard, and Norton.

Other similarities link various stories to one another and to earlier stories. There is a family resemblance between Julian in the title story, Wesley in "Greenleaf," Ashbury in "The Enduring Chill," and Thomas in "The Comforts of Home." The Wellesley girl in "Revelation" is related to all these and to the girl in "Good Country People." In the various mothers of the stories there are facets of Mrs. McIntyre in "The Displaced Person." Parker in "Parker's Back" has some of the traits of a latter-day Hazel Motes. The critic will note these recurrent types and situations. He will note too that the setting remains the same, Southern and rural as he will say, and that large classes of contemporary experience, as of industry and war and office work and foreign travel, are barely touched if touched at all. But in saying how the stories are limited and how they are not, the sensitive critic will have a care. For one thing, it is evident that the writer deliberately and indeed indifferently, almost defiantly, restricted her horizontal range; a pasture scene and a fortress wall of pine woods reappear like a signature in story after story. The same is true of her social range and range of idiom. But these restrictions, like the very humility of her style, are all deceptive. The true range of the stories is vertical and Dantesque in what is taken in, in scale of implication. As to the style, there is also more to say.

She would be sardonic over the word *ascesis*, but it seems to me a good one for the peculiar discipline of the O'Connor style. How much has been refrained from, and how much else has been cut out and thrown away, in order that the bald narrative sentences should present just what they present and in just this order! What counts is the passion by which the stories were formed, the depth, as Virginia Woolf said of Milton, at which the options were taken. Beyond incidental phrasing and images, beauty lies in the strong invention and execution of the things, as in objects expertly forged or case or stamped, with edges, not waxen and worn or softly molded.

If we look for pleasure of a secondary kind such as we take in the shadings and suffusions of Henry James, I suggest that this is given in these stories by the comedy. There is quite a gamut of it, running from something very like cartooning to an irony dry and refined, especially in the treatment of the most serious matters. John Crowe Ransom was the first reader known to me to realize and say that Flannery O'Connor was one of our few tragic writers, a fact that we will not miss now in reading "The Displaced Person" in the first volume or "The Comforts of Home" in this. But it is far from the whole story. On the tragic scene, each time, the presence of her humor is like the presence of grace. Has not tragicomedy at least since Dante been the most Christian of *genres?*

I do not want to claim too much for these stories, or to imply that every story comes off equally well. That would be unfaithful to her own conscience and sense of fact. Let the good critic rejoice in the field for discrimination these stories offer him. Before I turn them over to him and to the reader, I should like to offer a reflection or two on the late masterpiece called "Revelation." One of its excellences is to present through a chance collection in a doctor's waiting room a picture of a whole "section"—realized, that is, in the human beings who compose it, each marvelously and irreducibly what he or she is. For one example of the rendering, which is faultless, consider this:

> A grotesque revolving shadow passed across the curtain behind her and was thrown palely on the opposite wall. Then a bicycle clattered down against the outside of the building. The door opened and a colored boy glided in with a tray from the drug store. It had two large red and white paper cups on it with tops on them. He was a tall, very black boy in discolored white pants and a green nylon shirt. He was chewing gum slowly, as if to music. He set the tray down in the office opening next to the fern and stuck his head through to look for the secretary. She was not in there. He rested his arms on the ledge and waited, his narrow bottom stuck out, swaying slowly to the left and right. He raised a hand over his head and scratched the base of his skull.

Not only do we see this boy for the rest of our lives; for an instant we hear him think. But the greater excellence of the story is to bring about a rising and a convergence, a movement of spirit in Ruby Turpin that is her rising to a terrible occasion, and a convergence between her and the violent agent of this change.

The terms of the struggle are intensely local, as they will be in all such struggles, but we need not be too shy about seeing through them to the meaning that lies beyond at the usual mysterious depth. How else but at a mysterious depth can we understand a pretty notion like the Soul of the South? What the struggle requires of Mrs. Turpin is courage and humility, that is clear enough. Perhaps as a reward for these, her eyes are opened. And the ascent that she sees at the end, in an astonishment like the astonishment of the new dead, takes place against that field of stars that moved beyond Taulkinham in *Wise Blood* and that hold for a small boy, in another of these stories, the lost presence of his mother.

Vachel Lindsay:
A Springfield Memoir

In the photograph, the Lindsays occupy the living room couch, possibly a little nap-worn and therefore draped for the occasion with a fringed Oriental rug. Elisabeth at Vachel's left has her arm around small Susan; Elisabeth's gaze is gray and level under her smooth broad brow, her hair pulled back. Vachel holds Nicky, just coming out of a squirm, firmly against his chest and over Nicky's head has thrown his own head back, chuckling with half-closed eyes. It is the family that I knew and grope now to remember.

On perhaps half a dozen summer evenings in 1930 and '31, Vachel and Elisabeth were hosts to me and two or three of my friends in the Lindsay home at 603 South Fifth Street in Springfield. I had entrée, so to put it, in the first place because my Uncle Art had been a friend of Vachel since boyhood and made an appearance in his *Bryan* poem:

> Tom Dines and Art Fitzgerald and the gangs
> > that they could get—
> I can hear them yelling yet—

and in the second place because, on returning from Spokane to live in Springfield, Vachel had gone out of his way with a newspaper interviewer to praise my high school poems (put in his hands by Susan Wilcox, his English teacher in 1897 and mine thirty years later). So on summer evening walks with friends from high school days, talking life over as we sauntered under the elms through the sultry dusk of old neighborhoods, I sometimes ventured to lead the way to the Lindsay veranda and ring, or knock at the screen door. The children were by that time abed. We would be admitted out of the half-dark to the lamp-lit living room. Seated there perspiring with politeness and gaucherie, supplied by Elisabeth with cookies and lemonade, we would soon have the privilege of hearing Vachel read, or recite, poems of his choice. He could transmute what had seemed known on a page into something never

---

First published in *Poetry*, October, 1982.

known before. But he read almost none of his own things. The only one I am sure he did read was his tribute to Illinois' quondam Governor Altgeld:

> Sleep softly, eagle forgotten, under the stone . . .

He may have felt that the longer poems, the *Congo* poem, for example, and *The Chinese Nightingale,* were less suitable for the living room than for the auditoriums in which he performed them, sang them, with his bardlike range of tempo and tone. No, instead of Lindsay we heard Yeats and de la Mare and Hodgson. Vachel's voice was a great thing to possess: deep and clear and magical. His leonine head thrown back, his eyes shut under his bulging brow, he would make us imagine:

> . . . an old unhappy bull
> In the forest beautiful . . .

or:

> Picking a dish of sweet
> Berries and plums to eat,
> Eve in the bells and grass
> Up to her knees . . .

or he would thrill us with the Irishman's passion:

> But we have all bent low and low and kissed the quiet feet
> Of Cathleen, the daughter of Houlihan . . .

One evening he brought out smooth white cards and India ink and made us each an arabesque in his curling and sweeping calligraphic style. And I remember him saying, as he handed me mine, that this was for a love child. He must have had the story of my parents in mind, but the term also rang in my ears as touching my own nature, since in those days I forever pined for one faraway princess or another and at that very moment secretly adored his Elisabeth.

Kind and avuncular Vachel made me send some poems to *Poetry,* whence came in December 1930 a letter of acceptance in fine italic script from the associate editor, Morton Dauwen Zabel, of whose critical distinction I would have the benefit thereafter through years of friendship and correspondence. The poems appeared in August 1931. At Zabel's invitation I called at *Poetry*'s office, 232 East Erie Street, at lunch time when I passed through Chicago. The tiny and cordial but rather grim lady in dark garments was Harriet Monroe, and the shy but obviously able young lady in the background was Geraldine Udell, mistress of the files and ordered baskets. Miss Monroe and Mr. Zabel, he formal but quietly beaming in his gray homburg, took me out for lunch and showed interest in my future. What impended for me was Trinity College, Cambridge, where I had been admitted and would be expected in time for the Michaelmas term. At this prospect Miss Monroe became especially grim. She foresaw hazards for me across the sea. "I hope you find Cambridge of some use to you," she said in a letter a bit later. "It's all right to try England for a while if you don't get caught by the tyrannously snobbish English social system. Even Eliot succumbed, and Henry James and hundreds of Americans less distinguished. The way they look you up and down!"

No reflections of this kind came from the Lindsays. On the contrary, my voyage peculiarly excited Vachel. One of the chief triumphs of his life had been his reading and lecturing at Oxford in 1920, and now he saw another Springfield poet, much younger and in some sense his protégé, headed for comparable quads. It was as though the Gospel of Beauty might again be preached overseas; it was as though the majestic censer that in his drawing he had set swinging in the sky over Lincoln's tomb in *The Golden Book of Springfield* might get another toss from scapegrace me. So in the early fall he wrote notes to literati in England to herald my approach. Scarcely had I settled in my Cambridge digs in early October when a letter came from him written in India ink in his flowing looping hand.

My dear Robert, [he wrote] good wishes to you, and big vistas, on this year's adventure. I have the greatest faith in your past, your present and your future. It is eleven years since I saw England, and my last letters there, except two or three, were eleven years ago. I have therefore disturbed them so little that when I wrote to a handful of the poets, sending them also the August, 1931, *Poetry*, I felt I was springing on them a surprise they would like, after a long and thundering silence from Springfield.

These things are all chance—the man I had least hope of waking up may be having dinner with you this evening. I have suggested to one or two that I knew might like to make it the basis of a conversation to offer a book or two for review. The British like excuses like this. The understanding of course is that the real objective is incidental conversation. They are an amusing race indeed, and mean no harm. Make minute notes of all your sudden shocks and microscopic surprises, the first month. It is the only time to keep a diary, for after that in spite of Hell and Breakfast the visitor slips far enough into their ways to miss all the microscopic shocks. Then keep a diary no more but have a good time till the last month. Then annotate that first month's diary, a paragraph of comment for every sentence.

Of course you will not do this, in fact. But you will discover that you will do it mentally, in spite of everything. There has not yet lived the man who can draw the exact contrast between one good page of the New York Times and the London Times. But it is there—we all feel it—and it makes us full of dizzy wonder. Elisabeth is as eager over your fortunes as I am— we want to know all you want to tell us. We know you will not fail us in high adventure. With great good wishes, Vachel Lindsay.

In short order I heard from Wilfrid Gibson, John Drinkwater, T. S. Eliot, and (from Rapallo) Ezra Pound, all of whom I did in fact call on in the course of the year. But within two months Vachel Lindsay had by his own will departed from Springfield and from this world. There were to be no more evenings on South Fifth Street, where in the early hours of Saturday, December 5th, 1931, the beautiful voice had been finally and terribly stilled. "Sad," wrote Harriet Monroe, "that you and I have lost a friend, and the world a poet . . ." That was true. He merited the title more than most who aspire to it, and he had a great man's magnanimity. But the case was painful. The world's ways were not his, nor its wisdom, either. The town for which he had his visionary hopes of polity and beauty laughed up its sleeve at him. Those who hear no poetry and wish to hear none thought him eccentric merely. Literary authorities in the '30s had other interests, and literary fashion had turned from him long before he died. During the very time of his generosity to me, he lived, as later became clear, in greater and greater anxiety, until in the end it seems he did not know where to turn. There is lacerating pathos in his high-hearted words to me about high adventure. In January 1932, I had a remarkable letter from Elisabeth.

There is no thought of grief for Vachel [she wrote]. He had had everything he thought he wanted of life, and none of it was right. Now he is either at peace, or free in a realm to which he always belonged far more than to this small planet; and either way one can be glad for him. I wish I could have done more for him, but it was an impertinence to have attempted anything. The heart of the matter for me is complete and irrevocable defeat, with every banner struck, and tomorrow coming on just the same . . . There was a small margin of insurance over the debts, taken out just last spring; and Logan Hay [an honorable first citizen] is holding a subscription fund in reserve, in case we should need it; and Edgar Lee Masters in New York has been doing things in a big way with The Players and the Carnegies and others; so, bitter as it seems, I am less worried about money than for a long, long time. That doesn't seem right, and it rather hurts me; but I take it just the same, knowing that it is really meant for him. But how he should have had it! . . .

And I'm going on with the job I picked up in November, which is a superior culture racket, making the young business and professional woman safe for literature and Society, on a national scale, though I am responsible only for Illinois: in other words, organizing and sponsoring and getting most of the local grief for a sorority, Greek letters and everything, which derives appropriately from Kansas City . . . I bear it with a gusto which is truly appalling . . .

Such a strange thing: just a week before Vachel died, Harris and Ewing in Washington, D. C. took the most beautiful picture of him that I have ever seen. They evidently asked for the sitting, as people often did when he was in town; and then sent on the finished portrait as the customary thank you for the privilege. He hadn't thought to tell me about it, and when I opened the package, just a week after it had all happened, and saw him there, young, happy, strong, looking into the light, it was almost too much . . .

Then she wrote of how Vachel's sister, Olive Wakefield, had come for the funeral and stayed and one night insisted on talking until 4 a.m.

I finally fled and locked myself into the nursery and shuddered beside Susan till dawn, when, as usual, I could sleep. Susan took it calmly, woke up and said in a surprised sleepy voice, 'Why, Mother, you never did this before,' and went right back to sleep. Poor Olive, she wandered over the house and over the house, and kept calling Good Night, to what or whom I know not; but it was disconcerting. I think it must have been very hard for her . . .

I have seen Vachel's grave only once since that day. I had dreaded it so, though I don't believe in it; then Mary Morrison had to take me out to give him a medal Mother Michelle had sent. It had been blessed, and one couldn't leave it lying about. The place was very peaceful, and your laurel wreath still crisp and green under the winter sun. He told me when I first met him in Spokane that he wanted to be there. I couldn't be sure at the time. Now I know. And though he probably didn't want that, either, still he must have now whatever it was. He had waited so long . . .

Not the least of my fortunes as a fortunate young man was to have had the confidence of this touching and impressive letter. Elisabeth went to teach at Mills College in California, then to be a dean at a school in

Washington, and later at a school in Hartford, and she brought her children up. We kept in touch through correspondence for a decade, until the Second Great War, when so many people including ourselves lost track of one another. Now, after so many years, I hope it is no indiscretion to share with *Poetry* these memories and letters.

Randall Jarrell: A Memoir

If I could have my way in the matter, I would prefer to see Randall again in the quarry pool near Bloomington, Indiana, where we used to swim almost every afternoon in the summer of 1952. He and I and Leslie Fiedler were holding classes at the School of Letters there, and it was nice to have a swimming hole to resort to when the heat waves made our eyebrows crawl. The abandoned limestone quarry at the edge of town was filled with clear green spring water, always cool, and crossed by a smooth rock ledge a foot or so above the water, very handy for diving and sunning. You drove down a country road, walked a quarter of a mile or so, and found yourself approaching this place, which was off limits, we were told, for town and university people—and in fact rarely visited except by ourselves and our friends. Our friends were a few students, the most constant of whom were two bright and not at all uncomely girls. That sounds interesting, and it was, but it would have had very slight interest for the well-known Kinsey Institute at the university. If there had been no other considerations, I suppose the awful presence of the Institute would have been enough to make all three of us refrain from so much as brushing those girls with a daisy, in the fine Ransom phrase. Prelapsarian if not prenatal were our pleasures, cavorting in that pool with our naiads, whom I can still see pale and blurry underwater or emerging, hair streaming, to shake and bat the blearing drops from their eyes. And I see Randall just as vividly, coming up for air, his hair plastered over his forehead, his line of mustache dripping, eyes shut tight in the delicate sallow bony face that at those times and at others had what I thought of as a *Confederate* look—old-fashioned and rural and honorable and a little toothy or hungry. Once up and paddling and often laughing, he would talk about what had crossed his mind underwater, so to speak. Long ago he had done at least one passionate essay to wake people up to Robert Frost, but that summer he was still waking up, himself; hanging on a floating log in the quarry pool, he began one day to quote aloud the poem, "Provide, Provide," and to his growing astonishment and delight

First published in *Randall Jarrell, 1914–1965*, edited by Robert Lowell, Peter Taylor, and Robert Penn Warren (New York: Farrar, Straus & Giroux, 1967). Reprinted by permission of Farrar, Straus & Giroux.

succeeded in going straight through it from memory. "Why, *I* didn't know I had memorized *that!*" Randall is one of the few men I have known who chortled. He really did. "Baby *doll!*" he would cry, and his voice simply rose and broke in joy. As I say, I would like to see him again in that happiness, in the cool Midwestern water.

It is the chronological centerpiece in my memories of him. At Sarah Lawrence in the first year after the war we met as part-time teachers and became friends. Randall had agreed to edit the literary section of *The Nation* that winter while Margaret Marshall was on leave, so he was living in Manhattan as I was, and I could often give him a ride back from Bronxville in my olive-drab old Ford. We talked about poems and people on those trips, as the parkway unrolled before us back to the great Hudson scene, or we talked at lunch together in the college cafeteria or over coffee in the college tuckshop. I can see him plainly in that place, too: young and tallish and a bit gangling but with dignity, his long throat distinctly angled, his dark eyes in repose proud and solemn, the lids drooping slightly toward the outer corners. More often they were animated, exceedingly gay and bright, but in conversation they could shadow swiftly with recognition, looking less at you than at some depth in himself that had been stirred, becoming hooded eyes where memory and mockery lurked. He loved his job at *The Nation*, or at least he certainly loved the game of matching reviewers and books, and he did it so well that in Mr. Ransom's later judgment his editorship deserved a Pulitzer Prize. He made me aware of the work of his old Kenyon friends, Peter Taylor and Robert Lowell. He got me to do some reviews. It turned out that besides the vocation we had in common, Randall and I also shared a devotion to tennis. We would have liked, almost more than anything, to play well enough for national ranking, but we had been born to be only fair tennis players. In those days Randall used to remind people that he had been trained as a psychologist—at Vanderbilt, before he switched to English—and competitive tennis fascinated that side of him; then, too, he relished the craft and lore of the game, as of everything he took up. When he dropped the ball for his first forehand shot in practice, you saw a small ritual performed with attention and gravity.

I had the impression that for Randall this interest in tennis represented an attachment to common life, as later on sports cars did and later still professional football, and that he placed a peculiar value on these hobbies. He was, after all, precocious and a prodigy; he simply had genius; he must have known that at times he was not only lonely but faintly monstrous, as those who were fondest of him regularly agreed. Well, he wished not to be, and the wish was appealing. How many times he must have curbed his tongue! I never had to endure Randall's famous disdain, at least not the full brunt of it, but I have seen it rudely bestowed. The saving grace by which one forgave him in advance, and always, lay in his loyalty to his admirations and beyond them to the wisdoms and wonders of art.

Those were the first days of our acquaintance, in 1946–47. The summer in Indiana was six years later; six years later still, in 1958, after his term as Consultant to the Library of Congress, he brought his family to spend the summer in Liguria near the Peter Taylors and ourselves. He had acquired a full bushy beard and denied that it made his face hot. In some ways it proved to be an inharmonious summer. Randall and I were even outclassed in a local tennis tournament that we entered, both in singles and in doubles. But no incidental failures could outweigh the great pleasure of seeing one another again and exchanging our tidings and somewhat riper thoughts. One literary affection we were able to renew in company was that for Kipling. While reading the Jungle Books to my children in Italian, I had found, in the marvelous oceanic story about the white seal, a great and timely reminder of what may be done with sheer invention; the oaths that Kipling had thought up for that seal were somehow liberating to me at a moment when my own work demanded this. No one alive could have understood the case better than Randall. He may have been rereading the stories with a view to editing them for Anchor Books, because he remarked one evening that there wasn't a page of Kipling that he hadn't read, and most of them many times. He had been working on his translation of *Faust,* and as I was then working on Homer he made me a present of his Roget and, even more helpfully, of one admirable perception on the way diction can be modulated, but must not be abruptly changed, from high to low. After taking the Jarrells to the train one summer day, I was never to see him in this world again— except as I have been seeing him in the course of this reminiscence.

Lately in London I came across the new edition of Christina Stead's novel, *The Man Who Loved Children,* bearing Randall's long introduction, and it was like seeing a capstone fall into place, for it seemed to me that having done that essay, he had, in a way, completed the arch of his appreciative writing and had imparted to the rest of us the sum of his brilliant insights and delights. What he could do in poetry he did early and with prodigious security; he was one of our true poets for thirty years and practically the only American poet able to cope with the Second Great War; many of us both younger and older would acknowledge him as a master in one degree or another. It was this gift of true pitch as a writer that made his teaching voice, his critical voice, as penetrating as it was. I do not deny that he could be too chattery and too exclamatory; everyone can be too something. But his work again and again enhanced the life of poetry and gave the age, in its degradation, a great example of sensibility and wit. I hope that he has found his place of refreshment, as we found it in that quarry years ago.

Gold and Gloom in Ezra Pound

The first of Ezra Pound's verses that I remember seeing were in the volume *Personae*, borrowed when I was in school. In appearance this book had a style very distinct and rich. I admired, and found becoming to the poems, the generous, dense, and rough-edged white paper on which the black printing appeared luxuriously placed. A short poem called "Doria" seemed unforgettable to me, and has turned out literally to be so. The "Ballad of the Goodly Fere" moved me, and a little later I had to make an effort to understand why T. S. Eliot omitted it from his selection of Pound's poems. I thought nothing could be finer than some of the poems in *Cathay*, Pound's translations from the Chinese.

In one of his writings Ford Madox Ford said that *Cathay* was possibly the most beautiful book ever printed, and I found this a proper thing to say. But I liked everything written by Ford. When I was seventeen I had read his memoir and tribute to Joseph Conrad—picked out, I think, from a pile of library books on some lazy summer afternoon—a poorly bound, small, cheap book with no margins to speak of. "C'est toi qui dors dans l'ombre," said the first chapter heading, and the vivid, serious enchantment held to the last page. From Ford I learned how style might honor style in life and in writing—the clear line of style against the metaphorical shade. It is perhaps a sense of that background that makes one love with purity the art of writing. Ford loved it with purity, and I trusted him.

In those days a quiet interest in literature existed in the New York newspaper offices. The *Herald* had a weekly supplement, *Books*, edited by Stuart Sherman, who often found a woodcut and a poem to place on the front page, with an essay by someone who cared about works of the imagination. Ford's love poem, "My brown-eyed squirrel, my soft dove," appeared on the front page of *Books*. So did Ezra Pound's essay, "How to Read." Twenty-seven years of looking at literary supplements have not much blurred the emotions caused in me by these events—the

First published in *Encounter*, July 1956, and reprinted as "A Note on Ezra Pound, 1928–56," in *The Kenyon Review*, Autumn 1956; written at the request of *Nuova Corrente*, Genova, for an issue of that magazine devoted to studies of the poet.

first verse of Ford's that I had read, and the first prose by Pound. The gentle verse satisfied my ear; the prose rather opened my eyes. The writer gave a little list or curriculum of things that one should read as touchstones of literary art. Homer, Sappho, Cavalcanti, Dante. . . . A few things, each masterly in its kind. He put it with such spirit that I trusted him, too, though I felt a vague stir of callow resistance.

It is useful to learn things from someone who knows and imparts them openly with a view to instruct. But it is useful and also delightful to find things out for oneself, as it seems, even when in fact they are being suggested with courtesy and craft. So Pound's didactic writing never pleased me as much as Ford's anecdotes and reflections did. But in the authority they had for me at that early stage there was probably little to choose between the two men. I understood what each meant, and responded to it with confidence. Style was the essence that made literature precious, and the achievement of style would be a writer's proper concern. I do not think that either of them made me suspect how great a labor this might be, or how great a part of the labor might be extraliterary.

As for Pound's instructions, of course no one would have followed them doggishly, nor paid entire heed to his categories. I know now that generalities and rules in these matters, come as they will to mind, do not count for much in comparison with particulars—the morning's discovery, or the night's discontent. Nevertheless I think that Pound's list, beginning with Homer, has served me. A few things, each masterly in its kind. . . . At eighteen it seemed to me entirely possible that I was going to read everything ever written. This notion did not outlast the university where I learned what it meant. Works in Greek and Latin could not be read, anyway, in the casual sense; they mainly had to be studied, and I found that this suited me in other literatures as well. If you are not employed, you can read all day. If you are employed, you must work at your employment, and in particular if you are a writer you must write. You will do well, then, to read a few marvelous things until you half understand what they deliver and how it was done, and acquire other literary knowledge for yourself in the course of working. Pound's advice came to this in the end—a recognition of what the *métier* entails, or has entailed at least for me.

When *A Draft of XXX Cantos* appeared in the United States, my friend Dudley Fitts reviewed it for *The Hound & Horn*, concluding, I remember, that the *Cantos* were "a gallant and proud attempt to assert the positive value of experience." The phrase seemed to me rather desperate. As to the value of experience it appeared that there were graver doubts or

difficulties than I had realized. At any rate, now I went to the Poetry
Room in the Widener Library at Harvard, borrowed the *Cantos*, and
spent a day reading them. I went away in confused exaltation, as if
excited by whiffs of rare spices, drunk on rarities of liquor—a banquet of
style, or rather a vast sampling of styles in bits and pieces, here and there
conveying some magical strange image from an otherworld, distant or
past. Poetry may once have been *Hiawatha*, but there was no doubt that
in 1930 the *Cantos* were poetry. I could not tell what they asserted beyond that. I knew they were full of Protean life and music and hints of
the universe of possibility.

They did not, however, unfold or compose a world seen "steadily and
whole" in the manner of *Ulysses* and the great things that moved me
most. Where so much was given, should that, too, be asked? I should
have said, No; but I think I was disposed to say this too readily. The
point is difficult. It seems that poetic quality may be caught by the ear, or
by the specifically poetic sense, long in advance of the mind, and may
subsist for that sense long after the mind has finished with it. But can it
be complete unless the mind acknowledge it? When I use this word,
"mind," I understand something universal. As the Ephesian said, when
we dream we go apart each into a world of his own, but when we think
we have a world in common. Is the great work of poetry perhaps a
dream that may be held in common—a dream to that degree permeated
by mind? In the same season that I read the *Cantos* I read *The Wings of a
Dove*, in the same library, and I emerged from that reading likewise
affected in the higher sensory regions—mainly by a paradisal sense of
style. But the novel by James would later deeply engage and satisfy my
mind. The *Cantos* never could, because they did not have it in them. I do
not mean that they lacked the play of intelligence.

The point is indeed difficult, there being for example "Ash Wednesday" to consider. I have regarded this since I first read it as the best poem
of its length in English. There are nevertheless parts of it quite untouch-
able by the universal faculty I have mentioned. Why, then, is it satisfac-
tory? and would it be more so if there were no mystery in it? The answer
must be that it needs the mystery but that the mystery is kept in hand;
the song moves in a single direction, though with "steps and stops"
amid purely incantatory or dream material, and this movement is inti-
mately lucid for the mind. There are, again, the poems of St. John Perse.
In his preface to his own translation of *Anabase*, Eliot observed that there
is such a thing as a logic of images—a fact that the poem demonstrated.
But it could be said that the images interlocked within one overmastering

image, or imagined world, internally consistent and evoked in a consistent style. The *Cantos* were multiple, multiple in both respects. . . . They were not on that account dull. I bought them as soon as I could, and kept them by me.

Early in 1932, being in Switzerland, I sent a note to Ezra Pound and went down to Rapallo to see him. We walked a little in the long room in his top-floor flat on the Via Marsala, looking out over the esplanade and the sea. In this room he had taught Yeats to fence, he said. There was a letter from Hemingway on his table; he took out the snapshot and showed it to me—the sunblackened man grinning beside a shark he had caught off Cuba; the shark's belly, stripped open, displayed a man's undigested leg. Then he showed me his copy of *Ulysses,* inscribed at length and in gratitude by James Joyce. I felt numb with awe and with headache brought on by the chianti I had drunk on the train. The bearded and cat-eyed man before me had about him the hero light of the Irish. He had contended for good writing, for the making of it by himself and others, and he had kept clear of what was compromising and half-hearted. Moreover he was a workman; in his workroom he had an active filing system of cords strung overhead like clotheslines, to which he clipped or pinned envelopes or sheafs of material.

We walked out and around and down the *lungomare* in the damp January afternoon, Pound in a cape and widebrimmed hat which he swept away here and there in salute to a promenader. He gave me dinner at a restaurant, and we talked for a while before I went off to my train. I noticed that Ezra Pound, hero light and all, was quieter in talk and less positive than his writing; he did not impose himself, as the writing rather did. Two things he said were as "significant" as any man's casual remarks are likely to be. Of a trecento or quattrocento seal he was showing me, he said: "Here was a culture that got into every detail of life." Later on, I suppose in answer to some remark, he said in a troubled and reluctant way, as if to himself and as if it were an admission, "I live in music for days at a time." He did not mean the wordless music of the composers—Vivaldi, Antheil—who then interested him, but the music within himself, a visionary music requiring words. I knew that this applied to the *Cantos,* where the musical sense went free as a grasshopper among images and rhythms, styles perceived as tokens of culture or style in living.

Gallant and proud, in Fitts's words, this life and this work seemed to me then. I could only faintly register what was flawed and darkened in it, nor did I suppose that there would necessarily be something of the sort in every life and work. His tone when he said he lived in music might have warned me that in that beautiful intelligence all was not going well. I remember that I worried a little when it appeared that one thing I should do at his bidding was to write a review of his *Cavalcanti*, to be printed by Eliot or Orage. The implied confidence in my writing gave me pleasure, but my position was that one did not interest oneself in reviews of one's own work. To have to suppose that Pound did gave me a slight turn, as if he had asked me to hold a mirror for him while he put on his hat. The impression did not weigh upon me, however. Pound was certainly kind of me, as he is known to have been to many others. In any case I had soon to return from my premature excursion into the upper world of poetry.

In that year, 1932, Hart Crane dove into a ship's wake and drowned, Vachel Lindsay took poison and died halfway to a candle he had set burning at the top of a stair. I admired Crane's poems, and I knew and admired Lindsay. Not immediately but in the course of several years I understood something of the evil day that had come to each. All the life we knew was going round a turn in those years, or over a pass; from one side we looked back at the war of 1914–18 and from the other we looked forward to—no one knew what, but worse and more of it. The struggle to keep alive became grimmer and more humiliating. It was as if the very air of the world turned crass and bitter and lost its milder lights. So much experience now got shoved and hustled into the void that I could comprehend how the "positive value of experience" might be something to assert. The 1930s were years of complex trouble, and to allude to them is enough, for my point is only that they were killing or crippling for the arts; that few of us survived them undistorted or undiminished. It is clear that Ezra Pound did not.

In my own scrambling and mute existence of those years I did not keep in touch with him; I had nothing to keep in touch with him about. But I was aware of a gradual shift of attitude or orientation with respect to Pound, not only on my part but in general among people who cared for what he had cared for. In the exhortations from Via Marsala 12 his literary correspondents noticed the error of tone more often—the tone of a man no longer in touch, and the tone of presumption that dissipates the authority presumed. What had seemed high-hearted and really Olympian fun began to seem childish and beside the point. Then came the economic essays, the Social Credit campaign. As to that, I thought that no harm could come of a fresh mind in economics, and I certainly did not think that a poet should necessarily "stick to poetry." One had to respect Pound's effort to make these matters clear to himself, but the trouble was that he seemed to overestimate—to put it temperately—the objective value of the results. Only a man working in isolation, without criticism or ignoring it, could have failed to see the fretfulness and poverty of argument in some of these essays and those in *Kulchur;* his examination of Aristotle's *Ethics,* for example, was fairly alarming. By 1936 or '37 a considerable descent must have been accomplished, from my point of view, for I remember then feeling and saying with some heat that I preferred Eliot and Pound when they were young together, comparing verses in some restaurant in Soho, rather than in those later aureoles that in Pound's case had got so askew. The maker of *Cathay* and *Personae* and the handsomest Cantos was permitting himself too much license.

Let the purveyor of good judgment in mellow retrospect pause, however, and ask himself what *he* was doing, or what anyone else was doing, to redeem that period more impressively. I myself (not that I flatter myself, but to answer the question) was holding on to a stanchion, merely hoping to stay aboard; and the gate disconcerted my elders and betters. In Yeats's last work, it is true, no cheap or disheartened notes could be heard. Nor in Joyce's final revel with the powers of darkness. But weariness or suffering touched the lesser stylists. And the figure that comes to my mind as expressive of that time is Ford Madox Ford. In his last years the master sometimes came to the Jumble Shop, a restaurant on Eighth Street in New York where dinner was not expensive. During the meal he had to let his tongue hang out, panting like a dog. It was an affliction he owed to his having been gassed in the first war, but no other physical gesture could have told so well the extremity to which the fine stylist, the man of disinterested imagination, had come.

In 1940 I sat down one day to ponder the latest Cantos, those concerned with John Adams on the one hand and Chinese history on the other. In the latter sequence the poet had traversed the heavens for some magnificent panels of Imperial China, and much diversity of image and music. The Adams Cantos however were, to say the least, an overextended communion with Adams' style, excerpted from his journal and correspondence. Here dullness did finally set in; Pound had committed a monstrosity of composition, and it seemed a willful one by a man who held poetry to be the art of charging words with meaning. Then the war came, and I found one more thing to be depressed about when I heard what folly, as it seemed, had overcome the man in Rapallo. No one else had gone quite as crazy as that.

2

It is an impression that I have, and it can be no more, that in his early years Pound chose the difficult thing to do, but later chose the easy thing, or the easier for him, having by that time so much momentum of his own to ride on that it might have seemed merely intelligent to ride, rather than to make again those efforts with hands and feet that in reality alone bear us up. One has made oneself master of an art; one may forget that it is largely in making oneself master of something that mastery consists. With his gifts and energy Pound had led a war against dead fashions in perceptions and writing; he had helped to set a kingdom free, to open it up to communication. But then it was as if he did not know quite what to do next—like so many *condottieri* who have been left biting their nails in isolation or even in ignominy after some slashing campaign. If they take up the sword again it will be in a ridiculous cause. There is a simplicity in the militant, and it may bring them to this.

Pound, however, had not been simple, but multiple, and like Odysseus he should have prevailed. Perhaps the very multiplicity became too much for him and dispersed him, so that he lost the Odyssean compactness of heart. To live in music for days at a time will mean letting go of the public coherence that the mind requires. But this is a difficult matter to judge, this, too. One sees and hears many things that other men unquestionably neither see nor hear; one should not deny one's *daimon* or one's genius. It may be necessary to reject public coherence in the forms provided by this world—in the intellectual professions—for the sake of sheer poetry and its dangers, and we have seen more than one instance of the rejection and its fruits. But may one then undertake to join, or indeed to lead, the dialogue conducted by men trained in the public disciplines? Pound could never submit himself to the humble rigor and patience of thought that the university men and the lawyers and philosophers must practice. In a sense he did not have to; he comprehended at once much that they would acquire with labor. And he saw their fault—a kind of voluntary stupidity into which fear and malice entered. But he did not at first, and perhaps needed not ever, set himself apart from their community and overcrow them as he did. Saying to one's brother "Thou fool" may become a bad habit. The penalty—is it not that?—can be seen in a mild form in his sudden diffidence, in later years, before Santayana, who simply found his conversation too disconnected to follow.

Early in 1948 I heard a friend of mine read aloud the "Pull down thy vanity" passage from the *Pisan Cantos,* and I thought it sounded like good news. A quarter of a century before, Pound had been able with humility to address the God of waters in his little Venetian litany; perhaps what had now happened to him had brought him back toward some similar compunction, a human feeling of place and scale. I then read the *Pisan Cantos,* reread all the *Cantos,* and concluded that a new twinge had indeed occurred, though it had scarcely carried all before it: "Tard, très tard, je t'ai connue, la Tristesse. . . ." As to the *Cantos* taken all together, it seemed to me now that they were poetic sketchbooks, fixing in words at times evanescent but marvelous things in a fine economy, turning myth to something immediate:

> "It is Cabestan's heart in the dish."
> "It is Cabestan's heart in the dish?
> "No other taste shall change this."
> And she went to the window and cast her down. . . .

And then they would run into slapdash notation and revery, parenthesis within parenthesis, blurring the page. For the musical qualities of language—of a number of languages—rhythms, speeds, and texture, no one alive had an ear of greater range and delicacy. But the *Cantos* were not a composition in the exacting sense of the word. Of the best passages it would be true enough to say that no one could write so well; of the worst it would not be going too far to use the opposite superlative.

As you come to the final cantos of the *Purgatorio* of Dante you find that you have living within yourself a certain vision and a certain emotion that are well beyond anything to be experienced in Pound's or any conceivable sketchbook. This effect is due to what Pound mentioned, in "How to Read," as "architectonics, or the form of the whole." Let each kind of poem be valued for what it is, but let the difference, and the difference in value, be kept in mind. So, at least, I said to myself on the occasion of the republication of the *Cantos.* Then the admirable prose translations of Confucius were published, and in 1954 the *Literary Essays,* edited by T. S. Eliot with a just and faithful introduction. A number of these were first published long before my time; I had never read them; and I found them as exciting as if I had just opened *The Egoist* in 1914 or *The Little Review* in 1918—that is, quite exciting. In an American quarterly called *Shenandoah* I read Pound's review of *Ulysses,* reprinted in French from the *Mercure de France* of 1922, and it struck me as the best essay I had ever read on that mighty work. But the last essays in Eliot's selection were of 1934, and in them the frantic tones of the later prose had already begun to appear.

Now there are the verses of the *Chinese Classic Anthology* and the new-est *Cantos* of all, 85–95, published in Italy. The *Anthology* is a beautiful feat, which my soul delights to honor—the work of a great gift and of a lifetime spent in listening to the styles possible in English verse. Why is it so obviously, and so much, better than the recent Cantos, in one or two of which the Chinese written character has the lion's share of distinc-tion? Here again I venture upon critical speculation, if that is not a contradiction in terms. Farinta the Ghibelline, who stood up to the chest in hell, was endowed by Dante with clear vision of things distant in time; but he did not see the present, did not, as we say, know what the score was. With all proper reservations, the figure might do for Ezra Pound in his later condition. At the other end of historical time and terrestrial space he lives, in princely imagination, through texts with which he can be at ease; perhaps they are untouched by the tragic conviction and faith of the West. The case is too impressive and peculiar for easy moralizing. But I feel that I must take a further step now and inquire as to whether or not self-centered human pride at a certain point becomes incompatible with sanity or honesty or both.

Among the works of Ezra Pound is the transcript in about four hun-dred typewritten pages of his radio talks from Rome during the war. This transcript is published on microfilm by the Library of Congress, from which anyone who wants it can obtain it for about three dollars. It is certainly, from every point of view and all "politics" aside, one of the poorest productions ever thrown off by a man of genius. Few people seem to have read it, and I imagine few would care to. I went through this transcript last year with a kind of disbelief, the deliquescence of taste and style was so complete. I could take a great deal of rage against the snakes of finance, and I could well see the point of scorn for Roosevelt's public insincerities. Even anti-Semitism could be forgiven if it were what it had seemed to me in Pound before—an almost innocent vice partly echoing the Potash and Perlmutter era of comedy in America. But it was not like that, nor were the other contents in general anything but chaotic and unworthy. The style, the quality of feeling, in these radio harangues was abysmal. And style—why, the exactions of style were precisely what one had heard of long before from Ezra Pound.

So the irony that seems a constant in human affairs had operated in this case with singular power. He who had praised the sane construction, the clear moving line, the fine thing held in the mind, had ended in ramshackle and noisome fantasy, in a clogged and static obsession—no fine thing held in his mind but the most vulgar and violent of contemporary passions. The offence for which Pound had been indicted by a grand jury in the United States was no more serious than the offence he had committed against his own standards, against himself. I think that Pound at twenty or thirty would have thought hanging an entirely appropriate reward for the author of those radio scripts! By the mercy of contemporary psychology—to say nothing of common sense—the author of them would surely be held not responsible for his words; but here we come upon a further irony. When Pound was brought back to the United States in the fall of 1945 after his arrest and detention in Italy, he and his lawyer did not choose to stand trial and plead insanity as of 1941; they chose to avoid the trial by a plea of insanity as of 1945. Something had snapped, he is supposed to have said, in the cage at Pisa. The choice of this plea seems to have put Pound's head in a vise of pretence from which neither he nor anyone else has been able to wrench it. If he should be declared sane now, he is by implication committed to the position that he was sane when he wrote his scripts for Radio Roma, and on that premise he seems to have a choice of admitting his offence or of being convicted of it.

An intelligent man remarked to me not long ago that this situation reminded him of the one in Pirandello's *Enrico IV*, in which the principal figure must continue to play his own madness brilliantly because he cannot face a return to sanity. It is not that simple, of course, in either case: for one thing, the part to be played is no doubt partly genuine and extremely congenial. But it has been possible to suspect, in the last few years, that Ezra Pound in St. Elizabeths was not only being but playing at being Ezra Pound. This would comprise a certain repertory, as *Personae* and the *Cantos* years ago made clear to us. It would necessarily include the man who wrote the radio scripts with only an occasional inkling, I feel, of what he was doing. This would require, in support, another and not very sympathetic figure—one who perhaps put in his appearance ambiguously years ago—a cagey propagandist for himself. But amid the company, or perhaps apart from the company, there must be the great man upon whom I called when young, the generous spirit that discerned and loved and prompted good work in letters, the friend valued by Eliot and Yeats.

In the gloom the gold gathers the light against it.

Ezra Pound's place in the story of poetry is not in question, and with every year it becomes better discriminated and understood. In this note I have tried to suggest what it has been like to be a writer twenty-five years younger, and interested, during Pound's lifetime. It goes without saying that all of us who practice the art of poetry are indebted to him. The work I have been doing lately would have been done otherwise and not so well if it had not been for Pound's work and his critical stimulus. Reading over what I have written here, I am aware of its inadequacy; but I hope that it is a truthful tribute, and not without affection.

THE STYLE THAT
DOES HONOR:
THE POET IN
THE CLASSICAL
TRADITION

tu se' solo colui da cu' io tolsi
lo bello stile che m'ha fatto honore

Inferno, Canto I

The best translation is the one which best uses the
resources of our own language to communicate the
nature of that work of the imagination which so enthralled the people for whom it was made.

Interview with David Stern

Herald! here, take this to Demódokos:
let him feast and be merry, with my compliments.
All men owe honor to the poets—honor
and awe, for they are dearest to the Muse
who puts upon their lips the ways of life.

Odyssey, Book VIII

Generations of Leaves:
Studies in Homer,
Virgil, and Dante

1

In the sixth book of the *Iliad* of Homer, the clever and formidable Greek fighter Diomedes sees a young Trojan whom he does not recognize coming out from the ranks of the other army to stand up to him in single combat. It is in the Homeric fashion, and in Diomedes' personal style, to call out to the advancing challenger and ask him who he is: is he one of the immortal gods, perhaps? for in that case Diomedes will retire; but if he is a man and mortal, then let him come nearer and reach his appointed destruction. To this address the young man, whose name is Glaukos, replies in a leisurely speech that begins this way, in the English of Richmond Lattimore's translation:

> High-hearted son of Tydeus, why ask of my generation?
> As is the generation of leaves, so is that of humanity.
> The wind scatters the leaves on the ground, but the live timber
> burgeons with leaves again in the season of spring returning.
> So one generation of men will grow while another dies.

This passage of Homer appears to have been as moving as you might expect to his early auditors and readers, and the later Greek poet Simonides thought it the most beautiful thing that the man of Chios—that is, Homer—ever said. I should suppose that the elegiac poet Mimnermus had been acquainted with it when he wrote his own lines to the effect that we are like the leaves that the flowering season of spring puts forth, and it may have been in the back of Pericles' mind when he said of the young Athenians killed early in the war with Sparta that it was as if the spring had been taken away from the year. I do not suppose Homer underrated the passage, either, for he chose to introduce with it one of

First published in *Perspectives*, Summer 1954. This essay was published twenty years before Fitzgerald's own translation of the *Iliad*.

the most appealing of the short episodes in the *Iliad;* but I think we have
to study that episode a little if we want to interpret our passage more
fully and place it correctly in the art of Homer.

First of all, of course, Simonides was only half right in attributing the
lines to the man from Chios, for they were not spoken by Homer. They
were spoken by the young Trojan, Glaukos. Homer is a dramatic artist, a
creator of men acting and speaking for themselves, and here we have
young Glaukos presented on the battlefield, face to face with the terrible
Diomedes yet able to meet his adversary's harangue coolly with a general reflection on mortality followed by an elaborate speech. And the
speech, as so often in Homer, is itself a story. For he goes on to say that if
Diomedes would really like to know, he will tell him his genealogy; and
he does tell him, dwelling particularly on the adventures of his grandfather Bellerophontes, who slew the Chimaira and performed other godlike feats. The effect of Glaukos' speech is wonderful, for Diomedes of
the great war cry drives his spear into the ground and proclaims that
Glaukos and he are guest friends from the time of their fathers, since
Diomedes' grandfather had been host and friend to Bellerophontes.
Then Diomedes proposes that they avoid each other in combat and
exchange their armor so that Greeks and Trojans alike may know of their
special relationship. The two men spring down from their war chariots
and grip each other's hands.

At this point we may notice that the general reflection I quoted, the
one with which Glaukos begins his speech, is quite a little qualified by
the speech itself, for if the generations of men were entirely like the
generations of leaves one could not put such value as Glaukos does on
the glory of a forebear. I think we see, as Homer surely meant us to, that
the human gifts of piety and sense of the past weigh somewhat in the
balance against the universal fact of mortality. This implication is pleasantly enforced by the warm response of Diomedes, the hands clasping in
friendship in the midst of war, the exchange of armor. The passage about
the leaves seems all the more beautiful for what follows it, and we are
full of admiration and satisfaction. But Homer has not finished his episode. Here is how he does it:

> . . . but Zeus the son of Kronos stole away the wits of Glaukos
> Who exchanged with Diomedes the son of Tydeus armor
> Of gold for bronze, for nine oxen's worth the worth of a hundred.

. . . Surprise. We may imagine the moment of silence and then the
delighted laughter going up among the banqueters who were Homer's

first audience—laughter like the happy laughter to the gods. For Diomedes, the quick-witted warrior, the companion of crafty Odysseus, has won after all; and the young Trojan Glaukos, nobly as he has borne himself and eloquently as he has spoken, has had to pay a certain price for his inexperience in the ways of men.

2

In the sixth book of the *Aeneid* of Virgil the hero of the story is brought into the world of the dead by the Cumaean Sibyl and approaches in the gloom a wide river, Acheron, where the boatman Charon plies his skiff, the ferry of the swarming dead. This is the way Virgil describes the scene; the Latin first and then a free rendering in English:

huc omnis turba ad ripas effusa ruebat:
matres atque viri, defunctaque corpora vita
magnanimum heroum, pueri innuptaeque puellae,
impositique rogis iuvenes ante ora parentum,
quam multa in silvis autumni frigore primo
lapsa cadunt folia . . .

the whole crowd came streaming this way toward the riverside,
mothers and fathers and the husks of great men done with life
along with small boys and girls, and young men in their prime who died
before their parents' eyes: innumerable all these as leaves
that slip away and fall through forests in the first cold snap of autumn . . .

Now in the simile we were considering from Homer a general likeness was noted between the generations of men and the generations of leaves, both being numerous and both transient yet successive. Virgil of course knew Homer very well, and in this passage his vision of the dead owes something to the twelfth book of the *Odyssey*, but the thing I propose we should especially notice is that he had rethought this matter of the leaves clean through. He had rethought it, moreover, less from the point of view of the spectator, which is Homer's, than from that of the leaves themselves. The beauty of Virgil's simile is in the participle *lapsa*, which I've translated "slip away"—the leaves losing their grip. He saw that a dying man's weak hold on life is like a leaf's inability to hang on to a twig in the fall, and he saw the dead falling out of life as the leaves fall out of the air. In Homer's line the agent was the wind—"The wind scatters the leaves on the ground"—but in Virgil there is no wind, there is a cold spell, and the active verb belongs to the leaves themselves: *cadunt:* they fall. To see these things in this manner is no doubt distinctively Virgilian, or if it is not I do not know what is. And then, the placement of the simile is wholly different in Virgil. Homer had made one of his characters the poet, allowed Glaukos to say the beautiful thing. We cannot say that Homer is not serious about it. He is aware of the honor he has done to Glaukos by giving him that lyric to speak, and he is aware, too, of the honor the young poet wins, in the event, from his appreciative adversary, Diomedes; but it is Homer's dramatic sense and storyteller's humor that wins out and rounds off the episode with what we may take as a smile at lyric poetry and a suggestion that wisdom without practicality is incomplete. Virgil's seriousness is of a different quality and more personal; it is he who speaks in his simile and conveys to us his image of death and of the dead. Homer's simile was impartial; on the one hand the wind scattering the leaves in autumn, on the other hand the live timber bursting forth again with leaves in the spring. But Virgil here cannot have that impartiality, and not merely because it would be out of place in a description of the world of the dead, but because, as I have said, he has entered into the leaf's point of view and from the leaf's point of view the autumnal loosening and falling are final. It may be said that in Virgil's time and in other Roman writing we find the sense of death intimate and funereal; it may also be said that Virgil had the habit of close attention to landscape and seasonal change. However that may be, he has particularized and transformed the ancient simile and he offers his own vision—in passing—not as an introduction to an episode that will fill it out and comment on it dramatically but as a descriptive simile in narrative.

3

In the third canto of the *Inferno* of Dante, the narrator and his guide pass through the hateful region of those who in life had lacked all conviction, and they come to the shore of a great river where the souls of the damned are assembling, here too to make the crossing in Charon's boat. Dante does not tell us of these shades what Virgil told us of his: their varying ages and conditions in pathetic conjunction; no, these are undifferentiated, for the important point at the moment is that all are going into the dark, having lost forever the sight of God, the good of the intellect. At Charon's call, each flings himself from the bank into the ferry:

> Come d'autunno si levan le foglie
> l'una appresso dell'altra, fin che il ramo
> vede alla terra tutte le sue spoglie:
> similemente il mal seme d'Adamo
> gittansi di quel lito ad una ad una . . .

> As the leaves of autumn take off, one
> after another, until the bough
> sees all its spoils upon the ground,
> so one by one the evil seed of Adam
> cast themselves from the shore . . .

Dante of course knew Virgil, and from his references to the *Aeneid* it has been inferred that he knew that poem by heart. He also knew Homer— not in Greek but in Latin translation, a translation probably of selected passages from both the *Iliad* and the *Odyssey*. If this selection survives, the Dante scholars do not seem to know where, but it is reasonable to suppose that it included the passage we began with, the one that Simonides thought the most beautiful thing that Homer ever said. Dante's own simile of the leaves bears a certain obvious relation to Virgil's, and it is placed in a similar context in the underworld; but it bears an interesting relation also to Homer's, while being thoroughly different from either. The Dantesque image is of leaves on a single bough *rising—si levano*—in the straining wind of autumn and leaving the bough one after another. Dante is not alluding directly to human mortality but indirectly, through the mortality of the leaves. The wind which Homer mentioned blows again here after the still cold air of Virgil, but it blows only by implication, for the active verb belongs to the leaves that are said to rise. And this is wonderfully suggestive when we compare it with the Virgilian vision. To Dante's mind, it appears, the motion from life into death is not—or not necessarily, not at the instant of leaving one for the other—a downward motion but may be upward; moreover it is a motion that each singular leaf is seen to make in its own time. The picture of a forest full of leaves losing hold and falling is not here, and in its stead we have the leaves on one bough successively mounting, taking off in the wind until the bough, like the riverbank, is bare.

4

Let us take these three pieces of poetry together and see what is to be said of them. It may be useful to assert first of all that they *are* poetry. They were poetry when they were first conceived, they are poetry now, and if you think the time may come when they are not poetry, the burden of argument rests with you. Homer's simile is moving in itself, but it has its place and full significance in a narrative which is also poetry and is also in the clearest possible way entertainment, and this fact would seem to tell against some theorists who made the distinction hard and fast between poetry and entertainment; the works of Homer are like the plays of Shakespeare in being pretty plainly beyond that kind of distinction. The Virgilian and Dantean similes likewise play their parts in narratives, but their function in this respect is not dramatic in the Homeric way, not expressive of character; they bear the authority of the poet and are in differing degrees descriptive or evocative of action which the poet or narrator has under his eye. In differing degrees, for Virgil's simile comes in by way of the phrase *quam multa*—so many—the visual and logical analogy between the crowd on the riverbank and the autumn leaves being that both are numerous and both dead; but the action attributed to the crowd, a streaming and rushing, does not closely correspond to the action attributed to the leaves, a slipping away and falling. In Dante, as we have seen, there is a nearly exact correspondence: the leaves take off from the bough, the shades leap from the bank. It is an economy or an elegance, as they say in mathematics, and is Dantesque, but I don't think the behavior of autumn foliage as we know it is any the less sharply brought into view.

The three passages form a series, and if there is anything that we may call a classical tradition they should help us to understand what it is, or how to take it, which is perhaps the same thing. I said that the passages were simple, and they are, but analysis shows a richness in them and shows that each of the three poets had the ability to see things with his own eyes; that in the case of Virgil this ability suffered no impairment through familiarity with Homer, and that in the case of Dante familiarity with both Homer and Virgil had no disabling effect. On the contrary, by the evidence of the three passages, neither Virgil nor Dante might have been so original if he had not known in what originality would consist when making verse out of the mortality of leaves and men. In both cases, we may conjecture, firmness in the knowledge of previous masterwork has given them firmness in the definition of their own quite different images and meanings; and we might provisionally put it something like this: the classical tradition is observed when art is wakeful to reality in the fullest possible sense, including the reality of previous works of art.

That will serve if we keep thinking it over and remember that a first work of art is possible; that, so far as we know, Homer was the first to say anything in Greek verse about the generations of men and the generations of leaves, and that this originality may owe nothing whatever— except hexameter verse—to Homer's acquaintance with previous poetry. As for the passages from Virgil and Dante, there is no dead hand upon them but the mark of an essential originality as great as Homer's. I have not been tracing influences, but tracing rather, if anything, the way in which influences may be dominated by personal artistic force. We may make a slight shift of emphasis and say that the classical tradition is one in which previous work if any is chiefly a challenge, and the first requisite, wakefulness to reality, is the perennial lesson.

Now I come to an important question. What are we to think of in general when we speak of this reality to which the artist is attentive? Our criticism and our talk are apt to be remiss about this, and seriously so, and we are never going to get anything quite straight about poetry until we are in the habit of acknowledging at least roughly the complicated truth of the matter. Between Homer and Dante—that is, during more than two thousand years of life—there developed among Mediterranean people a self-corrected way of thinking, a philosophy, that was capacious and sensible enough to do justice to this complicated truth, and I will try—necessarily briefly and poorly—to suggest how.

5

Greek general thought, stimulated by Ionian speculation, humanized by Homer, made explicit by Plato, made methodical by Aristotle, and refined by the Arab and Latin thinkers of the centuries just before Dante, reached at length a profound epistemological humility. Contemplation made it clear that all abstraction was derived from things, and was tremendously inadequate to them; that in fact things—or events, as we might say—were an inexhaustible source of concepts and the words by which concepts are signified. Degrees of abstraction—of distance between concept and thing, between concept and concept—were recognized, and the highly abstract concepts of actuality and potentiality were arrived at as expressive of ultimate constituents of the real—the real that as plenum is ever characterized by change. We may say that within the actual the potential dwells like a charge; we may also say that within the full potential the actual is tiny and incomplete.

Now in being attentive to reality the artist is being attentive to a world that to general thought can best be described in these terms or their equivalent. Insofar as our criticism and our talk aspire to validity as general thought, they too must take account of the conditions of existence. And I would suppose this peculiarly easy in the case of general thought about the arts, for it is the nature of every art to bring into existence, to make actual, a reality hitherto potential or possible. The reality to which the artist is attentive is always in large part the reality of the thing he is about to make or is making. We are apt to speak as if the poet observed and wrote about things that happen—the fall of leaves or the way he feels when they are falling, for example—and that is all; but if that were all, we would not possess any of the three passages I have quoted and talked about, for in each of them the poet made something happen, or come to be, that had not happened before.

Perhaps what I am saying may become clearer if we pause and take stock of what is in our minds now—supposing that we have in mind everything we have been considering up to this point—and two minutes from now compare this with what will be in our minds then. For I am about to quote a fourth example in the classical tradition, this one in English, a poem by Gerard Hopkins:

> Margaret, are you grieving
> Over Goldengrove unleaving?
> Leaves, like the things of man, you
> With your fresh thoughts care for, can you?
> Ah! as the heart grows older
> It will come to such sights colder
> By and by, nor spare a sigh
> Though worlds of wanwood leafmeal lie;
> And yet you will weep and know why.
> Now no matter, child, the name;
> Sorrow's springs are the same.
> Nor mouth had, no nor mind, expressed
> What heart heard of, ghost guessed:
> It is the blight man was born for,
> It is Margaret you mourn for.

Here something has been made to happen that had not happened in Homer nor in Virgil nor in Dante nor indeed anywhere before, though here again memorable verse has been made out of the common mortality of leaves and men. If we ask ourselves what it would have taken for each of us to make such a poem we will realize pretty well what it took in the case of Hopkins. I will not paraphrase the poem but I will note that it is a self-contained dramatic monologue, that it is remarkable for artifice and elevation of metrical speech, and in short is a created thing such that attention to a pensive girl, a grove losing its leaves, a depth of sympathetic emotion, and much previous poetry may have preceded it but could not possibly have brought it to be. For that, it was necessary that it, the poem itself, be the object of attention.

Among the objects on which the poet lavishes his affection, then, is the literary object, the poem. This is a fact that may be confirmed empirically; we find, indeed, that the affection is scarcely less intense than in the case of any natural object of love. I am taking for granted that the literary object or poem is real and a part of reality, and like everything else that is real and a part of reality it will be different from all other things and related to them in different ways. But with a little care in abstraction we can make a few tactful general statements about some of these relations. I have mentioned the emotion of love felt by the poet for the reality he is making; but it is clear that other emotions get into poetry: heroic humor, strong melancholy, and sad scorn, respectively, are in the passages we considered from Homer, Virgil, and Dante. Now here again we are apt to speak as if the poet in his daily life felt an emotion, say of anger, that caused him to write a poem which would express that emotion. This may sometimes be the case in part, but again it may easily not be the case at all. The well-known dictum of T. S. Eliot about the "objective correlative" has become so well known that people have forgotten what he was actually saying in the little essay that the dictum comes from. He was saying that when a playwright wants a character in a play to express a given emotion he has to compose a speech or speeches for him that will contain or be an "objective correlative" of that emotion. Shakespeare did not first feel the emotions of Lady Macbeth and then write the play as an objective correlative; he first conceived the play, conceived her as feeling the emotions, and gave her speeches to express them. Both character and emotions were parts of the reality that he brought into being, and neither Lady Macbeth nor her emotions existed until be brought them into being.

No, the relationship between the poet's emotions and the poetry he writes—and I am still speaking of, and in, the classical tradition as I understand it—will be more remote and interesting. The poet is attentive to reality, and in reality actual and potential he discerns a qualitative range as, say, between ambrosial glory on the one had and terrifying void on the other, every shade in this spectrum arousing in him, if he is sensitive, an emotion appropriate to it. But it is the sense of the whole—of the potential fullness of the real—that moves him most; and if we want a general statement—not as to what makes him go to work in any specific instance, for that will be unpredictable and idiosyncratic—but as to the reason he goes to work at all, I suggest we shall be near the truth in saying that it is the desire to pay homage, to bring an offering, to the qualitative possibilities of existence. One of the best things Eliot ever said was also one of the flattest: that poems are written because the poet feels the need to write a poem. It is true, but it bears this interpretation—that the need in question is a need to make something as testimony, even as celebration.

6

A good deal may be learned as to the meaning of the classical tradition through considering the art of Virgil and the art of Dante together. Surely any view of the classical that omits or skips Dante is blinded in one eye, and sorely deprived of depth perception. The limitations of classicism and neoclassicism in French letters, for example, become more evident when we remember the general disposition from Ronsard to Voltaire to regard the poetry of Dante as crude. We are happily beyond that opinion, able to take both Virgil and Dante more nearly at Dante's own estimate, and I'd like to give one further example of the relationship between them as poets.

In the third book of the *Aeneid*, the priest Helenus tells Aeneas what he will find when he reaches the western coast of Italy, and he gives this description of the Sibyl at Cumae, the lonely priestess inspired by Apollo:

insanam vatem aspicies, quae rupe sub ima
fata canit foliisque notas et nomina mandat.
quaecumque in foliis descripsit carmina virgo
digerit in numerum atque antro seclusa relinquit.
illa manent immota locis neque ab ordine cedunt;
verum eadem, verso tenuis cum cardine ventus
impulit et teneras turbavit ianua frondes,
numquam deinde cavo volitantia prendere saxo
nec revocare situs aut iungere carmina curat . . .

there you will approach and see her, the touched prophetess deep in a cave
    in the cliff,
singing of what's ordained, and giving to fragile leaves her oracles.
And these songs that she writes on the leaves she puts in order,
secluding them in the cavern where each will rest in place,
unless perhaps a puff of wind from the open door scatters the light leafpile:
but then she will not bother to catch the leaves as they flutter around the
    cave,
or rearrange them, or make the verses fit together again . . .

An early scholar quoted in the commentary of Servius explains that
these were palm leaves, no doubt of the fan variety; but I see no particular reason for accepting the fact on his authority. The higher pedantry
will observe that Virgil does not specify, and we are free to imagine them
as oak leaves or what we will. It is a peculiarly haunting passage, and, as
we shall see, it haunted Dante. What it suggests is the fragility and
dispersion of knowledge, the precarious condition of all human wisdom
but perhaps especially of the highest and most clairvoyant, exposed to
the contingencies of life and time. Reality is big and continual, thought is
small and intermittent, and these are home truths with which one lives
in the classical tradition. Nevertheless the Sibyl's unconcern over the
scattering of her verses is a vatic resignation that those who visit her in
the hope of learning something are unable to share. Thought may be
intermittent, but what the mind perceives in reality is order, and order
once perceived the classical tradition wishes to hang on to—being in this
sense conservative—so that when the profounder order appears it may
be recognized as such. In the *Divine Comedy* we have a prolonged, subtle,
and beautiful struggle with these complexities and paradoxes of reality
and human intelligence. Everything in the poem bears witness at once
to the conservatism of the classical tradition and to its enormous capacity, since it is realist, for realizing new and profounder orders.
You remember that in the passage from Homer that I quoted at the outset the autumn fall of leaves and the spring burgeoning of leaves
were mentioned in the same breath; in the passages from Virgil and
Dante we had only the autumn scene. Spring hardly comes in the *Aeneid*,
which is a tragic poem; but spring does come in the *Divine Comedy*, only
there the image of multitudinous new leaves, which in Homer came in
the next line, does not come in the *Inferno* at all but is placed in the
twelfth canto of the *Paradiso*. Hell and purgatory have come between,
before the poet speaks of the new generation of leaves in a Western
land:

> la quella parte, ove surge ad aprire
> Zefiro dolce le novelle fronde
> di che si vede Europa rivestire . . .

> that region where sweet Zephyr blows
> to open the new leaves wherewith
> Europe sees herself dressed again . . .

But this is only an introduction, for it is the task of the *Paradiso* to bring us into a world on the other side of time and seasons, a world where order remembered and order foreknown are the same and eternal. In the eighteenth, twenty-sixth, and twenty-seventh cantos his heaven is presented as a garden, rooted in God, that blooms forever without dropping petal or leaf. These images in turn prepare us for the more symmetrical and fragrant image of the rose in canto thirty, whose petals, the seats of the blessed, are called *foglie*, leaves. But the most wonderful of all the leaf images are in the last, the thirty-third canto. Here the narrator strives to render for us his vision of God, the ultimate order and source of all order, and warns us how far his poetry must fall short; how far indeed his own mind comes short of recovering the order he had glimpsed, of which he retains little beyond the emotion, as one may retain little but the feeling of a dream. And he says:

> Cosí la neve al sol si disigilla,
> cosí al vento nelle foglie lievi
> si perdea la sentenza di Sibilla . . .

> Even so under the sun the snow melts away,
> even so on the wind in the light leaves
> the oracles of the Sibyl would be lost . . .

But the leaves the poet has in mind are not to be lost in this poem, for in God they are not lost. The Sibyl's unconcern was perhaps becoming in a Sibyl but would not be becoming in this poet, nor indeed possible to him in the ontological world of light.

> Nel suo profondo vidi che s'interna
> legato con amore in un volume
> ciò che per l'universo si squaderna;
> sustanzie ed accidenti, e lor costume
> quasi conflati insieme per tal modo
> che ciò ch'io dico è un semplice lume . . .

> Within its depth I saw there was ingathered
> bound together with love in one volume

> all that is scattered through the universe;
> substance, accidents, and their relations,
> all as if fused together in such a way
> that what I speak of is a single flame . . .

It will not be presumptuous to notice that the love of the poet for the volume he creates is here the analogy for God's love of the created universe. The poet, too, ties together, *legato*, leaves or verses that mortal contingency and distraction would diperse; the poet in the classical tradition does this. And Dante's *Paradiso* may perhaps stand as an example of how much of this he can do. If we recall Virgil's image of the Sibyl and realize fully what Dante did with it, as we say, we also have a means of understanding what the relation of one poet in the classical tradition may be to another.

7

Where do we ourselves stand with respect to this tradition? My final quotation will be from Mr. Eliot's "Burnt Norton":

> Footfalls echo in the memory
> Down the passage which we did not take
> Towards the door we never opened
> Into the rose garden.
> My words echo
> Thus, in your mind. But to what purpose
> Disturbing the dust on a bowl of rose leaves,
> I do not know.

This of course is among other things a statement that the garden—which we may and indeed are all too sure to identify with a sexual Eden but should also identify with the garden of Dante's paradise—is irrevocably in the past; that historically and in our individual lives we took the wrong turning away from it. The poet rather implies that if he were not reminding us of those forlorn footfalls we would be too far gone even to hear them, but he has—at this point—no particular confidence in his own echoing words. The rose of Dante's heaven is now dried petals in a bowl, preserved, one may imagine, by Charles Eliot Norton, but covered not only with the dust of time and gentility and neglect but also with the fine hard dust from the explosions which in two wars have pulverized the cities of Europe.

I am isolating this passage arbitrarily, but if it were all the Eliot we had, our inferences from it as to the quality of his classicism and his profound, pained sense of life would be substantially correct. We would say that the work is indeed, though tenuously, in the classical tradition, and we would trust the sense of life in it, but I think we would be right in thinking that the sense was more true of Europe than of ourselves.

In this country our original attachment to the Greek and Roman things was after the mode of the eighteenth century—the frigidity of the classic revival in design, Latin and Greek as the privileges of a gentleman. By the nature of the case, *that* tradition could not hold on here, and I think we can bear the loss. The Roman legionary eagle that we have on every quarter and the Roman lictor's axe on every dime inform the palms of our hands of a neoclassicism that our lives have repudiated. We owe some fine and graceful things to it, but it represented the full tradition pretty meagerly; and the same is true of the Paul Manship sort of thing in sculpture—all learning and exquisite finish—or of the marble purity—the Parnassianism—that in poetry we sometimes admire as classic. These graces appear decidedly pale when you think of the sustained elevation of the epics, the great force of the tragic plays, the terrible ironies of Thucydides.

There has never been anything you could call a renaissance in America and there may never be, but if there is, it will certainly be something very different from the fifteenth- and sixteenth-century events in Europe that the nineteenth century glorified under that title. Historical criticism and anthropology have made it unlikely that ancient nobleness will have an abundant life among us as a fashion in art or a privilege in society. Our sensibilities have become museums in which one expressive culture is on about the same footing as another, and now that all are accessible we are not likely to restrict our appreciation to what we consider Western. There is nothing especially Western, for example, about hot jazz music.

On the other hand, the grounds of what I have been calling Greek general thought, though discovered in the West, are not a Western property but by definition universal. It seems at least possible that the humanity, usefulness, and wisdom of that thought may grow in honor among Americans. General Marshall at Princeton some years ago said that no young man should think himself educated until he had read Thucydides—because, I take it, nowhere better than in Thucydides can you learn the best and worst to be expected from war and politics. The American sense of things, or savvy, confirms classical realism in many ways—in acknowledging the world as a plurality of distinct things each with its nature, in respecting the concrete, in looking toward the possible as realizable. It would be strangely fitting to our heterogeneous people if the American renaissance should be, or seem to be, a matter of placing that tradition—which I should call the plenary tradition—at the center of the sciences and arts and modes of knowledge. I do not mean that we are going to have something imposed on us by Mr. Mortimer Adler, but Mr. Adler's effort may be symptomatic of a much larger and more natural movement.

We are incorrigibly prone to talk as if some development that we fancy, granted it comes to pass, will be the end of human adventure, error, and endeavor. It is chastening to recall that the renaissance that took place in Europe in the twelfth and thirteenth centuries was something like the hypothetical one I have been thinking of for us. That one did not hold; in fact it lost out so quickly that almost until our own time its quality was forgotten. But the quality existed, exists, and is a standard of audacity and harmony in the ways of intelligence. I take it that men moved by concrete expectations create history; that our expectations are formed in consequence of what we know, and that one of the things *we* have begun to know is that standard. Surely we know it better than most recent generations could. We have also, it is true, some large and distressing and some beautiful kinds of knowledge peculiar to those recent generations. This is merely to say that reasonable expectations may be hard to form and the future they give rise to may be surprising. My point remains that from the American angle and to the American ear the Greco-Roman or classical tradition is not going to be found only in the Attic tragedians, the reasoning of the Academy and the Lyceum, the experience of the Peloponnesian War; nor only in the Roman erotic poets, the histories of Tacitus, or Roman administration and Roman Law. It will be found in greater fullness, and in strong irony, in the European summation of the thirteenth century; and for poetry that means in Dante.

You remember Edgar Lee Masters' epitaph for Pettit the Poet, the small-town American versifier in whom the art of poetry reached its last provincial attenuation. By contrast, the epitaph ended, "Homer and Whitman roared in the pines." I don't know that Whitman registers as high on the Beaufort scale as Homer, but I think Masters' classicism— like Ezra Pound's—was of the right sort for us in mentioning them together. We are not going to gain any ancient life by forgetting our own. But our own life may become something more than our own—and this is perhaps what did not happen in Whitman's case—when we have the luck and capacity to take the full tradition in. Dante was the kind of master who could do that. It is not to be wondered at that he drew so much from Virgil, for Virgil was that kind of master, too. Each practiced literature as an art and a profession, but it is noteworthy in both cases how deep a predilection there was for philosophy, not only in the professional but in the original sense, that is, of a clear-headed contemplation reaching through felt experience or the objective imagination to find and form something true in the mystery of being. Literary craft in both went to discovering in its own way the practical import of philosophy. That is why, I think, readers and writers might come at what I call the full tradition through them. But I have been thinking that we might come at it best through them both, through the relationship between them; for we should then see that the tradition I mean—the only tradition worth talking about—is a tradition of the mind's love and piety, not only before existence past but before existence present and to come: a tradition that helps to form the personal style and to enable the original achievement.

ΙΛΙΑΔΟΣ Γ

αὐτὰρ ἐπεὶ κόσμηθεν ἅμ' ἡγεμόνεσσιν ἕκαστοι,

Τρῶες μὲν κλαγγῇ τ' ἐνοπῇ τ' ἴσαν ὄρνιθες ὣς,

ἠΰτε περ κλαγγὴ γεράνων πέλει οὐρανόθι πρό,

αἵ τ' ἐπεὶ οὖν χειμῶνα φύγον καὶ ἀθέσφατον ὄμβρον,

κλαγγῇ ταί γε πέτονται ἐπ' ὠκεανοῖο ῥοάων

ἀνδράσι Πυγμαίοισι φόνον καὶ κῆρα φέρουσαι·

ἠέριαι δ' ἄρα ταί γε κακὴν ἔριδα προφέρονται.

οἳ δ' ἄρ' ἴσαν σιγῇ μένεα πνείοντες Ἀχαιοί.

ἐν θυμῷ μεμαῶτες ἀλεξέμεν ἀλλήλοισιν.

Robert Fitzgerald's worksheet for his translation of the opening of the Third Book of the *Iliad*.

Robert Fitzgerald at Harvard, 1974.

Postscript to a Translation
of the *Odyssey*

SOME GENERAL CONSIDERATIONS

1

An artist in narrative as we know it will have been interested in his art through reading, and he will expect to be read. It is difficult for us to realize what it means that the man who made the *Odyssey* may never have read anything at all. Five or six centuries before his time, in the heroic age of his poem, there had been a Greek syllabary at Mykenai and elsewhere, apparently used mainly for keeping accounts and lists. A memory of this may have survived in a line of the *Iliad*, but the syllabary itself had long gone out of use, and the world of Homer was illiterate. During the eighth century B.C. the people of the Greek mainland and islands imported a Semitic alphabet and began using it, at least for brief inscriptions. If Homer lived to see this, he probably thought of it as a new magic or amusement, almost certainly not as the medium of his work. We can surmise that we owe our text of *Iliad* and *Odyssey* not to Homer but to the importunity of some technician who "took them down," as nowadays a man would do with a tape recorder. Even in the unlikely event that Homer himself wrote out versions of one or both poems, the fact would remain that he and his audience were not readers but auditors of stories in verse.

Dozens of these stories had been told, or sung, among Aegean people for generations before Homer, forming a tradition possibly as old as English literature is now. We may imagine small communities of a feudal sort whose gentry found in the recitation or performance of these tales all history, all theater, and all that we think of as literary entertainment. The

First published in Robert Fitzgerald's translation of Homer's *Odyssey* (New York: Doubleday & Co.—The Anchor Press, 1963) then later by Random House, New York, 1983.

performers were no doubt sometimes amateurs, but more often as time went on they were professionals who spent a lifetime in a hard craft. Our poet came late and had had supremely gifted predecessors. He inherited a traditional art comparable in range and refinement to the art of the musical virtuoso in our day, but more creative and fluid, for in some degree it remained an art of improvisation.

Thirty years ago my teacher and friend Milman Parry showed how many Homeric lines were constructed out of metrical formulas, out of a vocabulary of metrical parts that with slight modification or none would serve in the context of various actions or descriptions. This vocabulary of phrases was like an Erector or Mecanno set for making verse as you went along. Parry and Albert Lord, who has continued his work, studied the similar technique of oral epic still practiced in our day in Yugoslavia. Professor Lord's important book, *The Singer of Tales* (Harvard, 1960), is an account of their researches and conclusions, and it is indicated reading for anyone who wants to understand the kind of art that Homer practiced. We appear to know more about this art than Plato did. It is a technique rather simply described: many formulas ready in the memory give the storyteller or singer a means of developing action and dialogue as the spirit moves him, with formulaic lines or passages to buoy him up when invention fails. A stringed instrument is indispensable. Meter is indispensable. What Lord calls the "phonological context," the alliterative and voweling pattern, to a certain extent determines invention.

I cannot refer to these studies without making one or two reservations. Parry thought Homer's vocabulary of formulas almost wholly traditional and conventional, but I could never see why originality in detail should be denied a poet to whom it was impossible to deny originality in the large—in conception and organization. I should suppose, too, that although his medium was suited to improvisation, it was no less suited to composition and rehearsal beforehand—an aspect of the matter rather slighted in Parry and Lord. Finally, while statements of the theory sometimes give us to understand that formulaic structure was all-pervasive in both *Iliad* and *Odyssey*, I have yet to see this proved. My own reading of both poems has left me with the impression that while there are many recurrences and reshapings, there are also many passages without echo or precedent—as we might infer from the fact that many Homeric words occur once and once only.

Our understanding of the Homeric poems, however, has been permanently altered and improved by Parry's work and Lord's, and the famous Homeric Question, the question of single or multiple authorship of

Iliad and *Odyssey*, will never be the same again. There is little doubt now that from the singers before him Homer had learned not only a rich metrical language but a large repertory of themes. Old themes, like that of the return of heroes, he handled again with joyous elaboration and cunning. It is likely that his compositions, from the nature of the case, varied from one performance to another. No doubt a tale might be told either briefly and broadly or at length and with subtlety, depending on audience and occasion. There was no canonical version.

As Professor Lord puts it: "The theme is in reality protean; in the singer's mind it has many shapes, all the forms in which he has ever sung it, although his latest rendering of it will naturally be freshest in his mind. . . . And the shapes that it has taken in the past have been suitable for the song of the moment. In a traditional poem, therefore, there is a pull in two directions: one is toward the song being sung and the other is toward the previous use of the same theme. The result is that characteristic of oral poetry which literary scholars have found hardest to understand and accept, namely, an occasional inconsistency, the famous nod of a Homer."

Our versions of *Iliad* and *Odyssey* must have originated in those versions that at the moment of dictation or recording the performer, whether Homer or a follower of Homer, happened to sing. He may have been more inspired on other occasions, but it is fair to assume that when it came to recording he did his best, and did well. Perhaps on this occasion he chose to record the "long songs" and to restore, so to speak, many cuts often made in performance. Neither poem as we have it could have been recorded at one sitting, and it is possible that long intervals elapsed between the recording of one part and that of another. Given the conditions, and given what Professor Lord calls the protean nature of the themes, we can no longer take inconsistencies in the poems as proof of multiple authorship.

Artist and writer know that any work, ancient or modern, even any masterwork, could easily have been very different from what it is. If you are curious about these matters, you can often see, in drafts and sketches, part at least of the sheaf or spectrum of possible forms of which the "final" version of a story or poem or picture represents a selection— not necessarily or invariably the best—or simply a terminus at which effort stopped. An element of the composite remains in all but the most perfect composition. Of this general truth the Homeric poems are special instances. It is not difficult to see in each poem traces of other stories, or of other versions in which the same stories were handled differently. For more than a century Homeric criticism devoted itself to spotting logical and linguistic discrepancies, discovering one or the other poem to be a "wretched patchwork," in the words of one eminent scholar. While I was engaged on this translation, Professor Denys Page's Bryn Mawr lectures, published as *The Homeric Odyssey* (Oxford, 1955), argued, or reargued, the case against "unity" with asperity and flourish. But many of his points were debater's points, and I doubt that Page realized all the implications of Parry's work or Lord's.

To sum up, the *Odyssey* could well have been composed by one singer, working with themes he had heard from others, in a medium developed by others; if single in one sense, the authorship was certainly multiple in another. There is no way of proving it single in any sense. An admirer, a son, an apprentice, a collaborator, may have contributed passages or sections—a final section perhaps, as many critics have thought—to the "long song" as we have it. But the contrary is also possible. The truth, I think, is that we are too remote in time and language to decide. These, roughly, are the considerations that ought to be present to our minds when we think of Homer. But it is not necessary to put the name in quotation marks.

2

A living voice in firelight or in the open air, a living presence bringing into life his great company of imagined persons, a master performer at his ease, touching the strings, disposing of many voices, many tones and tempos, tragedy, comedy, and glory, holding his auditors in the palm of his hand: was Homer all of this? We can only suppose that he was. If what we imagine is true, Homer must himself have been his poems, in a physical sense unequaled in the case of any poet since. Imagine *Henry IV* and *The Tempest* composed not for production by a company of actors but as solo performances by Shakespeare himself. Or imagine it in the case of either, not both. The notion is still astonishing, and it is difficult to believe it.

I learn from W. S. Merwin, in the introduction to his translations of *Spanish Ballads* (Anchor, 1961), that the wandering *juglares* of medieval Spain, who sang and recited the epic *cantares*, "might be accompanied in their performance by mimes, known as *remendadores*, and *cazarros*—a name which included clowns and most varieties of stunt man." Well, stunt men, or tumblers, are mentioned as performing along with a poet or singer at Meneláos' court in Book IV of the *Odyssey*. But no mimes assist any ἀοιδός in the Homeric poems. This of itself would not prove that Homer did his own impersonations. The ἀοιδός as Homer presented him was a figure of the heroic age, four or five centuries before his time. But so far as I know there is no evidence whatever that Homer himself, or the ἀοιδοί in his immediate tradition, or their successors, the rhapsodes, were accompanied by mimes or actors.

We have no perfect word for ἀοιδός, for the kind of artist Homer was. "Bard" was fairly exact but has become a joke. "Skald" takes us too far into druidical regions. "Minstrel" is better but still too slight, too trammeled with doublet and hose, and faintly raffish after Gilbert & Sullivan. The Italian compound word *cantastorie* is at least neutral and is a definition of sorts. Lord did well to adopt the English equivalent, "singer of tales." But I am not satisfied. The term does not do justice to the creative and inventive power of the ἀοιδός. It does not suggest his mimetic art. And there is a difficulty about "singer" as a term for the poet and performer of these things.

That the telling of a story, and the incidental acting of roles, should be called "singing"—this will strike us at first as affected or strange. We may indeed think of opera, disciplined and expressive opera like the *Orfeo* of Gluck, true lyric theater as the Italians call it; but the orchestra and the stage, the whole convention, are alien to Homer. Perhaps it is enough to recall certain fine acting voices. As a child I sat aloft in the second balcony of an old theater in Illinois while a traveling company played *Sancho Panza*, and I remember the beautiful voice of the late Otis Skinner rising effortless, malleable, and pure, or falling to a crystalline whisper, far off there below, in unhurried declamation, while the whole theater sat spellbound by that human instrument alone. There is no doubt that the master ἀοιδός had a gift like that, a trained voice of great expressive and melodic range.

By all accounts, too, the Homeric performer used a second instrument and depended on it: the κίθαρις, an affair of a few gut strings with some kind of resonator, possibly a tortoise shell, like the later lyre. It would be anachronistic to think of it as a guitar or lute, so I call it a "gittern harp" and sometimes refer to the performer as a harper. Homer describes him more than once as plucking or strumming an overture to a given tale or song, and he must have used the instrument not only for accompaniment but for pitch, and to fill pauses while he took thought for the next turn. No doubt the instrument marked rhythm, too.

We need not delude ourselves as to how far these generalities really take us. How in particular the voice, the metered verse, and the stringed instrument were related in these performances, and in the recital of poetry throughout antiquity, I do not well understand, and I do not think anyone does perfectly. In our own tradition the "music of verse" is one thing and "music" proper is another. A song is a song, not necessarily a poem. "The Peaceful Western Wind" and "Mistress Mine" indeed happen to be both, and I have heard Christopher Casson lean to a small Irish harp and sing "Oft in the Stilly Night" so attentively that it seemed twice the poem I had known before. But this is exceptional. Who would set to music the great lyrics of Yeats? Who could improve on *Lear* by scoring it? Here all is in the shape and movement of metered language. But we find the verse of Homer—and this is my point—as beautiful in itself as the verse of Yeats or Shakespeare. What we call a "musical arrangement" would disperse or confuse the effect of it. We can be sure, I think, that harp or κίθαρις played a very subdued part, however essential, in the original Homeric performance.

3

One of our first discoveries in reading Homer will be that he was a poet in our sense of the word, a man gifted at making verse. All the learning that we may later assemble, all we can know or guess of the artist as an improviser and entertainer, even our fugitive sense of him as the demiurge of a world transfigured, all this cannot supersede—indeed it is founded on—our pleasure in him line by line, the way we hear or read him. I will never forget how unexpectedly moved I was years ago when for the first time I heard Telémakhos in Book I speak of his father as

ἀνέρος οὗ δή που λεύκ' ὀστέα πύθεται ὄμβρῳ

Looking up, I said to myself, in effect, "Why, this really is poetry!" and I meant poetry as good as "Call for the robin redbreast and the wren." Many times afterward, in reading or translating Homer, I have again paused over a line or a pair of lines in recognition and homage.

Parry thought this incomparable medium, the formulaic hexameter, had been shaped through centuries of trial and error, a testing and refining process conducted on many occasions before generations of auditors so that in the end only the fittest language survived and the virtuoso had at his command the best words in the best order for anything he cared to relate or invent. I used at first to feel that the recurrent epithets and formula lines were a mere convention and a bore. In time I realized that they were musical phrases, brief incantations, of which the miserable renderings gave little or no idea. These formulas entered the repertory not only because they were useful but because they were memorable, I mean because nobody who had once heard them could easily forget them; and that is true to this day.

᾿Ημος δ᾿ ἠριγένεια φάνη ῥοδοδάκτυλος ῾Ηώς

It is possible that by Homer's time even he could not have said precisely what the two epithets in this line meant—and there are a number of others of which the same is true—but the line had been kept for its fragrance, a fragrance of Dawn, inimitable and unsurpassable, no more boring in its recurrence than Dawn itself. Because there are hundreds of lines like this and more hundreds of half lines and phrases, the very medium of Homer is pervaded by lyric quality. The simplest phrases have it. Hear Hektor saying (*Iliad* VI, 264), "Don't offer me any sweet wine, dear Mother:"

Μή μοι οἶνον ἄειρε μελίφρονα πότνια μῆτερ

How could you render that? Consider the voweling, and consider how the first epithet, after the ghost of a pause, hovers between "wine" and "mother." There is, besides, a peculiar cleanliness and lightness of movement, as often in Homer, and there is something else that I call the cut or sculpture of words. It is easiest to be aware of this in the last two feet of certain hexameters: νόστον ἑταίρων and ἔνδον ἐόντων. These are rounded shapes.

I am not being what Professor Irving Babbitt used to call "fanciful." If you will make the effort to imagine this Greek as still virgin of any visual signs at all, associated with no letters, no Greek characters, no script, no print—as purely and simply expressive sound, you will be able to perceive it in the air, its true medium, and to hear how it shapes and tempers the air by virtue of stops and tones. I will quote two more lines, one for consonants, and one for vowels. The first is Aphroditê saying in *Iliad* V, 359,

φίλε κασίγνητε κόμισαί τέ με δός τέ μοι ἵππους

in which we hear the light tongue of the goddess of love herself in three coquettish particles, τε . . . τε . . . τε . . . My second example is the first line sung by those temptresses of the sea, known to Homer as Seirênês, and it is a typical triumph of formulary art since it is a modified version of a line that occurs in the *Iliad* in quite a different context, and in the mouth of quite a different personage. Here it is, XII, 184:

Δεῦρ' ἄγ' ἰών, πολύαιν' 'Οδυσεῦ, μέγα κῦδος 'Αχαιῶν

There is a rhythm of anapests, and intricate rhyming: Δεῦ and σεῦ on the beat, λύ on the offbeat and κῦ on the beat, αιν' and αι on the beat, ῶν on the beat and ών on the offbeat, and ἄγ' turned round widdershins on μέγα: this is a conjuring kind of echolalia. But more: the crooning vowels are for low seductive voices, rising in mid-line with αιν' and then rising and opening with a savage shout in 'Αχαιῶν at the end.

You might call this sort of thing "phonetic wit"—though it may have come to the artist without calculation. Along with it, in Homer, there is a lot of verbal wit enjoyed for its own sake and also syntactical wit, a quality of style that Chapman and Pope could appreciate. Chiastic order is a favorite form, and the *Iliad* especially teems with it. Book IV, 125:

λίγξε βιός, νευρή δὲ μέγ' ἴαχεν, ἆλτο δ' ὀϊστὸς

I could go on indefinitely, but I should cut this short and say that we are not meant very often to stop and consider so curiously. The narrative pace does not encourage it. You can be a connoisseur of the single line if you like, but this is only the beginning of appreciation. Homer is lyric but rarely indulges the lyric, he keeps his surface alive but keeps it moving; the line is only the medium, as I began by calling it, and as such it is subordinate to practically everything else. It is subordinate in the first place to the passage, to the effect created by the placement of lines in succession. Continuous prose cannot achieve the switches and surprises that you get by playing on a regular meter, a measured base. Of these effects Homer, formulas and all, was a master. We have often heard how the movement of the hexameter line itself could be varied by pauses, lightened by dactyls, retarded by spondees; but we have heard less of what could happen in the movement from line to line and in the course of action or speeches. A change of pace, a change of mood, an ironic aside, a quick look into the past or into the distance—we find all these between one line and the next.

Homer's humor, too, in the *Iliad* rather grim or slapstick, in the *Odyssey* more subtly comic, often dawns on us at the unexpected swerve of a new line. In *Iliad* VIII there is a crash of lightning against the Akhaians and the best charioteers give way: Idómeneus retreats, Agamémnon retreats, big Aias and little Aias retreat, but Nestor? Nestor alone stood fast, we hear, and just as we begin to admire the veteran the next line says (81),

οὔ τι ἑκών, ἀλλ' ἵππος ἐτείρετο

"Not that he wanted to in the least, but one of his horses was disabled." In *Odyssey* IV, after Helen's story of how virtuously she kept Odysseus' secret when she had recognized him spying in Troy. Meneláos cannot refrain from a pointed story to keep the record straight. There is a march of hexameters extolling Odysseus' courage when he and the Akhaian captains were waiting in the wooden horse to bring death upon the Trojans. Then abruptly, in 274, ἦλθες ἔπειτα σὺ κεῖσε. The words make a trochee and two amphibrachs: "Who should come by there but *you* then"—and he goes on to tell of the peril she put them all in by mimicking the voices of their wives. You can see this trick of the sudden change of movement and tone played by Eurýmakhos in *Odyssey* I, 405, when after several lines of hearty assurance to Telémakhos he looks at him harder, ἀλλ' ἐθέλω σε, φέριστε, περὶ ξείνοιο ἐρέσθαι, and the sneer becomes, yes, audible.

Another thing, more highly dramatic, is of course the calculated and gradated heightening of tone or energy throughout a longer passage. For a crescendo of passion, I suppose Akhilleus' great tirade in *Iliad* IX, 307 sqq., cannot be matched, but Odysseus, among his other gifts of gab, has a way of beginning mild and ending deadly. In XVIII there are two examples, a relatively brief one in his reply to Iros, 15 sqq., and a longer one to Eurýmakhos, 366 sqq.

Now all these that I have mentioned are tiny applications of a principle everywhere at work over the expanse of both poems. Narrative art lives as a river lives, first by grace of tributaries—in Homer by the continual refreshment of invention and unlooked-for turns—and second by the direction of flow. If in the line and passage the poems are interesting, as they are, heaven knows they are even more interesting in the ways they take as their currents widen. Not that Homer is free of *longueurs:* Phoinix' tale of Meleagros in *Iliad* IX strikes me as windy, and in the slow movement of the *Odyssey* at least one of the digressions and retards—the pedigree of Theoklýmenos—was too much even for this virtuoso to bring off. He nods, and we nod with him. But almost always the attention of the audience is courted and held. The earliest critics noticed how Homer varied his effects: for an offhand example, Telémakhos arrives off Pylos by sea at dawn, arrives at Sparta by land at nightfall. The battle scenes in the *Iliad* are sometimes thought monotonous; in fact they are prodigiously inventive and differ one from another not only in general shape but in detail: time after time, it is true, a man falls and his armor clangs upon him, but either he or the man next to him has just been killed in an entirely new way. The formulas give the narrative musical consistency; the innovations keep it alive. The more it is the same, the more it changes. In the very use of the formulas themselves, remarkable effects are got by slight additions or modifications. Penélopê's visits to the banquet hall in the *Odyssey* are formulary: she appears with her maids, she draws her veil down and across her face, she speaks, she retires, weeps, and goes to sleep. The first time (I, 365) after she is gone the suitors make a din, they all swear they will have her; the second time (XVI, 413) she appears and retires as before but there is no din, no swearing; the third time (XVIII, 212) there is no din, but on her appearance (not on her withdrawal) a new line is added to the formula, telling us that the suitors knees were weakened with lust for her; then comes the swearing line from Book I. Someone has called this trick of style "incremental repetition." It can be, as it is in this case, very powerful.

4

A probable rate of Homeric performance was about five hundred lines an hour. So far as I know, nobody has gone very far with deductions from this fact. The first four books of the *Odyssey* are obviously a narrative and dramatic unit, so are the next four, and so are the next four. These are three successive waves of action, and each runs to about two thousand lines or about four hours of performance. There is no reason for not regarding this as the duration of a formal recital. If we look again at the second half of the poem we will see that these twelve Books, too, fall into three divisions of about the same length: XIII through XVI, XVII through XX, and XXI through XXIV. These six divisions could well be considered the true Books of the *Odyssey*, within which the traditional Books are like chapters or cantos. Please understand that I have no positive authority for this suggestion; it merely accords with units of probable performance and with the organization of the poem. I would not discard the traditional twenty-four sections, made by Alexandrians who were perhaps following a still earlier tradition.

My six divisions, at any rate, will help us to see the entire poem in outline. In the first performance (I through IV) the last is of course foreshadowed if not determined, Olympian decisions are taken, we are introduced on the scene to the situation that is to be remedied, the conflict to be decided, and we are prepared to meet the famous man who has it all to cope with. In the second (V–VIII) we find him in a distant setting and see him in action, facing other situations, other challenges, making his way back toward the big one that awaits him. In the third (IX–XII) he himself takes over the narration and interests us directly in his past adventures, as though he were now the poet before us. In the fourth or "slow movement" as I call it (XIII–XVI) we see him at last near to his home and battleground, gathering information, testing a likely helper, and reunited with his son. In the fifth (XVII–XX) he enters the scene itself, comes to grips with his situation, suffers it, and sizes up the persons involved in it at close hand. In the sixth (XXI–XXIV) he fights and wins, remedies and recomposes everything.

That is an outline in the most general terms. If I tried to follow and comment on the narrative in detail I would never finish. But there are a few matters. . . . One is this: the universe of the *Odyssey* is subject to moral law, and in the first few lines briefly, or amply in the first few hundred, we are informed of this law, of how it may be violated, and how badly, sooner or later, the offenders come off. The poet was not Plato, Augustine, or Immanuel Kant, and we need not bother to pick flaws in his thinking. He tells us that Odysseus' crew perished for their ἀτασθαλίῃσιν, and then Zeus remarks that Aigísthos in particular and mortals in general have aggravated their lot by the same misdemeanor. What is this misdemeanor? Presumption, impious and reckless: a folly of greed. It is more than taking what belongs to a vague "someone else"— for you are permitted some raids and wars of conquest; it is claiming and taking more than your share in your own commonwealth, without a decent respect for the views of heaven or the opinions of mankind. Wife-stealing and murder, usurpation and insolence: these are the crimes against private and public order on which the Olympians meditate as the poem opens. Specific objects of meditation are two Akhaian kingdoms left masterless by the war. Mykênai succumbed, now Ithaka is threatened. The two casts of characters are paralleled, as they will be often again, openly or by implication, throughout the poem: Aigísthos and the suitors, Klytaimnéstra and Penélopê, Agamémnon and Odysseus, Orestês and Telémakhos. The present action will stand out more sharply by contrast with the dark action in Mykênai years before.

A very learned and close student of literature, Erich Auerbach, was led by the argument he was making at the time to assert that "the Homeric style knows only a foreground, only a uniformly illuminated, uniformly objective present." It would be better to remove the word "only" and to add that the Homeric style knows a constant background of retrospect and allusion to the past. It is so in the *Iliad*, and more so in the *Odyssey*. In fact, that past of which the events of the *Iliad* form a part stands everywhere behind the events of the *Odyssey*, the perspective in which the *Odyssey* takes place.

The relationship between the two poems is fascinating. Clearly, both are drawn from the same great fund of stories about the heroes of the expedition against Troy, both are composed in the same formulary tradition, and the *Odyssey* was second in order of composition. Besides a great many lines of the *Iliad* adapted or even playfully parodied in the *Odyssey*, there is one curious bit of evidence that I do not remember seeing noticed. The audience of the *Iliad* had to be kept straight at every point as to which of the two armies was being referred to, hence a great number of formula lines ending with the Greek for "Akhaians," a short syllable and two longs in any of the plural cases. These line endings were so convenient metrically that they were kept throughout the *Odyssey*, even in contexts where they were no longer functional, where it was unnecessary to distinguish Akhaians from anyone else. But no single incident or event of the *Iliad* is so much as referred to in the *Odyssey*, and this is so striking (there are also a few odd differences of vocabulary) that it has been possible to argue that the composer of the *Odyssey* did not even know the *Iliad*. We will be sensible to conclude that he not only knew but leaned on it familiarly; that he, like Odysseus, did not hold with twice-told tales; and that he wanted to complete and complement the *Iliad* by working into his background events that took place after the funeral of Hektor, the close of that poem.

Of these events the fate of Agamémnon, as I have said, is from first to last the pattern of tragedy against which the *Odyssey* is played to a happy ending. In the successive appearances of the Mykênai theme, something is added each time—here is incremental repetition for you—until the climax in Book XI when Agamémnon himself tells his story. There is also a coda, in Book XXIV. But of course Mykênai is only a part of the background richly given in the first four Books and kept in view later, a background not only of depth in time but of the wide world beyond Ithaka. To make clearer the disorder of that realm there is first the order of Nestor's kingdom, where sacrifice and prayer are duly offered before meat (the suitors in Books I and II neither sacrifice nor pray) and then the splendor of Meneláos' court. In the discourse of the two great gentlemen there are echoes of battles long ago, and there are also images of other seas and lands far to the east and south. Most important of all, from one Book to another in the "Telemakheia" the figure of the absent Odysseus grows more vivid in what is said about him. We are being prepared for an entrance. We are even prepared thematically, in Meneláos' story of seafaring, of detention on an island, of the nymph Eidothea and the Ancient of the Sea, for the adventures of Odysseus.

5

The *Odyssey* is about a man who cared for his wife and wanted to rejoin her. In the resonance of this affection, and by way of setting it off, the poem touches on a vast diversity of relationships between men and women: love maternal and filial, love connubial and adulterous, seduction and concubinage, infatuation superhuman and human, chance encounters lyric and prosaic. There are many women, young and old, enchantresses and queens and serving maids. In the "society," as we say, of the *Odyssey*, women can be very distinguished: Athena is powerful in the highest circles, Arêtê holds equal power with her husband in Phaiakia, Helen has been re-established in the power of her beauty, which if I am not mistaken she makes Telémakhos feel. The honor roll of lovely dead ladies in Book XI is fully appropriate to this poem. Three of the principal adventures of Odysseus are with exquisite young women of great charm and spirit, and during each of these episodes the audience must wonder how he can possibly move on. He wants to regain his home and kingdom, it is true. But besides that, as Kalypso inquires, what is it about Penélopê that draws him homeward? Her distinction is often mentioned, but do we ever see it overwhelmingly demonstrated?

I believe we do, or should. The demonstration, however, is dramatic and has been missed by many people, though not by all, through a failure to grasp the nature of the *Odyssey* as performance. Let me again insist upon it. More than half of this poem is dialogue. We know that in the first centuries after the Homeric poems were written down, they were presented as performances by rhapsodes who had them by heart, and we know from the *Ion* of Plato that such performances could be histrionic, highly and effectively so. There must have existed among these professionals a tradition of interpretation, nuance, gesture, and "business" in general that may easily have descended from the ἀοιδοί, the inventors, from Homer himself. Into later and literary ages none of this survived. The French Homerist Victor Bérard noticed years ago that our text of the *Odyssey* often resembles an acting script. But no stage directions are included, and if we ask how to play any particular scene we find that there has been no Harley Granville-Barker of Homeric studies.

Well, let us at our leisure look into one situation and one big scene that will answer Kalypso's question.

The purpose of Odysseus, determining the action of the poem, is to get home and to prevail there. Once he lands on Ithaka his problem is a tactical one: how, with his son and two fieldhands, to take on more than one hundred able-bodied young men and kill them all. By the end of Book XVI he has thought his problem through to a certain point: Telémakhos is to precede him to the manor, he is able to follow as a beggar, and at a signal from him the young man is to remove all shields, helmets, and throwing spears from those racks in the banquet hall where, as we remember, they were located in Book I. To be exact, not all are to be removed; a few are to be put aside for use against the suitors. My first observation is that this is as far as Odysseus ever goes, by himself, in planning the final combat. He goes no farther in the course of Book XVII and Book XVIII, and as if to fix this in our minds the poet at the beginning of Book XIX has him repeat his previous instructions about removing the arms; in fact he and Telémakhos do the job together. (This repetition used to be thought an interpolation; the arms, at any rate, are removed.)

Let us now consider what *does* happen in Books XVII and XVIII. If I am right in dividing the poem into six performances, these Books with XIX and XX make up the fifth. Early in XVII Telémakhos leaves the swineherd's hut, goes home to the manor hall, and passes on to his mother the news given him by Meneláos at Sparta—that Odysseus is not dead but alive. The words are barely out of his mouth before his supercargo, the diviner, swears to Penélopê that her husband is not only alive but on the island at that very moment. Since the first piece of news is certainly authentic, the second—though it may seem fantastic—must at least quicken her interest in any stranger who appears. The only stranger about to appear is Odysseus in his rags. We may or may not recall Helen's boast of having recognized him through a similar disguise in a similar situation at Troy; if we do—and after all we heard the story only the other evening—our feeling of suspense may be heightened. Presently, strange to relate, Odysseus is in fact recognized just outside the manor. A dying old hunting dog who hasn't seen him for twenty years knows him by the sound of his voice.

Odysseus now enters the hall, begging, and one of the suitors banqueting there hits him with a footstool. Pénelopê has heard the scene from her room. She orders the swineherd to fetch the beggar in case he has news of Odysseus, and the swineherd tells her the beggar does indeed have news, at least he has sworn that Odysseus is nearby on the mainland and will soon be home. "If Odysseus comes, he will repay the violence of the suitors," she says, using the future tense for that eventuality in the most hopeful speech she has yet made. At this point Télémakhos, downstairs in the hall, sneezes, and Penélopê laughs at the good omen—the first time she has laughed in the *Odyssey*. She goes eagerly to the door, but Eumaios returns without the beggar, who wishes to put off a meeting until the young men have left the hall for the night. In spite of her impatience, the lady concedes that the stranger is right and is no fool.

Are we to suppose here, at the end of XVII, that it has even crossed her mind who the stranger might be? For the audience, this is already a very interesting question. The answer is, probably not—though it is clear how excited she has become.

In the next Book, XVIII, Penélopê feels impelled for reasons she cannot analyze to go downstairs among the suitors, to dazzle the young men with her beauty, and to be solicitous of the beggar, who has come off well in a fist fight. She is now in the beggar's presence. Is it his presence that prompts her to a rather gratuitous speech, a speech with an air of being "to whom it may concern," recalling her husband's instructions when he left for the Trojan War? Her point is that she cannot hold out much longer against marriage with one of her suitors. She induces the young men to give her some gifts (to the amusement of Odysseus) and then withdraws until the evening is over and the suitors have left the place. We come to Book XIX. It is after dark. From the empty banquet hall Odysseus and his son remove the arms and put them back in a storeroom. Before they do this, however, Telémakhos has the old servant, Eurýkleia, temporarily lock all the maids in the women's quarters. Why? Because among these women there are a dozen mistresses and accomplices of the suitors, who are only waiting until the house is quiet to slip out and join their lovers in the town. We already know one of these girls, Melántho, mistress of Eurýmakhos. When Penélopê comes down to interview the beggar by firelight, this girl is with her, as the poet carefully makes us see. The whole interview is conducted in her presence. If she should suspect the identity of the beggar, Odysseus' tactical plan—to catch the suitors in the hall without spears and trust to Athena—will miscarry, to say the least.

As the interview begins, Penélopê follows the usual formula and asks the stranger who he is. His reply is evasive, though it is moving if we remember that these are the first words he has spoken to her in twenty years. She proceeds to explain to him—to him, a stranger and vagabond—what her predicament is. She tells him of the famous feat of weaving and unweaving by which she had kept her suitors waiting for more than three years. It is as if she were justifying herself aloud for being, as she tells him she is now, at the end of her resources. Justifying herself to her husband? That is the fact, but it may still be something of which we are meant to be aware while she is not. In return for her confidence, Odysseus confides that he is a grandson of King Minos of Crete and that he once entertained Odysseus at Knossos. The lady weeps. She dries her eyes and asks him to prove it by recalling how Odysseus looked. He does so, very accurately, describing a brooch and tunic that Penélopê had given him. He adds, with a typical Odyssean touch, that the Cretan women had found him a fine sight in his tunic. The lady weeps a second time and remarks that *she* will never lay eyes on Odysseus again.

The beggar now contradicts her. He now ventures a speech that, taken along with all that has led up to it, looks like a serious effort to impart information. He not only repeats what he has already told the swineherd and the swineherd has relayed to her—that Odysseus is on the mainland and coming home—but he swears very solemnly that Odysseus will arrive (306)

$$\text{τοῦδ' αὐτοῦ λυκάβαντος}$$

"this very λυκάβας" and "between the waning and the new moon." Nobody can be sure what λυκάβας means, but it may well mean "the going of daylight" and the phrase could have the sense "before another day passes." As to the phrase about the new moon, there is very little doubt that this is precise. The next day, as we will hear in Book XX, is a feast day to Apollo, and that would be the festival of the new moon awaited in the evening. So he is telling her twice, cryptically and elliptically for the benefit of the maids in earshot, that her husband will be home tomorrow.

Now we, the audience, must suppose that this lady, who has been represented often as extremely intelligent, will be asking herself with some urgency how the vagabond before her could possibly swear to anything so definite. She is controlled, as usual. She answers that if he were right he would soon know her love, but no, he can't be right. Odysseus cannot return. She offers him a footbath, and he declines it unless there is an old maid-servant to give it to him. Penélopê says there is in fact an old woman who nursed Odysseus in infancy, and she tells Eurýkleia to bathe him. Here is an actor's line (358).

νίψον σοῖο ἄνακτος

"Bathe your master's—" the line begins, and a shiver runs through the audience. The next word, however, is not πόδας "feet" but ὁμήλικα "coeval" or "contemporary." (I think that Sophocles, for one, noted this feat of brinkmanship in a single line.) Now we have the well-known episode of the footbath during which Eurýkleia recognizes Odysseus by his scar, but he throttles her and keeps her quiet. This has been generally held to be the only recognition that takes place in Book XIX. At the climax when the old woman glances toward Penélopê as if to reveal Odysseus, the poet tells us that Athena has turned the lady's mind elsewhere so that she doesn't notice. Penélopê, in other words, is lost in thought, and we are aware of all that she has to think about. I find the outcome of her thinking very impressive.

When Penélopê speaks again, she tells the beggar that she has a dream for him to interpret—the dream of her pet geese killed by an eagle who professed to be Odysseus. In this there is a remarkable little confession that she had grown fond, in a way, of having the suitors about her, but there is more to it than that. When she says that on waking she saw the dream geese still there, what can she possibly mean except, "It is a dream to think that you can kill them; they are so many, they will survive and you will not." This at any rate is what the beggar answers. He assures her that there is no other way to interpret the dream than as Odysseus, in the dream, has already done: the suitors will be killed. Assuming the presence of the unfaithful maid—or maids—he takes a serious risk here in order to make it clear to her that he is ready for battle. She now remarks that dreams are not to be counted on, but that she has one more thing to tell him: listen carefully. She has made up her mind that *tomorrow* will be the day of decision as to whom she will marry, and the decision will be reached through the test of the bow. In reply to this the beggar says in effect that that will be excellent and tomorrow will not be too soon.

I agree with the late Philip Whaley Harsh, of Stanford, that this is one of the most interesting recognition scenes ever devised. Part of my argument was anticipated by Professor Harsh in the *American Journal of Philology*, Vol. 71 (1950). It is possible—though I think barely possible—to read the scene in the previously accepted way as involving no more communication between the man and woman than is compatible with their respective roles of lady and beggar, the roles they stick to, though so precariously. On this reading all evidence of understanding between them is coincidence and irony. But that is simply not consistent with the situation as a whole—a situation built up for the audience in the course of this performance. During the day, before the evening, Penélopê has been told first that her husband is alive, second that he is on the island, and third that he is coming soon. She has been waiting for ten years with no such authentic news and no such startling expectations and had made the suitors wait for nearly four. Are we, the audience, to believe that she wouldn't wait a few days longer to see if her husband turns up? Is it conceivable that, instead of waiting, the woman so distinguished for tenacity would this very evening give up the waiting game and seriously propose to marry the next day? How could she come to this abrupt decision in the course of her evening scene with Odysseus unless she realized that the stranger before her was indeed her husband?

Why, in short, underrate the high and beautiful tension of the scene and the nerve, the magnificence of Penélopê? Not Kalypso, not Nausikaa, not Kirkê could have played this scene. Consider what she bestows on Odysseus. Up to now his plan of action, as I have noticed, has been fairly desperate. Now it is she, not he, who remembers the big hunting bow that has hung in an inner room since he left Ithaka. Archery against men who have no missiles is in fact the only practical way of beating the numerical odds. Penélopê supplies the weapon for the suitors' downfall, and she does so for that purpose and no other. At the opening of Book XXI when Athena sends her for the bow, the goddess is said to prompt her to this as "the contest and start of slaughter"—a phrase that goes naturally by the syntax with what is in Penélopê's mind. In the course of that Book it is Penélopê who insists at the crucial moment that the beggar be given a try at the bow; she all but literally places it in his hands. I conclude that for the last and greatest of Odysseus' feats of arms his wife is as responsible as he is. The reasons for his affection should now be clear.

If in other Books, especially in XXIII, there are details inconsistent with the interpretation I have given, we may regard these as instances of what

Professor Lord has called the varying "pulls" of previous versions. But I am not sure there are any real inconsistencies. There is a certain mystery, if you like, but so is there mystery in *Daisy Miller*. Harsh explained Penélopê's affected incredulity and hesitation in XXIII as due to emotional exhaustion (she had been terribly afraid that Odysseus couldn't do it) and to the need to collect herself before resuming a marriage interrupted for twenty years. Twenty years is no trifle. If you left home to take part in the Second World War, imagine yourself lost to view afterward and only now returning; or if your father went to the war, imagine it of him. One difference between Homer and many of his commentators is that Homer could imagine people in situations. Some commentators even call it an "inconsistency" that the shade of Amphímedon in Book XXIV credits Odysseus with having thought up the archery contest—as though Amphímedon could have known any better, or made any better assumption.

As I noted earlier, Book XXIV has often been regarded as a later addition to the poem. This is mainly because two early critics, Aristophanes and Aristarchus, are said to have called line 296 of XXIII the "goal" or "end" of the *Odyssey*. This line, on which Odysseus and Penélopê retire to bed, could have been the conclusion of an old-fashioned movie but not of a poem like this. It is true that there are also some linguistic grounds, but they do not appear to be probative. Even if they were, I could only say that in substance Book XXIV is fully "Homeric" and that whoever composed it knew what he was doing. The many references to Laërtês throughout the poem require Book XXIV; so do at least two previous allusions by Odysseus to the aftermath of the fight with the suitors. In this Book the comparison between Penélopê and Klytaimnéstra, recurrent throughout the poem, is rounded off by Agamémnon himself. But there is another artistic reason for Book XXIV, and a great one. If Homer's incidental purpose in the *Odyssey* was to complete and complement the *Iliad*, XXIV in effect completes both poems at once. The Akhaian antagonists of the *Iliad*, Agamémnon and Akhilleus, are here reconciled among the dead, and as the *Iliad* closed with Hektor's funeral, the *Odyssey* does not come to a close until the funeral of Akhilleus has been described.

A page or so more and I will have done with my reflections. I have named Professor Lord's book and Professor Harsh's article, each illuminating in its way. Two more books that I have valued are *Homer and the Monuments*, by H. L. Lorimer (Macmillan, London, 1950) and *The Poetry of Homer* by S. E. Bassett (University of California Press, 1938). Rhys

Carpenter on *Folk Tale, Fiction and Saga in the Homeric Epics* (University of California Press, 1946) is full of interesting arguments. So, as I have said, is Denys Page's book on the *Odyssey*, though I read it rather as a brief than as a judgment. His later book, *History and the Homeric Iliad* (University of California Press, 1959) is more brilliant still. The most recent good annotated edition is W. B. Stanford's (Macmillan, London, 1947). D. B. Monro's annotated edition of Books XIII–XIV, with its long Appendix (Oxford, 1901), is a superb monument of scholarship and good sense in its time. I am indebted to it for my excision of lines 275–78 in Book I, an excision that obviates one of Page's chief criticisms. I like Monro's statement about the "Telemakheia": "It secures that gradual heightening of interest which is the chief secret of dramatic art." I also owe to Monro, and to J. D. Denniston's wonderful book, *The Greek Particles* (Oxford, 1954), confirmation of my sense that the colloquial entered into Homer's style in the *Odyssey*.

A word about "translation." The *Odyssey*, considered strictly as an aesthetic object, is to be appreciated only in Greek. It can no more be translated into English than rhododendron can be translated into dogwood. You must learn Greek if you want to experience Homer, just as you must go to the Acropolis and look at it if you want to experience the Parthenon. There is a sense, however, in which the Greek poem was itself a translation. It was a translation into Homer's metered language, into his narrative and dramatic style, of an action invented and elaborated in the imagination. This action and the personages involved in it were what mattered most to poet and audience.

It might be possible to translate, or retranslate, this action into our language. We may assume that Homer used all the Greek he knew, all the resources of the language available to him and amenable to his meter. Three or more Greek dialects and perhaps half a millennium of Greek hexameter poetry contributed to Homer's language; so did a wide spectrum of idiom from the hieratic to the colloquial. Anglo-Irish-American provides comparable linguistic and poetic resources, a spectrum of idiom comparably wide. If you can grasp the situation and action rendered by the Greek poem, every line of it, and by the living performer that it demands, and if you will not betray Homer with prose or poor verse, you may hope to make an equivalent that he himself would not disavow.

Why care about an old work in a dead language that no one reads, or at least no one of those who, glancing at their Rolex watches, guide us into the future? Well, I love the future myself and expect everything of it:

better artists than Homer, better works of art than the *Odyssey*. The prospect of looking back at our planet from the moon seems to me to promise a marvelous enlargement of our views. But let us hold fast to what is good, hoping that if we do anything any good those who come after us will pay us the same compliment. If the world was given to us to explore and master, here is a tale, a play, a song about that endeavor long ago, by no means neglecting self-mastery, which in a sense is the whole point. Electronic brains may help us to use our heads but will not excuse us from that duty, and as to our hearts—cardiograms cannot diagnose what may be most ill about them, or confirm what may be best. The faithful woman and the versatile brave man, the wakeful intelligence open to inspiration or grace—these are still exemplary for our kind, as they always were and always will be. Nor do I suppose that the pleasure of hearing a story in words has quite gone out. Even movies and TV make use of words. The *Odyssey* at all events was made for your pleasure, in Homer's words and in mine.

SOME DETAILS OF SCENE AND ACTION

1

The ship on which I sailed from Piraeus one summer night approached Odysseus' kingdom from the south in the early morning. Emerging on deck for the occasion, I saw a mile or so to the west the bright flank of a high island, broadside to the rising sun. This was Kephallenia, identified by tradition with Samê of the *Odyssey*; in fact the port where we presently put in is called Samê. Beyond it to the north and dead ahead rose another island mass, lying from northwest to southeast and therefore visible only on its western side, all shadow, a dark silhouette. This was Thiaki or Ithaka.

Now, one of the innumerable questions never quite settled by students of Homer is the intended meaning of these two lines, concerning Ithaka and neighboring islands, in Book IX of the *Odyssey* (lines 25 and 26):

αὐτὴ δὲ χθαμαλὴ πανυπερτάτη εἰν ἁλὶ κεῖται
πρὸς ζόφον, αἱ δὲ τ᾽ ἄνευθε πρὸς ἠῶ τ᾽ ἠέλιόν τε.

Uncertainties ramify handsomely in the first line, but let me confine myself here to the second, which literally means, or appears to mean, that Ithaka lies "toward the gloom, while the other islands lie apart toward the Dawn and the Sun." Long before my Ithakan landfall I knew that this line has been thought simply inaccurate. But when I saw the islands with my own eyes in the morning light I felt at once that I had discovered the image behind Homer's words. He, too, I felt sure, had looked ahead over a ship's bow at that hour and had seen those land masses, one sunny and one in gloom, just as I saw them. An overnight sail from Pylos would have brought him there at the right time.

This notion was, of course, highly exhilarating. I am sorry that further consideration has more or less deflated it. One trouble with it was that Homer (or Odysseus, the speaker in this passage) did not describe Ithaka as being itself shadowy or gloomy but as lying in a certain direction, "toward" the "gloom." If the contrast between Ithaka and Samê at sunrise had been in his mind, he could have put it more distinctly. Not that Homer is always lucid grammatically, but "toward the gloom" for "in gloom" is not his kind of vagueness. Then, too, the word ζόφος in Homer does not mean simply gloom; it means the gloom of one end of the world, one quarter of the compass, generally held by the ancients to be the west. ἤδη γὰρ φάος οἴχεθ' ὑπὸ ζόφον says Athena in Book III, 335, "The sun has gone down already under the gloom [of the west]," and Odysseus asks Elpênor in Book XI, 57, πῶς ἦλθες ὑπὸ ζόφον ἠερόεντα,"How did you come down under the cloudy gloom [of the world's end]?"

It would be excellent if these clear instances were also conclusive, and πρὸς ζόφον were to be translated "toward the west" or "toward the western gloom." But here precisely is the difficulty. Ithaka does not in fact lie "west" of the other islands in the group. Neither does Leukas, the more northerly island that some students have believed to be Homer's Ithaka. So far as Ithaka itself is concerned, the fact is that the northern horn of Kephallenia, across a channel a mile or so wide, reaches up along the length of the island to the west. How now?

Well, it must be recalled that Homer knew no other west than the direction of sunset, and in midsummer, in that latitude, the sun goes down at a spot on the horizon far north of true west. Whether the poet was an Ionian or an Athenian, he is unlikely to have visited the islands except in the sailing season. Homer's sunset quarter could have been roughly northwest by west. This very nearly solves the difficulty, but perhaps not quite. If we are still a few points off, so to speak, I am glad to say that recourse may be had to the later Greek geographer, Strabo.

According to Lord Rennell of Rodd, in the Annual of the British School in Athens, No. xxxiii, Session 1932–33, Strabo "entertained no doubt" that in the line I have quoted, ζόφος "indicated the north, as the Sun does the south." That is to say, Strabo and Lord Rennell pass lightly over the antithesis between ζόφος and Dawn in that line of Homer in order to embrace the antithesis between ζόφος and the Sun, whose usual path in north latitudes passes south of the zenith. Most of Kephallenia does indeed lie to the south of Ithaka, and so does the island now called Zante, very likely the Zakynthos of the *Odyssey*. As for Doulikhion, Rennell and others rather desperately identify it with one of the small Ekhinades to the east.

Pondering this argument, I asked myself why each of the antitheses noted in the phrase should not be given equal value, or half of full value. Granted that Ithaka is "west" with respect to Doulikhion and "north" with respect to Zakynthos and Samê-Kephallenia, then πρὸς ζόφον could be briefly rendered "to the northwest," and the other islands πρός ἠῶ τ' ἠέλιόν τε could be said to "lie east and south." Here I left this question.

2

If you will do an hour or two of hard climbing on Ithaka you can reach the spinal ridge of the island and there, while you cool off, you can look across the blue channel to the west at the steep side of Samê a mile away. Close in to the other shore you will see a tiny islet known as Daskalion. This, with no great satisfaction, the commentators identify with Asteris, the small island behind which the suitors in their long boat lay in wait for Telémakhos at the end of Book IV. This identification in turn depends on another, that of a small round cove on the west side of Ithaka, somewhat north of the islet, as the harbor from which Telémakhos put out on his evening voyage. The longer I looked at this setting the more quarrelsome I felt with received opinion. It is true that at first glance all the requisites are there: the channel, the islet, the harbor. I am afraid, of course, that received opinion may be right. But on this point I have remained cranky and fond of my private reasons for dissent.

It appears that Polis Bay, as the round cove is tendentiously named, was once larger, and that it was a port of call in the classical period for

Greek ships passing up the channel, outward bound for Italy. This fact of itself seems to me irrelevant if we are concerned to find the port of Ithaka at the time of the Trojan War, long before colonization or commerce with Italy, or even in Homer's time, late in the eighth century, when voyages to the western Mediterranean had just begun. The harbor described in the *Odyssey* serves, above all, ships that ply to and from Elis, the mainland of the Peloponnesus to the southeast, and Thesprotia, or Acarnania, to the east. It was from the southeast that my ship, the *S. S. Miaoulis*, arrived, and the *Miaoulis* put me ashore at Vathy on the deep harbor of the same name (it means "deep"). This is the longest and best sheltered of three bays opening southward off the wide Gulf of Molos, which runs inward from east to west and almost cuts Ithaka in two. Along the quay of Vathy in the evening I saw open caïques from the mainland unloading cattle in slings. From pasture land to the stony island, pastureless, the caïques had brought these cows to be slaughtered for Ithakan markets. Here was a ferry service exactly like the one alluded to in Book XX, 187, of the *Odyssey*. As the Gulf of Molos is the roadstead of Ithaka, Vathy is its natural harbor—or at least so it seems to the ferrymen, to the Greek steamship company, and to me.

But how could Vathy have been the port from which Telémakhos sailed, if on leaving it he would have had to issue eastward by the Gulf of Molos into the open sea, passing through no channel between Ithaka and Samê? This objection would be insuperable if Homer had been an Ithakan. Since he surely was not, but was a visitor like myself, I think it worth reporting that on the day after my arrival I had another visual revelation. From high ground on the north part of Ithaka I saw a small island, perfectly satisfying Homer's description of Asteris, that seemed to lie between Ithaka and Samê to the south. I said to my guide, "What island is that?" "Oh, that is Attako," he said. I looked at my map, which showed Attako lying in the sea to the east of Ithaka. "Are you sure?" said I. "Of course, I'm sure, I've been fishing there many times." No one would have guessed from the map that from the northeast height of Ithaka, looking south, you see this islet against the background of what appears to be another island mass but is in fact the southern part of Ithaka. What looks like a "channel" is the mouth of the Gulf of Molos.

My surmise is that Homer on his peregrination over Odysseus' island made mistakes like mine, that he confused the Gulf of Molos with the channel between Ithaka and Samê, and that his islet "Asteris" is the island Attako, not the tiny rock called Daskalion. Do not suppose that my theory lacks textual support. Attako has high ground from which the suitors could have kept their watch (XVI, 365); Daskalion has not. Moreover, to bear out my identification of Vathy with Telémakhos' harbor, I can refer to at least one detail of his embarkation. Athena is said to have moored his ship "at the harbor's edge," in Book II, 391 ἐπ' ἐσχατιῇ λιμένος, and once he had shoved off she sent him a following wind that took him out to sea. From what quarter blew this wind? From the west, for it is expressly called Ζέφυρος, the west wind, in II, 420–21. This is just the wind you would need astern if you wanted to put out from the mouth of Vathy Bay, but if you were putting out from Polis Bay it would blow you right back in.

It can be urged against me that the stern wind supplied by Athena lasted all night and took Telémakhos' ship all the way to Pylos. A steady wind from the west would have taken him not south to Pylos, but east, let us say, to Missolonghi. Perhaps, as I have myself argued that Homer's west lay in a more northerly quarter, his Zephyr also blew from that quarter and would serve a ship sailing from Polis Bay down the channel between Ithaka and Samê. I do not, of course, see why it could not have been the west wind at the start and have changed direction during the night, but in the end I compromised in deference to the established view. It is a northwest wind in my text. I may add that on my second evening at Vathy the wind freshened from that direction and, blowing over open water, made a fluttering and percussive effect in my eardrums—not entirely agreeable—like the noise of Homer's line for it:

ἀκραῆ Ζέφυρον, κελάδοντ' ἐπὶ οἴνοπα πόντον.

3

These notes may suggest some of the pleasures and complexities of going to see for yourself. I would be a fool to plume myself on my dip into those studies on ancient sites that have occupied good men and women for years. But I am forever grateful for my days on Ithaka as I am for other days, few but moving, in Athens and elsewhere in Greece. A rendering for the opening of Book III,

'Ήέλιος δ' ἀνόρουσε, λιπὼν περικαλλέα λίμνην

came into my head in the Saronic Gulf, and a week later at sunrise in Heraklion I found words for the next phrase, οὐρανὸν ἐς πολύχαλκον. By these and other keepsakes I am reminded that if I had never listened to the cicadas and drunk the resined wine I would have done the job differently, if I had done it at all. But most of it was what all writing is, a sedentary labor, or joy, sustained at a worktable. At one elbow, in this case, there were always those lines and parts of lines that have been pored over by so many for centuries. Of the puzzling ones I will give a few more examples, two at least of them notorious, with some account of the elucidation I think they demand. Multiply these cases by a thousand, and you will see what the preliminary or incidental work was like. As befits a dramatic poem, the first case is a tiny detail of action.

In Book XI Odysseus hears the shade of Agamémnon tell how Aigísthos and Klytaimnestra murdered him on his return from Troy, and with him his companions. They were all butchered, he says bitterly, like swine. I take it that he means what he says. The way you butcher a pig is by piercing or cutting his throat, and it does not seem unreasonable to imagine here, and to bear in mind elsewhere, that this is what happened to Agamémnon. He describes the banquet scene, the laden tables, and the floor fuming with blood where the victims lay. Then, in line 421, he says he heard a most piteous cry from his royal slave and mistress, Kassandra,

> τὴν κτεῖνε Κλυταιμνήστρη δολόμητις
> ἀμφ' ἐμοί, αὐτὰρ ἐγώ ποτὶ γαίη χεῖρας ἀείρων
> βάλλον ἀποθνήσκων περὶ φασγάνῳ

and great difficulty has been found in grasping precisely what action this passage was meant to convey. Klytaimnestras was in the act of killing Kassandra, so much is clear, and Kassandra was close beside the fallen Agamémnon. But what does he say he himself was doing? Consider it word for word in the order in which it appears: "but I upon (or against) the ground lifting my hands / was throwing [them] while dying around the swordblade." Half the problem is to divide or punctuate this.

On one prevailing interpretation we should divide or punctuate after βάλλον and must therefore take ἀποθνήσκων περὶ φασγάνῳ to mean "dying around the swordblade," that is, with a blade left in his body. This is contrary to slaughtering procedure, but Professor W. B. Stanford in his annotated edition of the *Odyssey* tells us that there are many precedents for taking it so. He refers to four passages in the *Iliad* and to one in Sophocles' *Ajax*. With all respect I must say that none of these makes a good precedent for Stanford's reading, because in none of them does anyone die "around a swordblade" left in him by anyone else. Ajax has, of course, impaled himself on his own sword. Of the cases cited in the *Iliad*, one is concerned with an arrow and two with spears, weapons often left sticking in tenacious parts of the foe. It is otherwise with a sword; a sword in these poems was something a killer held onto if he could. The fourth case in the *Iliad* might be a better precedent, not for Stanford's notion of Agamémnon's wound but for mine (since it is an allusion to slaughtering), if the preposition used were not ἀμφὶ instead of πεϱὶ. In short, the evidence is inconclusive.

Moreover, if you adopt this awkward reading, you are left with a clause that represents Agamémnon as lifting his hands and throwing them. With what purpose? Or perhaps I should ask, with what aim? Victor Bérard imagined that he meant to shield Kassandra. A. T. Murray, the Loeb translator, thought he tried to hit Klytaimnestra. Butcher and Land, W. H. D. Rouse, and T. E. Lawrence accepted "let fall" as a translation of βάλλον: he lifted his hands and helplessly let them fall. Others, including Stanford, take ποτὶ γαίῃ as "against the ground" with βάλλον and suggest that he beat his hands against the ground to invoke vengeance from infernal powers.

I cannot myself hear the shade of the hero saying any of these things, except possibly what Murray has him say. But it is quite possible to punctuate the lines in another way, like this: "But I upon the ground, lifting my hands, was throwing them—while dying—around the sword-blade." Or to put it in English, "As I lay on the ground I heaved up my hands and flung them with a dying effort around the swordblade." There is a scholion in which the lines are so understood, but the scholiast adds πϱὸς ἐκσπάσαι τὸ ξίφος, "to pull out the sword"—no doubt in order to die more quickly. G. H. Palmer, one of the few translators to follow the scholiast, settled for "clutched" as a rendering for βάλλον. This was logical, since Palmer, like the Alexandrian and like Stanford, conceived the blade as embedded in Agamémnon. A man with a blade in his midriff would not "fling" his hands around it when all he had to do was, precisely, to clutch it. But βάλλον is stronger than "clutch," and the sword was not in Agamémnon, in any case. He would have had to heave up and fling his hands around the blade if the blade were a short distance away, within reach but still requiring an effort. This is where the sword of Klytaimnestra must have been while she slashed or poked at Kassandra. Therefore I prefer to think that as Klytaimnestra used the sword, Agamémnon, reckless of his hands, tried to get it away from her. Alone among modern translators, so far as I can discover, E. V. Rieu adopted this reading. It not only satisfies all the conditions, syntactical and verbal, but it makes all possible dramatic sense of the line.

4

If you think of the poem as a play or a cinema—inevitable if not irresistible thoughts—you will find many problems for the set designer and the property man. There are two fine ones in the big closing scenes. How precisely are we to visualize the contest with Odysseus' hunting bow, announced by Penélopê in Book XIX and carried out in Book XXI? And in Book XXII what precisely is the layout of the great hall and adjoining passage by which the suitors, for the moment out of sight of Odysseus, are given throwing spears at a crucial point in the fight? The Greek is ambiguous or sketchy.

In XIX Penélopê tells her interesting new confidant of a sudden decision: next day her suitors will be challenged to perform an old feat of her husband's, and she will be the prize. It is a feat (line 573) with πελέκεας, axes,

> τοὺς πελέκεας, τοὺς κεῖνος ἐνὶ μεγάροισιν ἑοῖσιν
> ἵστασχ' ἐξείης, δρυόχους ὥς, δώδεκα πάντας.
> στὰς δ' ὅ γε πολλὸν ἄνευθε διαρρίπτασκεν ὀϊστόν.

"those axes that he used to set up in his hall all twelve in line like a ship's ribs (or props), then he would take his stand far off and shoot an arrow through." The prize will go to that suitor who most easily strings her husband's bow and "shoots through all twelve axes." To this Odysseus replies in effect that tomorrow is not too soon; her husband will be there before any of the younger men can string the bow διοϊστεῦσαί τε σιδήρου "and shoot through the iron." It need not escape us that this phrase is rather an addition. We might imagine shooting through twelve axes if they were arranged in a line slightly staggered, leaving an interval of an inch or so for the arrow to pass. The alternative is to imagine apertures in the axeheads, and the phrase of Odysseus, repeated by Telémakhos in Book XXI, inclines us to that. He speaks with familiarity, not to mention his remarkable confidence. It is not the speech of a man still interested in concealing from his wife how well he knows her husband.

If the arrow is to pass "through the iron," and we interpret this to mean through apertures in the axeheads, then what apertures are meant? D. B. Monro in his edition of the *Odyssey*, Books XIII–XXIV, printed drawings of two perforated ancient axeheads, one from a Mycenean excavation, another from an early classical metope, and a third drawing of the very late classical *bipennis*, a double axe whose crescent blades form by their inner edges two circular openings, the one above the haft open and unobstructed. An arrow could pass through any one of these types of axeheads. With archaeological backing, then, we may imagine twelve pervious axes in alignment for the contest. Penélopê's phrase, "like a ship's ribs (or props)," in fact makes us see twelve axes stuck in the ground by their helves.

Oddly enough, there are quite serious objections to this reading. When we say "axe" we mean axehead and helve together. But it seems more likely that the word πέλεκυς to Penélopê meant "axehead" alone. In Book V when Kalypso gives Odysseus a πέλεκυς for cutting timber, she must complete the gift with a στειλειόν, or helve of olive wood (line 236). In all the references to the gauntlet Odysseus' arrow had to run, there is no illusion to a στειλειόν, though a closely related word appears. On the contrary, when Penélopê brings the bow back from the storeroom in XXI, 58, her maids bring along a basket full of iron and bronze "accessories of the contest," certainly axeheads without helves. Any normal axehead, then as now, had an aperture: it had the socket hole where a helve could be fitted. Is there positive evidence that this was the aperture in question? There is indeed.

When Odysseus finally makes his prize-winning shot in XXI, 420 sqq., we hear that

$$\text{πελέκεων δ᾽ οὐκ ἤμβροτε πάντων}$$
$$\text{πρώτης στειλειῆς, διὰ δ᾽ ἀμπερὲς ἦλθε θύραζε.}$$

"he didn't miss the πρώτης στειλειῆς of all the axeheads, and the arrow went clean through and out." Confusion about the word στειλειή appears to be ancient and inexhaustible; it was taken very early to mean "helve" or "haft"—that is, to be a synonym for στειλειόν—and translators in torment have tried to make sense of a shot that did not miss the first axe helve. But if Homer had meant that, if he had meant πρώτου στειλειοῦ, he could have said it. It is metrically equivalent and phonetically a little better. Professor Stanford thinks, and with excellent reason, that the difference in gender may be significant. He agrees with the twelfth-century Archbishop of Thessalonica, Eustathius, that the feminine form, στειλειή, meant "socket" as στειλειόν meant "helve." What Homer intended to say was very simple: that Odysseus didn't miss his bull's eye, the first socket hole in the line of twelve.

It is a perfect conclusion, but it lets us in for other difficulties. If the axeheads were without helves, if each was turned so that its socket hole faced the archer, how were they set up and supported? In what respect was the line of axeheads comparable to "a ship's ribs (or props)"? The second question is easier to answer: the point of similarity could have been merely that in both cases there were equal intervals between one and another. As to the way of setting up the axeheads, all we have to go on are two lines and a half, XXI, 120 sqq., in which Telémakhos prepares the contest:

> πρῶτον μὲν πελέκεας στῆσεν, διὰ τάφρον ὀρύξας
> πᾶσι μίαν μακρήν, καὶ ἐπὶ στάθμην ἴθυνεν,
> ἀμφὶ δὲ γαῖαν ἔναξε

Literally, "first he set up the axeheads, after digging a trench through for all, a single trench, a long one, and he trued [it or them] to the line, and he pressed earth on both sides." It is pertinent to remember that in Homer's "additive" style items are not always given in any particular order. That is, the pressing of the earth could have preceded or accompanied the truing, and we may understand that he trued the axeheads, not the trench. If we held the theory that axeheads fitted on helves were being set up, a trench would bed the helves, around which earth could then be pressed to hold them upright. I have given the evidence against that. On the other and better theory that axeheads alone were used, is there anything in the context to suggest how they were held up?

Well, a byproduct of a trench is a long pile of loose earth. If the loose earth beside the trench were "pressed" up in a narrow ridge, with peaks at equal distances, the axeheads could be stuck in these, one blade in the earth and one out, since the πέλεκυς was double-bladed. The verb νάσσω that appears here in the aorist active, ἔναξε, "pressed," had the sense "be piled" in the passive in later Greek. The very point of digging a trench could have been to supply enough earth for this purpose; if it had been a matter of embedding axe helves, they could have been planted in a line of holes like fence posts or fruit trees. It is a good deal to read into these lines, but I am willing to risk it because I see nothing else for it. Telémakhos made a bedding of earth for the axeblades and trued them ἐπὶ στάθμην, "to the line," by the wall builder's immemorial technique, a stretched cord. One more question: if set up in this way, could the axeheads have been high enough for the bowshot from the door? Odysseus made the bowshot while seated on his stool. He held the bow horizontally in the usual ancient style. If he shot from the hip just above knee level in a flat trajectory, the axeheads as I see them could have been at the right height.

5

If those passages needed unfolding, more unfolding still must be done to render with clarity the several lines beginning at 126 of Book XXII—a sketch for a ground plan or a stage set. Odysseus has been doing execution with his bow while Telémakhos has brought arms from the storeroom; now all the arrows are gone, and father and son and the two herdsmen arm themselves for combat with spears. The narrative continues:

> ὀρσοθύρη δέ τις ἔσκεν ἐϋδμήτῳ ἐνὶ τοίχῳ.
> ἀκρότατον δὲ παρ' οὐδὸν ἐϋσταθέος μεγάροιο
> ἦν ὁδὸς ἐς λαύρην, σανίδες δ' ἔχον εὖ ἀραρυῖαι.

"There was a certain ὀρσοθύρη in the well-built wall. And at the edge [or along the top] of the threshold of the hall there was an entry way into the passage, and well-fitted folding doors kept it closed." This is all baffling, and the editors have left it so. We wish to know what the ὀρσοθύρη was and in which wall it was located. We also wish to know what if anything the ὀρσοθύρη had to do with the passage, where the passage ran, and where precisely the "entry way" opened into it. These lines do not tell us. But we can learn some of the answers from the action that now takes place.

First, Odysseus tells the swineherd to stand over near the "entry way" and guard it, μία δ' οἴη γίγνετ' ἐφορμή, "for there was only one way in." Why guard it? Because it must be a possible exit for the suitors who have been under fire at the other end of the hall—the only possible exit, we gather, besides the main door where Odysseus and Telémakhos have taken their stand. Now one of the surviving suitors, Ageláos, says to the others,

> ῏Ω φίλοι, οὐκ ἂν δή τις ἂν' ὀρσοθύρην ἀναβαίη
> καὶ εἴποι λαοῖσι

"Friends, why doesn't someone climb up by the ὀρσοθύρη and tell the townsmen?" From this it is clear that by climbing through the ὀρσοθύρη you could get into the passage and out by the door where the swineherd has been posted. Out where? If ἀκρότατον δὲ παρ' οὐδὸν is taken to mean "along the top" of the threshold inside the main door, any man issuing at that point would run into the arms of Odysseus and company. It must mean "at the edge" of the threshold outside the entrance. If this were not the meaning, the swineherd would not have had to move to be in a position to guard the "entry way." His movement, incidentally, seems to have escaped notice by Ageláos, who has also failed to see that Odysseus has no more arrows. The goatherd, Melánthios, answers him:

οὔ πως ἔστ', 'Αγέλαε διοτρεφές: ἄγχι γὰρ αἰνῶς
αὐλῆς καλὰ θύρετρα καὶ ἀργαλέον στόμα λαύρης.
καί χ' εἰς πάντας ἐρύκοι ἀνήρ, ὅς τ' ἄλκιμος εἴη.

"It can't be done. The fair door of the courtyard is terribly near [or the fair door is terribly near the courtyard] and the mouth of the passage is hard [to force]; one man alone if he were strong could hold off all of us." If the mouth of the passage is hard to force, it must be a narrow passage, narrow as a catwalk. Melánthios' remark that one strong man could hold it suggests that he has seen Odysseus order the swineherd outside. All this is fairly clear. But precisely what is "terribly near" to what? That is not so clear.

Monro and Stanford thought Melánthios meant that the gate into the courtyard from the road was near—near to Odysseus, or near to the exit from the passage. Since the gate is in fact on the other side of the court-yard, these editors thought it could be called "terribly near" only from the point of view of a man in fear of archery as he crossed the courtyard. I find this interpretation strange. A man thinking of making a run under fire would complain of how far the gate seemed, not how near. It may be irrelevant that there can be no more archery, anyway, for Odysseus is out of arrows; Melánthios, like Ageláos, may not have noticed this (nei-ther Monro nor Stanford appears to have noticed it, either). But I doubt that αὐλῆς θύρετρα necessarily or even possibly means the gate from the road into the courtyard. The word θύραι has been used for this. Here is a different word whose proper meaning is certainly "door" and not "gate." It could mean the door from the passageway into the court-yard, and I think it does. To what or whom is that door terribly near? To Odysseus, who has already posted a guard there. On this interpretation these lines cohere.

Melánthios proposes to bring the suitors arms from the storeroom, and he climbs

ἐς θαλάμους 'Οδυσῆος ἀνὰ ῥῶγας μεγάροιο

"up the breaks of the hall and into the storeroom of Odysseus." The ῥῶγας or "breaks" have been thought to be steps, but steps are κλίμακες. A closer reading would be "fissures" or chinks in the wall, toeholds for a goatherd. Although it is not expressly mentioned at this point, there is no doubt that the aperture to which he climbs is the ὀϱσοθύϱη, and I should now note that etymologically this word almost certainly means a "raised door" or window. Since his destination is the storeroom, it follows not only that this window-opening gives on the passage by which Ageláos thought someone might get out, but that the passage itself leads to the storeroom at the back of the house. It is the same passage by which at the beginning of the slaughter Telémakhos ran to get arms for his father and friends. From the passage, through the window, Melánthios can hand out arms to the suitors.

Where is the ὀϱσοθύϱη? At the far end of the hall from the entrance, as stands to reason and as we learn explicitly later on in line 333 from the position of Phêmios, the harper, when the fight is over. It must be a window in one of the side walls, for two reasons. First, the passage that it lights and ventilates runs along the side of the hall from front to rear. Second, one of the side walls could have a recessed part like a shallow transept, not visible from the entrance. The context requires this. The ὀϱσοθύϱη and all that happens there are out of sight of Odysseus. The young men harried by his shooting would have huddled on the other side of any angle in the wall that offered shelter, and there the ὀϱσοθύϱη would have come to their attention. Odysseus may well have had this in mind when he ordered the passage guarded. But why didn't one of the suitors use the ὀϱσοθύϱη instead of letting the goatherd work for them? The question as framed almost answers itself: they were accustomed to service. There may be another reason, too. One of the scholia on the ὀϱσοθύϱη informs us that

ὑψηλοτέϱα ἦν ἐφ' ἧ ἦν ὀϱοῦσαι καὶ ἀναθοϱεῖν

"it was quite high; you had to make a jump to get up to it." Perhaps jumping for a hole in the wall was beneath the dignity of Akhaian gentlemen with flowing hair.

6

Details like these may turn out to be self-consistent, but what of the poem as a whole? Does it hang together? Did a single composer hold it all in his mind? Whatever opinion we may hold on the famous Question, we may accept at least one modest principle: when proof to the contrary is lacking, any given passage should be interpreted in consonance with the rest. Take the eagles.

During the assembly scene in Book II, Zeus launches two eagles from a ridge, either τῷ δ' or τώ δ' according to the alternative readings. The Oxford editor, T. W. Allen, reasonably chose the first, meaning "for him," that is, for the last speaker, Telémakhos. The eagles are to be an omen for him. When in their gliding flight they reach a point over the center of the agora they wheel and beat their wings, and then we have two more alternative readings, ἐς δ' ἰδέτην πάντων κεφαλάς or ἐς δ' ἱκέτην πάντων κεφαλάς, that is, either the pair "looked at the heads of all [below]" or they "came down on" all the heads. Again Allen chose the reading more charged with life and sense: "came down on." In the next clause, ὄσσοντο δ' ὄλεθρον, the verb has changed from the dual form, used when the pair of birds was the subject, to plural form. Does this mean a change of subject? Not necessarily; Homer often uses plural verb forms for dual subjects; indeed he has already done so once in this passage, though not in this sentence. If it does mean a change of subject, then the "heads," or men in the crowd, are said to behold death or doom in the diving eagles; if it does not mean a change of subject, the diving eagles are said to make doom visible to the men, or in a word to menace them with doom. "Death was in their glare," as Murray ingeniously puts it, making perhaps the best of both alternatives. Perhaps, but wait. The next line presents us again with a dual form, this time in a middle participle. It goes:

δρυψαμένω δ' ὀνύχεσσι παρειὰς ἀμφί τε δειρὰς

"tearing, this pair, with talons, cheeks and all around necks (or throats)."

Now, the received interpretation of this, cited by Liddell & Scott and followed by Murray and practically everyone, takes the middle voice of the verb as reflexive here, meaning they tore *each other's* cheeks and throats. But first let me observe that the middle may or may not have this shade of meaning. It is the voice you would use in Greek if you wanted to say, "We cut ourselves a slice," and you would not be referring to a knife fight. Second, if the two eagles are a sign, what after all do they signify? What future event do they portend? The old augur Halithersês has no doubt, and neither have we: they stand for the return of Odysseus and the doom of the suitors. Why two eagles? In order that the sign, a sign for Telémakhos, may give him, or at any rate ourselves, to understand that he and Odysseus together will attack the suitors. The two eagles correspond to the two royal assailants. Why then should they assail one another? What would any intelligent augur make of that? No, no, surely; they assail the suitors, who have been arraigned by Telémakhos in the assembly, and if this were not the case there would be no point in their having "come down on the heads of all," for an eagle fight would have been as well or better conducted high in the air. A scholiast says, τὸ δὲ καταδρύψαι τὰς παρειὰς τὸν τῶν μνηστήρων ἐσήμανε φόνον, and *he* does not use the middle but the active voice: "that business of tearing the [suitors'] cheeks signified the suitors' violent death." We are to see the eagles' portent not merely "in their glare" but in their ripping talons.

Between Book II and Book XV no eagles fly, or at any rate no significant ones, but in Book XV, 160, as Telémakhos is taking leave of Menelaos and Helen, just as he is saying how fine it would be to meet his father on Ithaka so that he could tell him of their hospitality, ἐπέπτατο δεξιὸς ὄρνις, αἰετὸς ἀργὴν χῆνα φέρων "a bird, an eagle, flew up on the right, lugging a white goose." This portent is quickly interpreted by Helen. It means, she says, that just as the eagle flew from the wild mountain of his birth to pounce on the domestic bird, so Odysseus will appear out of the rough world of his wanderings to avenge the wrongs done him at home. Near the end of the same Book (525 sqq.) the motif is repeated. Again the omen appears as if in comment on a speech by Telémakhos, who has just been wondering aloud whether anything will prevent his mother's marriage to Eurýmakhos. This time the portentous bird is not an eagle, αἰετός, but a hawk, κίρκος, carrying a captured dove. And this time the interpretation is not given immediately; it is given to Penélopê in Book XVII (152 sqq.) by the diviner, Theoklýmenos, who tells her it meant that Odysseus had already landed on Ithaka. Again there is an interval of two Books, and in XIX (535 sqq.) the motif comes to a kind of flowering when Penélopê recounts her "dream" to the beggar, who is Odysseus. This time there is a more exact correspondence between the terms of the equation; Penélopê was in a position to be exact. Upon the geese feeding at her house

ἐλθὼν δ' ἐξ ὄρεος μέγας αἰετὸς ἀγκυλοχείλης
πᾶσι κατ' αὐχένας ἧξε καὶ ἔκτανεν

"coming from the mountain a great eagle with crooked beak broke their necks and killed them all."

Thus in four passages the descent of Odysseus on the suitors has been foreboded or foreseen in strikes made by birds of prey. In three cases the attacking birds are eagles; once it is a hawk. The appearance of the motif twice in Book XVII and once again in Book XIX harks back to its introduction in Book II. It also anticipates the climax of the fight in Odysseus' hall in Book XXII. At that point Athena unfurls her storm cloud, the aegis, overhead, and the surviving suitors break and run like cattle stung by gadflies. Now (302) comes the simile:

οἱ δ' ὥς τ' αἰγυπιοὶ γαμψώνυχες ἀγκυλοχεῖλαι
ἐξ ὀρέων ἐλθόντες ἐπ' ὀρνίθεσσι θόρωσι, κτλ

"But the pursuers, like αἰγυπιοί with hooked talons and crooked beak issuing from the mountains to dive on flights of birds, etc." We had expected eagles, αἰετοί, or hawks, κίρκοι, but the word is αἰγυπιοί, and I am distressed to say that the usual translation of that is "vultures." Liddell & Scott give "vulture" for αἰγυπιός. But let us consider the case patiently. We have not met the word before in the *Odyssey*. Liddell & Scott and the Homeric lexicographer, Autenrieth, cite three occurrences in the *Iliad*. In Book VII, 59, when Athena and Apollo are represented as taking their seats on the oak of Zeus as Hektor challenges the Akhaians,

ἑζέσθην ὄρνισιν ἐοικότες αἰγυπιοῖσι

"They perched like birds, like αἰγυπιοί." In Book XVII, 460, Automedon making chariot forays among the Trojans is likened to an αἰγυπιός among geese. Most interesting of all is the case in Book XVI, 428, when Patroklos and Sarpedon clash in battle—for here the first line of the simile is the very same line that we find repeated in the *Odyssey*:

οἱ δ' ὥς τ' αἰγυπιοὶ γαμψώνυχες ἀγκυλοχεῖλαι
πέτρῃ ἐφ' ὑψηλῇ μεγάλα κλάζοντε μάχωνται

"like αἰγυπιοί with hooked talons and crooked beak/on a high rock, crying loud, they fought."

Now, it seems to me that on the Homeric evidence there is something wrong with translating this word as "vulture." A vulture as we understand the term is a carrion bird rather than a hunting bird, and in every context of both *Iliad* and *Odyssey* where a vulture in our sense is clearly indicated Homer uses the word γύψ. In no instance, as we have seen, is αἰγυπιός used of a carrion bird; on the contrary, in two cases, one in the *Iliad* and one our climactic simile in the *Odyssey*, it is used of a hunting bird, and in one of the two remaining cases it supplies a simile for two gods at rest on a bough. If Homer had meant γύψ he could have used γύψ, a handy word and one he used often enough elsewhere. But he used another word, and used it because he unquestionably meant another thing. He meant a bird like a hawk or an eagle, a killer, a threat to geese, a hunter of small birds in general. He did not mean the stinking buzzard that feeds on corpses left by others.

In the first edition of my *Odyssey* I translated αἰγυπιοί in Book XXII as "eagles" to go with the eagle passages that lead up to it. I went too far. If the poet had wished to say "eagles" he could have used the word for eagles, αἰετοί. Instead, he lifted a line from the *Iliad*, as he often did, presumably because it would suit his purpose here. How, then, should αἰγυπιοί be rendered? Well, I see that John Moore, in his recent excellent version of Sophocles' *Ajax* (The Complete Greek Tragedies, ed. Lattimore & Grene, Chicago), encountering this problem in line 169,

μέγαν αἰγυπιὸν δ' ὑποδείσαντες, κτλ

translates

But fear of the huge falcon, etc.

possibly in view of considerations like those I have been expounding. In revising I have followed his example. I hope Homer would be better pleased. No doubt the four attackers in Book XXII are more justly likened to falcons than to eagles if, as I suspect, falcons more often hunt in company; the wild eagle, unless paired by Zeus, I imagine hunts alone.

An Introduction
to Dryden's *Aeneid*

The version of the *Aeneid* that we might have had in English poetry was never written. By this I do not mean merely that there is no complete *Aeneid* in English as good as Gavin Douglas's *Eneados* in Scots of the fifteenth century; I mean that during two periods, very roughly from 1570 to 1650 and from 1800 to 1880, someone might have done justice to the poem, but no one did. It is easy to conceive an *Aeneid* by Keats, who had read Virgil in school and whose power over language resembled Virgil's, or by the Tennyson of *Milton* and *Ulysses*. From these poets and their century, however, we do not have even any partial attempts that are really memorable. From Tudor times we do; an English *Aeneid* of the sixteenth century exists in fragments, so to speak, or potentially. It can be so present to the imagination that we can almost reconstruct it or make a composite. There is the dignity and sonority of Surrey:

> "O Queen, it is thy will
> I should renew a woe cannot be told,
> How that the Greeks did spoil and overthrow
> The Phrygian wealth and wailful realm of Troy. . . ."

And there is the motley splendor and kick of Stanyhurst:

> Now manhood and garbroyles I chaunt, and martial horror.
> I blaze that captayne first from Troy cittye repairing
> Like wandring pilgrim too famosed Italie trudging
> And coast of Lavyn; soust with tempestuus hurlwynd . . . .

And the élan of Marlowe:

> Not moved at all, but smiling at his tears,
> This butcher whilst his hands were yet held up,
> Treading upon his breast, struck off his hands . . .

Spenser, an avowed Virgilian, could have made an admirable *Aeneid*. But the poet most capable of the full Virgilian range was probably John

---

First published in John Dryden's translation of Virgil's *Aeneid* (New York: Macmillan, 1964).

Milton. Suppose that on his return from Italy around 1640 Milton had taken up Virgil and had spent the next years not in controversy but in retirement, translating the *Aeneid*. Our literature would have been handsomely—and very usefully—enlarged. Just as Marvell wrote the one truly Horatian ode in English, Milton might have written the one truly Virgilian long poem.

It was John Dryden, however, who produced the English *Aeneid;* and at the time he did so neither he nor any other Englishmen, it seems, could manage, except briefly, the kind of poetry required. They were too interested in improving on it. I do not say this entirely in malice, but with some sympathy for the criterion of "sense" and with respect for the cultivated and sometimes noble energy of Dryden's writing. If anyone then living could have done a great *Aeneid*, Dryden could. He was not narrowly a man of his time in the way Rochester was, for example. He admired and drew upon Spenser, Shakespeare, and Jonson. He appreciated Donne's *Satires*, and the Metaphysical poets contributed something to his style. But after the Restoration in 1660 urbanity and abstraction overcame English letters, and Dryden himself wanted an English Academy, on the order of the French, to "purify" the language of poetry. In the exploration of the physical world the Royal Society, of which Dryden as Poet Laureate was a nominal member, had succeeded Raleigh and Drake. Likewise in poetry, discussion and wit now flourished at a certain remove from discovery and experience.

It we think only of prosody, it may appear that the blank verse masters, Shakespeare and Milton, had exhausted one great form for generations. It is certainly impressive and odd that long before the end of the seventeenth century the rhymed couplet had swept the field in English verse. We might imagine that the couplet itself diminished the range of poetry, but in fact pentameter couplets had been used by Douglas for his *Eneados* and by Chapman for his *Odyssey*. An *Aeneid* in blank verse would not necessarily have been any better than in couplets like these:

> Buskins of shells all silvered usèd she,
> And brancht with blushing corall to the knee;
> Where sparrows pearcht, of hollow pearl and gold,
> Such as the world would wonder to behold . . .

or these:

> When Evening grey doth rise, I fetch my round
> Over the mount, and all this hallow'd ground,
> And early ere the odorous breath of morn

> Awakes the slumbring leaves, or tassel'd horn
> Shakes the high thicket, haste I all about,
> Number my ranks, and visit every sprout
> With puissant words, and murmurs made to bless,
> But else in deep of night when drowsiness
> Hath lockt up mortal sense, then listen I
> To the celestial Sirens harmony,
> That sit upon the nine enfolded sphears,
> And sing to those that hold the vital shears,
> And turn the adamantine spindle round,
> On which the fate of gods and men is wound.

In fact, each of these examples could be called Virgilian: Marlowe's for the image and sound and Milton's for the running syntax and resourceful diction, culminating in his superb "adamantine spindle."

Dryden's predicament, then, was not that of being enslaved by the rhymed couplet; it was the enslavement of the couplet itself by a certain style. The example of the French Alexandrine had had much to do with tidying and balancing the English couplet, though Dryden himself remarked on the variety that the alternation of masculine and feminine endings gave the French couplets and on the lightness that made the French language fall easily into logical symmetries. He realized that the genius of his own language might be cramped by them, but they charmed him and his contemporaries, and in place of greater touchstones Dryden was fond of quoting Denham's lines on the Thames:

> O could I flow like thee, and make thy stream
> My great example, as it is my theme!
> Though deep, yet clear, though gentle, yet not dull,
> Strong without rage, without ore-flowing full.

He was also fond of alluding to Waller as the man who taught smoothness to English numbers, by which he meant rhyming without wrenching the natural order of words, disposed as in "the negligence of prose." It is perhaps a revealing phrase. Engaged as he was in breaking ground for English criticism and in developing English critical prose, Dryden in practice wanted the discursive merits, a little negligence included, in verse as well.

At any rate, a new realm of possibilities had opened for English poets to explore, and we know the refinement to which in due course Pope would bring the couplet. But now another fact comes in for consideration: before this couplet became "heroic," its chief triumph was in satire.

Dryden wrote *Absalom and Achitophel* and *Mac Flecknoe* in his prime, years before he thought of translating the *Aeneid*. Another way of putting this is to say that his couplet was mock heroic first. The satires owe their savor partly to a deliberate use of epic convention or allusion for topical burlesque. In *Mac Flecknoe*, for example, there are a number of lines that parody well-known passages in Virgil:

> At his right hand our young Ascanius sate,
> Rome's other hope, and pillar of the State.
> His brows thick fogs, instead of glories, grace,
> And lambent dullness played around his face . . .

The pleasure given by this sort of thing was about all anyone wanted of the heroic under Charles II, apart from theatrical heroics, another genre. Could a style so ingeniously employed in making fun of epic be effectively used for epic? The same sequence occurred and the same question arises a generation later in the case of Pope, who wrote *The Rape of the Lock* before he translated Homer.

In 1689, under William and Mary, Dryden, a Jacobite and a Catholic, lost his Laureateship and his income and faced relative adversity. Among various shifts to support himself, he gave thought again to writing a heroic poem, an enterprise that his former royal patrons had not encouraged. He must have realized that by this time it was beyond him; even for the translation of Virgil, upon which at length he settled, he doubted his powers and his poetic means. Insofar as chief among these means was the couplet trained in verse satire, it is curious to see him dragging his favorite Virgil into a discourse on satire that he prefaced to a book of translations of Persius and Juvenal in 1692. Noting Martial's remark that Virgil could have written better lyrics than Horace, Dryden went Martial one better: "Virgil," he said, "could have written sharper satires than either Horace or Juvenal, if he would have employed his talent that way." As evidence, he supplied a well-chosen quotation from the Third Eclogue. The notion of Virgil as a satirist has the elation of some great figure of speech, a sublime chiasmus, when proposed by the author of *Mac Flecknoe* just before he girds himself for the *Aeneid*.

Before Dryden, the art of translation had been a gentleman's diversion or a scribbler's piece work, but Dryden's Virgil was a business venture, a writing project of a distinctly modern kind. He arranged for it and eventually signed a contract with his Fleet Street printer, Tonson; and in a letter of December 12, 1693, he said: "I propose to do it by subscription, having an hundred and two brass cuts, with the coats of arms of the subscriber to each cut; and every subscriber to pay five guineas, half in hand, besides another inferior subscription of two guineas for the rest, whose names are only written in a catalogue printed with the book."

This may not have been the first publishing enterprise of the kind, but it was the most ambitious and successful until then ever carried out in England. One hundred and one subscribers were found for the "brass cuts"—deplorable engravings of neoclassic statuary—and three hundred fifty-one gentlemen paid two guineas to be enrolled in the "catalogue," or list. Thus the total amount subscribed appears to have been 1,229 pounds 8 shillings. Besides his share of this, Dryden received gifts from the three noble patrons to whom he dedicated, respectively, the *Pastorals*, the *Georgics*, and the *Aeneid*—"that no opportunity of profit might be lost," as Dr. Johnson observed more than eighty years later. According to a recent estimate,* the poet's income can be reckoned at about 1,600 pounds, or 400 pounds a year if divided equally among the four years—1694, 1695, 1696 and 1697—spent on the labor.

It probably came down to little more than three working years, as he himself counted it, for besides time lost to affairs or illness he took two months off to do a prose version of du Fresnoy's Latin poem, *De Arte Graphica*, and a preface for it. If we suppose Dryden to have worked 1,000 full days on his Virgil, he must have turned out an average of at least sixteen lines, or eight couplets, a day, for his *Aeneid* alone runs to 13,700 lines (for 9,896 Latin lines), and the *Pastorals* and *Georgics*, some of which he had only to revise, come to 4,358 lines more.

It seems that all England, or at any rate all Englishmen who had paid their guineas, awaited the result with impatience, if not with anxiety; the poet later complained that some grew clamorous. According to Johnson, "the nation considered its honor as interested in the event." Since Dryden felt under great pressure of time, his friends and admirers helped him as they could. Noblemen invited him to work at their country houses; a young barrister made him a gift of the principal annotated editions of Virgil; Addison, at twenty-four, undertook to write the prose "arguments" for the various Books; and Congreve, at twenty-seven, did Dryden the considerable favor of checking his *Aeneid* against the Latin text.

At the end of these exertions Tonson was able to bring out, in July 1697, in the pomp of folio, "The WORKS of VIRGIL: containing His

---

* By William Frost, in *Dryden and the Art of Translation* (Yale, 1955).

PASTORALS, GEORGICS, AND AENEIS. Translated into English Verse; By Mr. DRYDEN/Adorn'd with a Hundred Sculptures," etc. A few corrections and changes were made and a missing couplet supplied in a second folio edition in 1698. Dryden had been sixty-two when he undertook the translation; he was sixty-six when it was published. It was the longest sustained labor of his life. By his own account, his health suffered from application to it, and in any case he had but three more years to live. Although he may for a time have felt some hopes of royal recognition from their Protestant Majesties, he had refused to seek King William's favor and had resigned himself to his position as a veteran of a repudiated party and a vanished court—a court with whose vices he felt unfairly associated. He renounced satire, "for who gives physic to the great when uncalled?" and produced his Virgil as both a demonstration of his independence and a means of maintaining it. In his "Postscript to the Reader," he wrote:

> What Virgil wrote in the vigor of his age, in plenty and at ease, I have undertaken to translate in my declining years: struggling with wants, oppressed with sickness, curbed in my genius, liable to be misconstrued in all I write; and my judges, if they are not very equitable, already prejudiced against me, by the lying character which has been given them of my morals. Yet steady to my principles, and not dispirited with my afflictions, I have, by the blessing of God on my endeavors, overcome all difficulties; and, in some measure, acquitted myself of the debt which I owed the public, when I undertook this work. In the first place therefore, I thankfully acknowledge to the Almighty Power, the assistance he has given me in the beginning, the prosecution, and conclusion of my present studies, which are more happily performed than I could have promised to myself, when I labored under such discouragements. For, what I have done, imperfect as it is, for want of health and leisure to correct it, will be judged in after ages, and possibly in the present, to be no dishonor to my native country . . .

He was quite right. Few subscribers were disappointed, and the eighteenth century immensely appreciated Dryden's *Aeneid*. Pope called it "the most noble and spirited translation that I know in any language." There is no doubt that it gave Pope the idea for his own enterprise with the *Iliad* some fifteen years later. The heroic couplet had had the heroic thrust upon it by Dryden. We cannot call ourselves acquainted with English poetry in his age and in the next unless we have read his translation, and it is still fascinating to see his mind at play over his great original.

Whatever the incongruities between the two poets, between the shy perfectionist of Latin verse in his Parthenopean villa and the able Restoration wit in his coffee house, the fact remains that few English writers have ever known or admired Virgil as Dryden did. Amid the pages of flattery, interested pleading, and neoclassic aesthetics in Dryden's prefaces, we come upon nothing more genuine—and nothing more perceptive within a certain range—than his frequent references to Virgil. To some extent, of course, it was an interest that he shared with the age itself. Writers for whom Latin was still a living language knew what it was to make Latin verses and in this sense knew what Virgil had been doing. Aspects of the Virgilian lingered in their imaginations and took life again even in their candlelit theaters: Racine's *Andromaque* was first performed in 1667 and Purcell's *Dido and Aeneas* in 1689. Still, Dryden's devotion was remarkable. It began early and lasted all his life.

During 1665 and 1666, when London was being visited first by plague and then by the Great Fire, Dryden worked in Wiltshire on his Dialogue *Essay of Dramatic Poesy* and on a long poem, *Annus Mirabilis*. In the Dialogue he touched on Virgil as the "pattern of elaborate writing" and as Ovid's superior in restraint. In his preface to *Annus Mirabilis* he declared that Virgil had been his master in this poem, as, in a sense, anyone could see from the fact that some thirty passages in it were direct imitations or echoes. For example:

> All hands employed, the royal work grows warm,
> Like laboring bees on a long summer's day . . .

It is a baroque poem, in which Virgil as a pattern of elaborate writing served him only too well, but Dryden's critical remarks on Virgil are another matter. "We see the objects he presents us with in their native figures, in their proper motions; but so we see them, as our own eyes could never have beheld them so beautiful in themselves . . . the very sound of his words have often somewhat that is connatural to the subject . . ." Not only is this just, but the concluding remark is far from commonplace even now.

In his subsequent prose, Dryden refers often enough to Virgil to give us the impression that the text lay open on his table for thirty years. He praised "the divine Virgil" more frequently even than he did Waller's contribution to English numbers. His last insights appear to have come, naturally enough, during his work on the translation. One, particularly valuable, he found a place for in his preface to *De Arte Graphica* in 1695. "Virgil knew how to rise by degrees in his expressions; Statius was in his towering heights at the first stretch of his pinions." In the course of his long dedicatory preface to the *Aeneid* Dryden wrote with a craftsman's interest in Virgil's style. He had compared Virgil and Ovid years before, to Ovid's disadvantage, and now touched again on this subject. Speaking of French poets, he said: "The turn on thoughts and words is their chief talent, but the epic poem is too stately to receive those little ornaments. . . . Virgil is never frequent in those turns, like Ovid, but much more sparing of them in his Aeneis than in his Pastorals and Georgics.

Ignoscenda quidem, scirent si ignoscere Manes.

That turn is beautiful indeed, but he employs it in the story of Orpheus and Eurydice, not in his great poem. I have used that licence in his Aeneis sometimes: but I own it as my fault. 'Twas given to those who understand no better . . ."

As we read Dryden's *Aeneid*, we may find this passage recurring to us fairly often; it becomes a nice question, in fact, how much weight to give to the last sentence. Another passage of special interest in the light of the translation itself is that in which he remarks on "the sober retrenchments of his [Virgil's] sense, which always leaves somewhat to gratify our imagination, on which it may enlarge at pleasure . . ."

Of formal criticism, analysis of Virgil's composition in the large, Dryden had little to offer beyond a discussion of standard topics of neoclassic criticism (the relative greatness of heroic poetry and tragedy, piety versus valor as the virtue of the epic hero, the behavior of Aeneas toward Dido, the debt of Virgil to Homer, the elapsed time of the main action, etc.) that no longer seem to us of the greatest interest. He did notice that extended epic similes were introduced by Virgil after, not before, the crest of an action, and took as his example the one in Book I in which Neptune is likened to a respected Roman official calming a mob. A modern critic would not fail to see something thematic in this first simile of the *Aeneid*, but notions of that sort could not occur to Dryden. He wondered, oddly enough, why Virgil allowed Aeneas to be wounded toward the end of the poem—an episode that is not only obviously dramatic but makes for epic symmetry: the just prince's disablement balanced against that of the cruel exile, Mezentius, as the death of Pallas is balanced by that of Lausus. We hear nothing from Dryden of Virgil's architectonics and depth of suggestion, nor of the quality of his imagination—so supreme and terrifying when the Fury in the form of a small bird beats around Turnus' head in the final combat, so forced and awkward when Aeneas' ships are transformed into sea-nymphs and we are troubled for a moment by an image of nereids on that scale.

As to Virgil's way with language, however, I do not know any happier descriptions than Dryden's. "His words are not only chosen, but the places in which he ranks them, for the sound. He who removes them from the station wherein their master set them spoils the harmony. What he says of the Sibyl's prophecies may be as properly applied to every word of his: they must be read in order as they lie; the least breath discomposes them; and somewhat of their divinity is lost . . . he is like ambergris, a rich perfume, but of so close and glutinous a body that it must be opened with inferior scents of musk or civet, or the sweetness will not be drawn out into another language. . . . What modern language, or what poet, can express the majestic beauty of this one verse amongst a thousand others?

> aude, hospes, contemnere opes, et te quoque dignum
> finge deo.

For my part, I am lost in the admiration of it: I contemn the world when I think on it, and myself when I translate it."

Conscious as he was of the inferiority of his "coarse English," Dryden strove undaunted to correct it as well as he could. "I have endeavored," he said, "to follow the example of my master: and am the first Englishman, perhaps, who made it his design to copy him in his numbers [metrical excellence], his choice of words, and his placing them for the sweetness of the sound. On this last consideration I have shunned the caesura [elision]. . . . For where that is used, it gives a roughness to the verse, of which we can have little need, in a language which is overstocked with consonants. Such is not the Latin, where the vowels and consonants are mixed in proportion to each other." His tentative claim for himself may recall a wicked remark of Swift's to the effect that people would not have been so aware of Dryden's merit as a playwright if he had not told them of it so often in his prefaces. But it is true and highly pertinent that English is overstocked with consonants, while in Latin vowels and consonants are in better proportion.

With respect to diction, the translator knew from Horace that Virgil's secret lay in the placement of words and their subtle stress upon one another, a mutual energizing of words within a line or passage to achieve that "majesty in the midst of plainness" that Dryden so admired. The difficulty of rendering such effects is rather simplified in his account of it. In practice, he said, "I found the difficulty of translation growing on me in every succeeding Book. For Virgil, above all poets, had a stock, which I may call inexhaustible, of figurative, elegant, and sounding words. . . . Virgil called upon me in every line for some new word: and I paid so long, that I was almost bankrupt. So that the latter end must needs be more burdensome than the beginning or the middle. And consequently the Twelfth Aeneid cost me double the time of the first and second. What had become of me if Virgil had taxed me with another Book?"

Dryden's opinion of what a translation should be had already been expressed at some length in various essays, beginning with his preface to *Ovid's Epistles* in 1680. No part of Dryden's criticism seemed more important or more definitive to Pope and Johnson. It has been rejected by some later critics, to whom scientific scholarship and historical study have made differences of language and culture appear more nearly absolute, but it has continued to be the premise of poet-translators, including Ezra Pound. ("The best trans. is into the language the author wd. have used had he been writing in the translator's language.") In his preface to the *Aeneid* Dryden restated it. "The way I have taken is not so strait as Metaphrase [word for word] nor so loose as paraphrase: Some things too I have omitted, and sometimes have added of my own. Yet the omissions, I hope, are but of circumstances [incidentals] and such as would have no grace in English; and the additions, I also hope, are easily deduced from Virgil's sense. . . . I have endeavored to make Virgil speak such English as he would himself have spoken, if he had been born in England, and in this present age . . ."

There was nothing wrong with Dryden's command of Latin. It was better than ours is likely to be, and has been well defended* against imputations of ignorance. He used the latest edition of Virgil, prepared in 1675 by the French editor Charles de la Rue (Carolus Ruaeus) for the Dauphin of France (*in usum serenissimi Delphini*), one of a series referred to by Dryden as "the Dolphins." This presented to him on every page not only the best text available in his time but also a Latin prose paraphrase, or *interpretatio*, and notes. Dryden generally stuck to Ruaeus' interpretation and followed it in many of his expansions, but he occasionally insisted on his own interpretation and at least once left untranslated a line that baffled him in Ruaeus—though he later found a better reading in an edition by the Dutch scholar Nicolas Heinsius.

As he worked with all possible speed, Dryden used all possible aids to

---

* By J. McG. Bottkol in *Modern Philology*, Vol. XI, No. 3, February, 1943.

composition, including such previous translations as he could lay his hands on. He does not appear to have known the Scots translation by Gavin Douglas; he made no reference to Surrey's version (1574) of Books I and II nor to Stanyhurst's version (1582) of Books I through IV. He had the Italian translation by Caro (1581) and the French translation by Segrais (1668); he had Denham's version (1636) of Book II, Waller and Godolphin's version (1658) of Book IV, and Ogilby's version (1649) of the whole poem. He also received from Paris, in manuscript, a translation by the Jacobite Earl of Lauderdale, completed before his death in 1695 but unpublished until 1718. Dryden drew on all of these for rhymes, phrases, and even for lines. He took five lines of Denham and acknowledged taking one; from Lauderdale he plundered freely, taking about 800 lines with improvements or at least minor changes and about 200 lines without change and without acknowledgment. We would call this plagiarism, but an ambiguous reference to Lauderdale in Dryden's preface may indicate that that nobleman had consented to it, perhaps because on another occasion he had printed a great many lines of Dryden as his own. Dryden admitted his debt somewhat disingenuously by saying that "having his manuscript in my hands, I consulted it as often as I doubted of my author's sense."

It is plain from Dryden's own remarks that he felt the inadequacy of his verse and his diction. To break the monotony of his couplets he resorted to triplets and Alexandrines, often in combination. This provided what could be called momentary relief, but did not suffice in the long run. In certain Books, III for example, the habit of the closed couplet so hobbled the movement of his narrative that he himself seems to have become bored with it, and in the following Books we find him trying more successfully to make verse paragraphs beginning within one couplet and ending within a later one.

He also tried to extend his resources of language. The effort was not constant enough to save him from the curse of a number of poeticisms that were even then clichés. Reiteration does not convince us that shades were so frequently dusky, bosoms manly, seas briny, gore purple, night sable, skies vaulted and rent by shrieks—to name only a few. One recourse from this sort of thing would have been to look again at shades, bosoms, seas, gore, night, skies etc., but this would have been asking too much not only of Dryden but of the age. The role of vocabulary in poetry can be slightly misconceived, and Dryden slightly misconceived it. The "store of words" he found so inexhaustible in Virgil was first of all *copia* of imagination and feeling, and Dryden matched it best—as on occasion he did match it—from the same sources, not by using new words and Latinisms.

"He was no lover of labor," observed Johnson. "What he thought sufficient, he did not stop to make better; and allowed himself to leave many parts unfinished, in confidence that the good lines would over-balance the bad." This would be fair enough if it took account of Dryden's haste, probably as much to blame for his faults as aversion to labor. A number of his bad lines were doubly bad in that they introduced literal absurdities into Virgil's narrative. In Book I, 302 sqq., we hear that after the intervention of Mercury

> ponunt ferocia Poeni
> corda volente deo; in primis regina quietum
> accipit in Teucros animum et mentem benignam. . . .

The Carthaginians and their queen, so the Latin says, were put in a benignant mood toward the approaching Trojans. In Dryden, 414 sqq.,

> The surly murmurs of the people cease,
> And, as the Fates required, they give the peace.
> The Queen herself suspends the rigid laws. . . .

But at that point the Queen took no such action, and when later the Trojans appeared, they petitioned her to do so. In Book II, 52–53, a spear is hurled at the Wooden Horse:

> stetit illa tremens, uteroque recusso
> insonuere cavae gemitumque dedere cavernae. . . .

It stuck trembling, and from the blow in the belly the hollow interior gave a resounding groan. In Dryden, 68–69:

> The sides transpierced return a rattling sound
> And groans of Greeks enclosed come issuing through the wound.

Apart from the padded "come issuing," this misrepresents the situation to the point of farce. If any Greek had been heard groaning, the Horse would have had a short career. So it goes, too frequently, throughout the poem.

Faults of this kind were not necessary, and it may seem to us that they could have been corrected by a moment's thought. They betray the haste of the translator. But more than this, they suggest that Dryden did not really value fidelity in such particulars as we do. Though in theory he understood that his task was to do so and liked to think that he had, he did not consistently enter into the mind of the original artist to the point of seeing, hearing, and feeling the scenes that Virgil created. Most often he wished rather to make a literary artifact answering to another literary artifact, and this satisfied the taste of his contemporaries. Up to a point, of course, they were right. The *Aeneid* is not a realistic work of art. Nevertheless, Dryden himself had noted of Virgil that "we see the objects he presents us with," and this therefore was one of the qualities of Virgil that he must have hoped to emulate. If his failures mattered less to his own age than they do to ours, so much the worse for his age.

Minor effects of haste are occasional eccentricities like "herds of wolves" in VII, 21, or tangled syntax, as in VII, 92:

> This plant, Latinus, when his town he walled
> Then found, and from the tree Laurentum called . . .

or X, 752:

> The holy coward fell: and forced to yield,
> The prince stood o'er the priest . . .

or fatal asyndeton, as in XII, 414:

> And struck the gentle youth, extended on the ground,

meaning that he hit and felled him. Again, we are inclined to ask why Dryden could not have reworked lines like these, if not for the first edition then for the second. Johnson appears to have been struck by the fact that he did not do so. "What he had once written, he dismissed from his thoughts; and I believe there is no example found of any correction or improvement made by him after publication."

Johnson may be excused for thinking so, but in fact he was wrong about this. Dryden "bestowed nine entire days" on corrections for the edition of 1698. These are usually of a spelling, a single word, sometimes of a phrase or a line, and hardly ever represent an attempt to rewrite a passage or to revise it substantially. If, however, we look at certain parts of the *Aeneid* that Dryden had already done years before for a literary miscellany, *Sylvae* (1684), we find a few revisions of longer passages. At least one of these is worth close attention. For lines 459–61 of Book V, the earlier version had:

> A lion's hide, amazing to behold,
> Ponderous with bristles, and with paws of gold,
> He gave the youth. . . .

Ten years later Dryden wrote:

> . . . and from among the spoils he draws
> (Ponderous with shaggy mane, and golden paws)
> A lion's hide. . . .

Here several admirable motives were at work: to abandon the padding phrase, to let the syntax float and carry through the couplet, and to strengthen the image and "feel" of the lion's hide. The line in parentheses is masterful and typical of Dryden at his best. This revision shows what the poet might have done if he had been able, or had wished, to take his whole translation as a draft and to spend another three years rewriting it.

Dryden's good lines are often very good indeed, and they occur frequently enough to keep the reader on the alert for the next one. He was capable of lyric beauty:

> With branches we the fanes adorn . . .

> Not her own star confessed a light so clear . . .

> And rent away with ease the lingering gold . . .

But more often his peculiar excellence lay in a whiplike power of statement, swift and flexible but weighted:

> His holy fillets the blue venom blots . . .

> And on the shaded ocean rushed the night . . .

> See! Pallas, of her snaky bucklet proud . . .

> While the fierce riders clattered on their shields . . .

Lines like these may not "overbalance" the inferior ones, but they check the effect of them and contribute enormously to the vigor of the translation. So does Dryden's syntactical ingenuity within the couplet. Those "turns" that he regarded as Ovidian are indeed Ovidian in the sense that Ovid did them to death, but they are not quite so sparse in Virgil as Dryden suggested; in fact they occur here and there very naturally in the compact Latin (*nostro doluisti saepe dolore* . . . *una salus victis nullam sperare salutem*). Virgil was perhaps deliberately sparing of them, but Dryden certainly was not. Often they too give an effect of swiftness and concision:

> Through such a train of woes if I should run,
> The day would sooner than the tale be done . . .

> . . . All combine to leave the state
> Who hate the tyrant, or who fear his hate . . .

The truth is that structure of this kind had already become an essential characteristic of the couplet style that Dryden bequeathed to Pope. Dryden probably could not have translated Virgil or anyone else without "that licence" that he owned as a fault. What he meant by saying "'Twas given to those who understand no better," I am not sure, unless this is a unique reflection on the taste of his readers—surely not those who got their coats of arms on the brass cuts? Every so often, no doubt, it is chiefly interesting as a trick, a rhetorician's amusement:

> Her cheeks the blood, her hand the web, forsakes. . . .

There is also the point that since Dryden's wit in his satires depends partly on the balanced, antithetical style, the more we find of that style in his Virgil, the more we are reminded of the satires. We are reminded of them also by Dryden's gusto in many passages:

> . . . a thirsty soul,
> He took the challenge, and embraced the bowl . . .

> . . . the bleating lambs
> Securely swig the dug beneath the dams. . . .

Then there are moments when we perceive a tone of decided burlesque, as in the episode of Hercules and Cacus in Book VIII, or in this couplet given to Turnus in Book XI (658–59) on the subject of human fortunes:

> Some, raised aloft, come tumbling down amain;
> Then fall so hard, they bound and rise again.

That, I think, was for the boys in school. In general, though, Dryden's touches of the satiric gave variety to his style and kept it from being unrelievedly high-flown. Certain couplets seem to have come straight out of *Absalom and Achitophel*, and are none the worse for that:

> But cautious in the field, he shunned the sword:
> A close-caballer, and tongue-valiant lord.

In the altercation between Drances, so characterized, and Turnus in Book XI, Dryden was able to use the gift for verse debate that he had exercised for years in writing for the Restoration stage.

The attitude conveyed by Virgil's whole narrative of the war in Latium is cumulative and very complex. The way in which time and again violence gets out of hand, by malign force overcoming the will of peaceful leaders, makes us think that the iron of the Roman civil wars had entered into the poet. His laments for slain princes are overdone to the point of bathos. Slaughter interests him, of course, as a challenge to description, but he does not have Homer's evenhanded and rather superhuman gaiety about battle. Dryden could scarcely equal Virgil's massive effect of tragic ambiguity, but for all his heartiness he, who had lived through Cromwell's time and Monmouth's, looked with a reserve of his own on the heroic convention. In an occasional turn of phrase he implies it:

> The champion's chariot next is seen to roll,
> Besmeared with hostile blood, and honorably foul. . . .

That is neither heroic nor Virgilian, but it has edge and character, and a sophisticated civilization stands behind it.

These notes will perhaps have suggested how Dryden's *Aeneid* suffered from being a rush job and yet how brilliantly he brought it off. No one else, with no matter how much time, has yet achieved a version as variously interesting and as true to the best style of a later age as his was to his own. He allowed himself a complacent sentence or two about it, but the final judgment expressed in his Dedication was severe: "I have done great wrong to Virgil in the whole translation: want of time, the inferiority of our language, the inconvenience of rhyme, and all the other excuses I have made, may alleviate my fault, but cannot justify the boldness of my undertaking. What avails it me to acknowledge freely that I have been unable to do him right in any line?"

Too severe.

Postscript to a Translation
of the *Aeneid*

1

There once was a Troy, or Ilium, a walled city given over to fire and sword around 1250 B.C. You can see the fortress mass of stonework, unearthed during the last century, a few miles inland south of the Hellespont, looking west toward Tenedos and the Aegean. But the Troy of Homer was far less historical than mythical. Composing in Greek around 750 B.C., he imagined a heroic world drawn from the storytellers who preceded him and elaborated it in his *Iliad* and *Odyssey*. The Greeks were spellbound, and so later were the Romans. Composing in Latin in the decade after 29 B.C., Virgil chose the mythical age of Homer as the setting of his narrative.

Those were early days indeed, and there had been days earlier still, at the limit of Greco-Roman memory or reference, when the ancestors of Homer's heroes lived their primordial and shadowy lives near the gods. The god Atlas, both titanic personage and snow-covered mountain, had a daughter named Electra, beloved of the sky-god, Zeus, the Roman Jupiter. Their sons were Dardanus and Iasius. From the western land later known as Italy Dardanus journeyed to Asia Minor and founded Dardania.

Dardanus espoused a daughter of a neighboring king, Teucer, and begot Erichthonius. Erichthonius begot Tros, whence the name Troy. Tros had three sons, Assaracus, Ilus (whence Ilium), and Ganymede. Assaracus begot Capys, who begot Anchises. Ilus begot Laömedon, who begot Priam. In the royal house of Troy, accordingly, Anchises and Priam were second cousins. Their sons, respectively Aeneas and Hector, were cousins once further removed. Anchises had had the privilege of lying with the goddess Venus, who bore him Aeneas. Aeneas married Creusa, a sister of Hector.

First published in Robert Fitzgerald's translation of Virgil's *Aeneid* (New York: Random House–Vintage Books, 1984).

In Book XX of the *Iliad*, Aeneas faces Achilles in single combat and acquits himself well but not so well as to quiet the fears of the sea-god, Poseidon, who proposes to save him, saying to the other gods:

> ". . . Come now, we ourselves
> may take him out of danger, and make sure
> that Zeus shall not be angered by his death
> at Achilles' hands. His fate is to escape
> to ensure that the great line of Dardanus
> may not unseeded perish from the world.
> For Zeus cared more for Dardanus, of all
> the sons he had by women, and now Zeus
> has turned against the family of Priam.
> Therefore Aeneas and his sons, and theirs,
> will be lords over Trojans born hereafter."

According to this, Aeneas will escape not only the sword of Achilles—as he does when Poseidon spirits him off to another part of the field—but the doom already known to impend for Troy and the family of Priam. We hear further that not all Trojans will be killed or enslaved when the city falls but that there will be survivors, and Trojans "born hereafter," over whom Aeneas and his sons (the plural is worth noting) will be lords. Here is the germ of the *Aeneid*.

2

In post-Homeric storytelling the prophecy of Poseidon would be borne out with respect to the survival of Aeneas, a datum undisputed in otherwise differing versions. Perhaps Homer's authority prevailed to this extent, his poem foretold this much of the truth. The possibility of foreknowledge and accurate prophecy enthralled the ancient mind. So did its logical corollary, the notion of fate and fated events. It is not too much to say that the *Aeneid* is charged with notions of fate and instances of prophecy.

On his way back from Greece, where he had become ill, Virgil died at Brundisium in 19 B.C. with his work unfinished. He had hoped to spend three more years on his poem and then to devote himself to philosophy. If this were not known we might have guessed it. *Felix qui potuit rerum cognoscere causas* he had once written, and meant it, though perhaps with a shade of irony, of his predecessor, the atomist Lucretius: "Happy the man who has learned the causes of things." Things known and felt by

Virgil in his lifetime included extremes of experience almost as great as those of our own century. His mind certainly dwelt on the possible causes, or what later thinkers would call a Sufficient Cause, of those extremes. Seen from the outside, as it were, are events as unalterably fixed beforehand as they are in retrospect? If so, or nearly so, by what power, and to what end?

Virgil gave his poem the Greek title *Ainêis*, thus expressly invoking, as with his prior *Eclogues* and *Georgics*, the older poetry, the parent poetry, of Greece. He re-created a Homeric hero in the Homeric age; he also deliberately echoed Homer in many details of narrative, in many conventions and features of style. But his purpose was totally un-Homeric and drastically original: to enfold in the mythical action of the *Aeneid* foreshadowings and direct foretellings of Roman history, more than a thousand years of it between Aeneas and his own time. Most of all, the apparent Homeric pastiche, the ancient story, was to refer at times explicitly but more often by analogy to the latter centuries of that history, to the immediate past and present, and to such hopes and fears for the future as the record might suggest.

3

In the plain of Latium the city-state of Rome on the Tiber, a Latin-speaking community of farmers, first ruled by kings including some Etruscans, became a republic at the end of the sixth century B.C. The assembled people entrusted the *imperium* or high command to two annually elected consuls and maintained a senate or council of elders. Roman history for three centuries thereafter consisted of an internal struggle between the classes, patricians and plebeians, and of wars by which Roman authority bit by bit took over central Italy from Sabines, Etruscans, Volscians, Oscans, Umbrians, and other tribes; then southern Italy from Samnites and Lucanians. The Romans built roads and founded colonies, incorporated the conquered as citizens or allies, attracted neighboring peoples to Latin culture and the ceremonious Roman law. By the middle of the third century B.C. all Italy was in effect Roman and a world power with trading interests east and west in the Mediterranean.

By that time Romans had begun learning Greek from the Greek colonies in South Italy, at Cumae, Naples, Tarentum, and elsewhere. Romans crossed the Adriatic on errands of peace and war. In due course they conquered the Greeks and were conquered in their turn by Greek literature, philosophy, and art. And they grew fond, no one quite knows why, of tracing their origin to the emigration of surviving Trojans under Aeneas. Certainly the Aeneas legend had been Italian property for a long time; Etruscan craftsmen in the sixth century liked the image of Anchises riding on Aeneas' shoulders. If the first Etruscans had emigrated to Italy, as Herodotus believed, from Lydia or Maeonia, a region south of the Troad, who should say that the Trojans had not made a similar trek to Hesperia, the western land? What, after all, had become of the Trojans? The Roman clan of the Julii went so far as to claim as ancestors Aeneas and his divine mother.

A hundred sea-miles southwest of Sicily a harbor-site on a projecting spur of North Africa, long since colonized by Phoenicians from Tyre, had become the seagoing power of Carthage, dominant in the western sea, in Sicily, Sardinia, Corsica, and Spain. Now for a century and more the first and second Punic Wars between Rome and Carthage tested Roman stamina and strategy to the utmost. The Romans had to build ships, learn to handle them, and do battle with Carthaginian fleets. They won an early victory at Mylae but endured great reverses and wrecks at sea before driving the enemy from Sicily, which they made the first Roman province outside Italy.

In the second war the Carthaginian general Hannibal, marching from Spain, crossed with his African elephants the western Alps and invaded Italy. He crushed Roman armies in great battles, but though he remained to devastate Italy with his army for fifteen years he could not conquer Rome. Her leaders met the challenge. The consul Fabius Cunctator wore Hannibal down by harassment and delay, avoiding a pitched battle, and Scipio Africanus, a gifted general, finally defeated him at Zama in Africa. In the following years the testy Roman statesman Cato made *Carthago delenda est*, "Carthage must be destroyed," his refrain in the Senate, acted upon in the end when another Scipio in a third Punic War besieged, fired, and razed Carthage in 146 B.C.

All of this, and a great deal more, came to the mind of the Roman reader or listener as Virgil in his exordium told of the Tyrian settlement dear to Juno, implacable enemy of the Trojans, just as Carthage in days to come would be, year after year for many, the most dangerous enemy of Rome. The adventure of Aeneas and his people as guests of the Carthaginian queen would seem to the Roman reader as narrow an escape as that of Rome when beset by Carthage. Dido indeed in her final curse called for future strife without quarter between her descendants and those of Aeneas and prayed for one Carthaginian in particular, *aliquis ultor*, "someone to avenge me." At this the Roman reader murmured "Hannibal."

So far as we can see, there are no comparable historical resonances in the Homeric poems; this dimension of meaning is entirely Virgilian. And it is enriched by literary echoes that no educated Roman ear could miss. Concentrated in the role of Dido, for example, are those feminine distractions of Odysseus, Calypso, Circe, and the princess of Phaeacia. Virgil's simile introducing Dido is almost identical with Homer's simile introducing Nausicaa. Dido then takes the part of Nausicaa's father in welcoming and feasting the stranger and inviting him to tell his tale.

4

Homer's greatest display of virtuosity, it may well be, lay in handing over to his hero his own job, his art as *aoidos* or singer of tales, for 2,232 lines, a good sixth of the *Odyssey*, Books IX through XII of his twenty-four. Virgil followed suit, giving to Aeneas' tale about the same proportionate length but placing it earlier, in Books II and III of his twelve. As a hero, Aeneas has not always had a good press in modern times, but it would be hard to deny the power lent him by Virgil as a narrator of Troy's fall. In *The Confessions*, Saint Augustine reproached himself for overlooking his own *errores* when young in favor of the romantic but fictive wanderings of Aeneas, *Aeneae nescio cuius*, "some Aeneas or other." Reading this in Augustine's passionate Latin when I was seven years out of college, I exhumed my Virgil, read Aeneas' tale, and perceived for the first time that those pages down which I had clambered from construction to construction as a toiling schoolboy were in fact a masterpiece of narrative art.

Beginning with Aeneas' first lines in Book II, like long and shuddering bell-notes on the gay banquet scene, the story moves from memory to memory in a steady progression of effect. Aeneas' account of Sinon's performance has the qualities of a big scene in a play—a Greek play, complete with at least one daring touch of dramatic irony. And the attitude of the narrator is that of an honest Roman before his time: grim wonderment at Greek trickery, with a sense that the Greeks are too clever by half, too brazenly good at histrionics and dissimulation.

But here Aeneas' tale itself is dramatic and could hardly be more so: first the parley, touch and go, of the Trojans; the misread omen of the sea-serpents and Laöcoön; the clang of arms inside the wooden horse, four times jarred to a halt on the city threshold; the festal celebration and repose of the Trojans; the tremendous night through which the Greek fleet glides . . . ; Aeneas' dream of the ravaged Hector; the glare and seething of the fires; the tumult and fighting in the streets; the giant glittering figure of Achilles' son, Neoptolemus or Pyrrhus, breaking through into the palace where terrified women wail and cling . . .

It has been said that in the rhythm of Virgil's composition scenes of intensity or violence are succeeded and relieved by quieter scenes. That is to take the matter hindside before. Time and again throughout the *Aeneid* we see a repetition of the very first pattern in Book I, when a sunlit scene, a squadron happily under sail, provokes Juno to send, through Aeolus, her wild hurricane. Refuge and welcome at Carthage bring on Dido's deathly passion and Aeneas' reenactment of Troy's ruin. In Book III a promise of settlement in Thrace turns to horror at Polydorus; fresh Creteward sailing, in hope stirred by the oracle at Delos, brings the Trojans to famine and plague; the windfall of beef and goat-flesh in the Strophades is befouled by the Harpies . . . In Book V, successful games, peaceful hilarities, trained horsemanship proudly on display— all this had its climax in disaster when the Trojan women fire the ships. This is the rhythm of composition in the *Aeneid,* and in the second half of the poem episodes that are literally hellish make it bitter indeed.

5

The composer of the *Aeneid,* following his Homeric models, surely planned no falling off but rather a progressive heightening of interest from middle to end of his poem. He says as much himself at the opening of Book VII:

> A greater history opens before my eyes,
> A greater task awaits me . . .

Among other misfortunes, the *Aeneid* has had to suffer from a relative neglect in the schoolroom and elsewhere of Books VII through XII in favor of I through VI, with special attention to II and IV—the two books, for example, chosen by the Earl of Surrey in the sixteenth century for translation into the first English blank verse. It could be said, and has been, that this is faulty composition. It might seem less so if we could, even for an instant, put ourselves in Virgil's phantom shoes. In this half of the *Aeneid*—and it really begins with Anchises' review of Roman souls in Book VI—the poet was on home ground, his action at last ranging along the river and in the countrysides that he cared for, north, east, and south, among places named and folklore handed down by the fabulists and annalists of Rome. But during his century this land of Italy, this vital culture, defended and built up by the fortitude and political enterprise of generations, had been torn by civil wars between big armies, conducted not only on the peninsula but from Spain to Thessaly over the breadth of the Roman world.

The very success of the Romans in holding and unifying Italy, creating in effect a nation out of a city-state, had brought expanded Roman power too quickly to the conquest of the whole Mediterranean basin. Provinces—and magistracies—were organized in one conquered territory after another, Sicily, Spain, Africa, Macedonia, Asia, Narbonese Gaul, Cilicia, Bithynia, Cyrene, Crete, Syria, Cyprus, finally Gaul, and in too many cases Roman officers and tax gatherers plundered these countries for the enrichment of the capital and themselves. At the same time, sophistication, intrigue, and venality weakened the old Roman virtues of patriotism and probity, on which, at least in the later Roman view, the old institutions of the Republic depended. Those institutions, overburdened in any case, more and more often refused to work.

Powerful men, inflamed by ambition and arrogance, manipulated parties in assemblies and Senate for consulships and military commands. Gaius Marius broke the invading hordes of Cimbri and Teutones in North Italy, but under him a citizens' army in which it had been a privilege to serve the state became a professional army loyal to its general. Lucius Cornelius Sulla led such an army for the first time into Rome itself to claim a command that had been denied him. Later after two years of civil war he became dictator and resorted to proscription, setting up lists of enemies in the thousands whom it was then lawful to kill without trial. Murderers and informers flourished. Romans had endured this much before Virgil was born in 70 B.C. There would be more.

Statesmanship and generalship were now too often the same thing; if you could not command troops, it almost seems, you stayed out of politics. After Marius and Sulla came greater examples: Gnaeus Pompeius, Marcus Licinius Crassus, and Gaius Julius Caesar, who in 60 B.C. formed the first triumvirate to share consular and military power. Crassus had defeated the big slave insurrection led by Spartacus, Pompey had swept the Mediterranean of pirates and triumphed in the East. By their consent Caesar as proconsul for ten years carried out the campaigns that subdued the Gauls in France and Belgium and made Rome's presence felt in Britain and beyond the Rhine. But Crassus lost his life when defeated by the Parthians, and Pompey, estranged after the death of his wife, Caesar's daughter Julia, joined Caesar's enemies at Rome. Caesar chose to lead his formidable legions from Gaul into Italy at the river Rubicon in 49 B.C. and thus to initiate the Civil War. In Book VI of the *Aeneid* Anchises beholds these two among the shades:

> What war, what grief, will they provoke between them—
> Battle lines and bloodshed—as the father
> Marches from the Alpine ramparts, down
> From Monaco's walled height, and the son-in-law,
> Drawn up with armies of the East, awaits him.
> Sons, refrain!

The next year Caesar brought Pompey to battle and routed him at Pharsalus in Thessaly, proceeding to Egypt, where he had Cleopatra as mistress; then he moved with his usual velocity to other victories in Syria, North Africa, and Spain. As dictator this versatile genius ruled and reorganized the Roman world, but barely for four years before Brutus and Cassius on behalf of the old republican order killed him in the Senate house. Plutarch and Shakespeare, each in his day, would tell or stage the story.

The old order and republican rule could stave off only briefly the next round between the party of the tyrannicides and the Caesarians, followers and emulators of Julius: his lieutenants, Marcus Antonius and Marcus Aemilius Lepidus, good soldiers both, and his twenty-year-old grandnephew and adopted son and heir, Gaius Julius Caesar Octavianus. In 43 these three contrived official appointment as a second triumvirate. The tyrannicides were outlawed. The *triumviri* proscribed their enemies as Sulla had done. In 42 Julius was formally deified. In the same year Brutus and Cassius, defeated by Antony at Philippi, took their own lives. The victor, married to Octavian's sister Octavia and allotted the East, took Cleopatra as mistress and year by year made himself more openly monarch of Egypt. Meanwhile Octavian outmaneuvered Lepidus and forced him to retire, thus gaining sole power in the West. Antony finally divorced Octavia and declared Cleopatra's son by Caesar the future ruler of the Roman provinces in the East. At Rome this at long last brought a declaration of war against Cleopatra. She and Antony, with her Egyptian fleet and his Roman and Hellenistic army, met Octavian's host by sea at Actium on the eastern shore of the Adriatic and were decisively defeated in 31 B.C. Within a year Antony committed suicide and Octavian entered Alexandria. At thirty-three he held the reins of power over Rome and her dominions.

Octavian had many gifts, including one perhaps denied his great foster father: along with a sense of what the time demanded, a keen sense of how far, and at what pace, he could go. He appears to have been cool, immensely capable, assiduous, and farsighted. As head of state, he had what we call vision, and to his taste and patronage in literature we owe some of the best poetry ever written. He is beyond doubt one of the principal shapers of the world we still inhabit. Making use of inherited political and legal forms that had in fact grown corrupt and undependable, he called himself *princeps*, roughly "first citizen," to placate the old Roman sentiment against kings. His triumph did not obscure for him the poor condition of Italy, her people in city and countryside worn out by a century of fear, discord, and conflict, by the marches and quarterings of armies. Regions of once productive farmland were deserted or handed over to discharged veterans ill-suited to work them. Impoverished countrymen had joined a proletariat housed in tenements in the cities. Long before Actium, Octavian may well have put his mind on the establishment of peace and the reform of Roman life. Like the strong men before him, he had an assisting circle or entourage, in this case a credit to his judgment of men. One member of it was the poet Virgil.

6

Publius was his given name, Vergilius that of his clan, Maro that of his family, and he was a Northerner, perhaps as much Celtic as Italian or Etruscan, born in a rural small town near Mantua. His father owned a farm. Men of this region did not acquire Roman citizenship until Julius Caesar accorded it, in 49 B.C., when the poet was in his twenty-first year. By that time Virgil had studied at provincial private schools in Cremona and Mediolanum (Milan) and finally at Rome. His schooling trained him in Greek and Latin. The pupil with a stylus made his letters on a wax tablet which could then be smoothed. He listened to the teacher's lesson and read or recited his exercise aloud. He wore the Roman *tunica*, a sleeved shirt reaching the knees, and after his fifteenth year the Roman *toga*, a white woolen full-length robe, passed over the left shoulder, brought from behind under the right arm, and then thrown again over the left shoulder. Trousers were Gaulish, therefore outlandish, and were worn only by legionaries in wintry regions. One could wear a hood, or cover one's head with a fold of robe.

At Rome Virgil studied rhetoric, the construction and delivery of speeches, a part of the education of young Romans for public affairs. When Drances and Turnus debate before the Laurentine Senate, when Venus and Juno debate before Jupiter, their creator is drawing upon such rhetoric, though no doubt these and all the speeches in the *Aeneid* owe more to the poetic precedents in Greek theater. At Rome, also, Virgil became a friend of Gaius Asinius Pollio, an honorable politician and a gifted literary man who had known Catullus and shared with him—as now with Virgil—an admiration for the polished Alexandrian Greek poets, whose famous dictum that a big book is a big headache their Mantuan admirer had it in him eventually to flout. Tall and dark-haired, with a dark complexion, Virgil retained in Rome a shy and countryfied air. He had a fine reading voice. He was not robust.

During the Civil War, Virgil retired from the fever of the capital to Naples and the study of philosophy with an Epicurean, Siro. After the *triumviri* triumphed at Philippi, among Italian lands confiscated and given to veterans by Octavian was the poet's patrimony near Mantua. Octavian, to whom his trusted friend Maecenas introduced Virgil, may later have restored this land, as Virgil's *Eclogue I* suggests.

The works by which Virgil's art first became known to others besides his immediate friends were the ten brief *Eclogues*, "Selections," on which he probably worked from 45 to 37 B.C. Imitating the Greek Theocritus often, but almost as often no one at all, these pastoral inventions charmed Roman ears. Maecenas encouraged him to a larger enterprise, that of the *Georgics* in four books on the labors and beauties of husbandry, composed between 36 and 29 B.C. and read to Octavian in the latter year on his return to Italy from Egypt. Octavian heard among others the following lines:

> Let not this young man fail to rescue us,
> To rescue the torn world! . . . So many wars,
> So many kinds of wickedness! No honor
> Rendered the plow, but the fields gone to ruin,
> Countryfolk made homeless, and their scythes
> Beaten to straight swords on the blowing forge!
> War from the Euphrates to Germany,
> Ruptured engagements, violence of nations,
> Impious Mars raging the whole world over . . .

For so, no doubt, it still seemed before the finality of Actium and the difference between Octavian and the dictators who preceded him had been fully realized. Virgil had already, however, meditated a poem on Octavian, either an annalistic poem or one curiously figured in Book III of the *Georgics* as an elaborate temple wherein the conqueror would be enshrined among pictured triumphs. This plan underwent a true metamorphosis. Soon after Octavian accepted from the Senate the title of "Augustus" (we might say "The Blest") in 27 B.C. Virgil had freed his imagination for his mythical story of Aeneas, not precisely—and certainly not overtly—a poem on Octavian, but one that dramatized, on an ancient stage, toils and choices as difficult as his and sometimes analogous.

Achilles and Odysseus in Homer were not without communities. The cause of the Achaeans engaged Achilles when it suited him, Odysseus tried to bring his shipmates home and, once there, surgically removed a threat to his island folk and family. But Virgil's hero, Aeneas, had to bring the surviving people of Troy by sea to the unknown land of Italy and to settle them there, united with an indigenous race, to undertake what would be the world-governing task of Rome. The man whom Virgil imagined had to orient himself, as we say, and to go through tests and temperings. His heroism was by no means flawless. *Il débute par un évanouissement*, as Sainte-Beuve put it, when the storm at sea makes him shake and despair. We are embarrassed for him when he shirks his interview with Dido and tries to deny to her the obvious truth. But his *pietas*, responsible care for his father and son and his people, with their household gods and greater gods, distinguishes him in the mind of his creator from the start.

Aeneas is the son of a goddess and gets a great deal of supernatural attention, good and bad. On the last night of Troy the shades of Hector and Creusa appear to him with their strange admonitions. His divine mother in majesty recalls him to his duty. Promissory tongues of divine fire lave the brow of his young son. When he literally does not know where to go at sea, the oracle at Delos tells him; then the Larës and Penatës, Troy's figurine gods of Hearth and Larder, tell him more precisely. Helenus, the old Trojan warrior and seer at Buthrotum, gives him sailing directions and advice on consulting the Sibyl. At Carthage, Mercury makes two eerie appearances with commands from Jove. In Sicily the shade of Anchises urges him onward. His greatest privilege, shared with godlike heroes of the past, is to pluck the golden bough and visit in trance the world of the dead and the still unborn, where his father's shade passes in review for him the souls of Roman worthies in centuries to come. His confidence, his grasp of his mission, cannot fail to be confirmed by all this portentous experience.

Now see him in Book VII leaving behind the nocturnal magic of the Old World for the virgin forests of the New, sailing past Circe's island by night to head in for Tiber mouth in the morning, like our first explorers at the mouth of the Hudson or the James. All seems auspicious here at first in a land at peace recalling the Saturnian peace of old, and the king, Latinus, is disposed by local portent and oracle to welcome the new-comers. Here are the new Latin traditions, effigies, and names: Italus, Sabinus, Janus, Picus, semidivine figures of woodland and vineyard. The elated Trojans break ground for the walls of a settlement. Only look upward, though.

Often it must have occurred to men that the forces ruling their affairs from above—or below—are not merely punitive or angry but malevolent on a grand scale. It has occurred to us amid the exterminations and abysses of our century. It must have occurred to the Romans during the terrors and massacres of the first century B.C. Juno in the *Aeneid* answers to this nauseating sense of things. The storm at sea in Book I was nothing compared with what she now engineers in Book VII, calling up from hell her hideous Fury to madden Queen Amata and Prince Turnus and to provoke a fray between Italians and Trojans. In a ritual well known to Romans of Virgil's day, the goddess herself pushes open the closed gates of war. Now the Homeric Muses are invoked and there is a big Iliadic passage as the detachments of the home army from their differing regions pass in review, concluding with the splendid figures of Turnus, commander of Rutulians, and Camilla, the Volscian amazon.

Book VIII opens with one of Virgil's tender natural scenes, another hopeful time, as Father Tiber, hoary and magical in a dream vision, comes to Aeneas with reassurances, and selected ships go upstream under oars to the Arcadian realm of Pallanteum. Where one day the imperial city will stand, Aeneas finds hospitality among the penurious and humble huts of origin. His diplomatic mission has good fortune. Not only will King Evander entrust his horsemen and his only son to Aeneas' cause, but he will also mount a troop of Trojans to ride with them into Etruria for alliance with Tarchon's Etruscans, already under arms. Thunder and flashing armor amid the clouds announce to Aeneas his mother's intervention. The book ends with a description of the divine armor that Vulcan has made for him at her request, especially the shield with scenes from Roman history, and the centerpiece picturing the vast seafight at Actium. But now with Book IX war as martial magnificence gives way to essential war, war as combat and slaughter.

I first read through all twelve books of the *Aeneid* in my Oxford Classical Text in the spring, summer, and early fall of 1945, the closing months of the Second Great War, when I was stationed on an island in the western Pacific. Living and working in commodious Quonset huts on neat coral driveways amid palms regularly treated by DDT sprayed from a slow biplane, staff officers had little to suffer but boredom off duty, and Virgil remedied that for me. Our navy's Actium had been fought long before at Midway. But the last island fighting continued, first at Iwo, then on Okinawa, where kamikaze season got into full swing. There we were on our island in our fresh khakis, laundered and pressed, the little bars gleaming on our collars and caps, saluting the old admiral with his snowy Roman head and the urbane operations officer who held in his crystal mind the location, course, destination, and speed of every least landing craft over thousands of miles. The scene could not have been more imperial or more civilized. APO mail from the States came fast. We played tennis, skipped rope, and worked out on the heavy bag. At night at my neat desk in the B.O.Q. I read Virgil by the light of a good lamp. I heard young submarine skippers, the finest Annapolis products, give their lighthearted accounts of shelling poor junks to smithereens in the China Sea. Meanwhile, offshore of the big Japanese island to the north, picket ships were having their prows or upperworks and the men who manned them smashed into flaming junk by Japanese fighters aflame; ashore, men with flamethrowers were doing what I had heard a briefing officer in San Francisco, with an insane giggle, refer to as "popping Japs"; and a good many young and brave of both sides were tasting the agony and abomination that the whole show came down to, in fact existed for. The next landings would be on Honshu, and I would be there. More than literary interest, I think, kept me reading Virgil's descriptions of desperate battle, funeral pyres, failed hopes of truce or peace.

More than literary interest surely moved the first Roman readers of these books of the *Aeneid*, for war, the Roman specialty, had within their memories gone fratricidal and got out of hand. If Virgil intended, as he almost certainly did, an analogy between the task of Aeneas and that of Augustus, the hardest and hugest part for both was waging war to end war, to work out settlements so magnanimous as to challenge no more strife but to promote *concordia* and the arts of peace. This is the meaning of Aeneas' promise in Book XII:

> I shall not make Italians underlings
> To Trojans. For myself I ask no kingdom . . .

—just as Augustus, after defeating his flamboyant Turnus, Antony, had asked for himself no kingship or dictatorship, and (possibly bearing the *Aeneid* in mind) he never did.

One thing is poised against another, however. Take the matter of mercy, *clementia*. Augustus prided himself on showing it as *princeps*, but in his early days he had been capable of great cruelty. Aeneas is eloquent in his expression of *clementia* to the Latin emissaries in Book XI, but at the very end of the poem he cannot help his murderous anger and, though appealed to in the name of his father, kills the suppliant Turnus.

Take the matter of cities. City founding, city building, completed or aborted, and the seige, defense, and destruction of cities: these are recurrent themes in the *Aeneid*. Now and then Trojan enemies recall the dishonesty of Priam's father, Laömedon, who had cheated Apollo and Neptune of their fee for building the massive walls of Troy. Thereupon a sea-monster sent by Neptune plagued the city until the superman, Hercules, killed it on the promise of being given Laömedon's prize horses. Defrauded in his turn, he captured Troy and sacked but did not destroy it, an event remembered by Anchises in Book II as the Greeks and the dread immortals carry out their fiery, and final, destruction. We notice that this conflagration, so fully realized that we can feel the scorching breath of it on our skin, is echoed in Book IV, when the wave of lamentation in Carthage after Dido's fatal stroke is likened to billowing fire—as though in forecast of the fire that conquering Romans centuries later will set to burn the Libyan city to the ground. And the *Aeneid* will not end until the flames of Troy and the imagined flames of Carthage are echoed again in the flames that Aeneas' torches light to enwrap the city of Laurentum. The fire's victim at Troy becomes the incendiary now.

Take, finally, the matter of Fate and those spinners thereof known to the Romans as the *Parcae*. Jupiter, father of gods and men, is privy to the fated future. Venus is not, until he discloses the drift of it to her in Book I. Juno knows it but also apparently knows that the drift of it does not exclude her own ability to twist and retard it. Vulcan remarks that though the fate of Troy was fixed, the city might have held out for another ten years. Jupiter permits Juno to prolong Turnus' life, though briefly. There is a certain amount of play in the inevitable. The free choices of the mortal and immortal actors count for something. Aeneas is

free to neglect his mission or to live up to it, though he cannot change it
in the long run.

7

What was a *liber*, a book, at Rome? A roll of papyrus on which the text
was inscribed in ink with a reed pen. Publication consisted of the preparation and sale—or presentation as gifts—of copies made by hand. A
wealthy man would have copyists on his household staff. There were
bookshops, and Augustus founded a public library on the Palatine.
Books were valuable, not owned by everybody, and by our standards
hard to handle and to read. Words were not set off from one another by
spaces but appeared in an unbroken line. You held that scroll in your
right hand and unrolled it with your left. This is what Jupiter does
metaphorically for Venus in Book I, unrolling the scroll of fate, and in
Book IX, line 528, the poet calls on the Muse of Epic to unroll with him,
as though on a scroll, the mighty scenes of war. In the first case the text is
the future; in the second it is the past.

Virgil had a prose outline and worked at pleasure on one part or
another, not necessarily in sequence. He would compose and dictate
lines in the morning and later revise and eliminate. In early years he
seems to have tried various forms, but in his prime he stuck to the
hexameters of which he was a master. Many passages of this could be
called, in Yeats' phrase, "ingenious, lovely things," and they are not
more lovely than they are ingenious. Dryden observed, and one does,
that they could embody or enact what they described or narrated. Here is
one:

> Intonuere poli, et crebris micat ignibus aether.

(Book I, line 90) Thunder rolls in the first half of the line, and an electric
storm crackles in the second. Here is another:

> Vertitur interea caelum et ruit Oceano nox,
> involvens umbra magna terramque polumque
> Myrmidonumque dolos . . .

(Book II, lines 250 sqq.) The density of echoing sounds conveys the density of this darkness, especially in the nine successive long vowels of the
second line. The poet worked his language to make it appropriate and
memorable, whether or not he did so in terms of an analysis like mine.

On his deathbed Virgil asked that his unfinished poem be destroyed. Augustus overruled this and had it "published"—i.e., edited and copied—with no improvements or additions. Incomplete lines appear here and there, and there are other lines that though complete are clearly provisional. There are also inconsistencies in the story, such as Aeneas' attribution to Anchises in Book VII of Celaeno's prophecy in Book III that famine will one day reduce the Trojans to gnawing their tables. One Trojan ship goes down in the storm in Book I, four are destroyed by fire in Book V, and at least two vanish, for the ships that ascend the Tiber to Pallanteum in Book VIII and are then dispatched downstream again to "bring Ascanius news" never do so, never reappear. On these occasions we hear nothing of the anxiety that Cybelë, the great Phrygian mother goddess, is said in Book IX to feel for the ships built of her sacred timber. It is only in IX, when Turnus threatens the remainder, that Jupiter carries out his promise to change them into sea nymphs. The size of the nymphs, incidentally, if it corresponds to the size of ships, may strike us as a bit Brobdingnagian. Finally, Turnus' lieutenant, Messapus, is named with Trojan company—Mnestheus and Asilas—in Book XII, as though the poet had momentarily forgotten in which army he belonged.

Even at our distance in time, it is easy for us to understand the poet's bitterness at not having been able to perfect his work. But we can join many past generations in gratitude to Augustus for giving us this poem. It is a unique story, freshly imagined and often masterfully told. At the core of it is respect for the human effort to build, to sustain a generous polity—against heavy odds. Mordantly and sadly it suggests what the effort may cost, how the effort may fail. But as a poem it is carried onward victoriously by its own music.

The Style That Does Honor:
In Tribute to Dante

Sapientis est ordinare: the wise man's gift is for putting things in order. It would be a relief if this were commonly and firmly established as a criterion of art, as well as wisdom. There is an old connection between the two. In the Greek usage, at least in some of Plato and in some passages of Aristotle that may be exoteric—popular, as we should say, rather than technical—we find the notion of wisdom as a "skill" in a sense closely recalling that of the artist. And of putting in order as a skill expected of the artist the *Poetics* tells pretty clearly.

By order we should first understand serial clarity, the succession of distinct things placed so as not to confuse each other. By putting in order we mean doing this, and we also mean observing a certain principle in the succession: first things first, second things second, and so on. And then we must mean applying a consistent rule—or ruling sense—for determining what things are first, what second, and so on. If one rule were applied at the outset and another adopted midway we should find items already in place clamoring for a second admission. The mind of its own nature assents to propositions like these as holding good of whatever work the mind proposes; the conduct of a business or a home, a military operation, a theatrical production, a medical examination and diagnosis, the preparation and pleading of a case. By general consent, it is better that we perform these tasks in an orderly way and that order reign visibly over the results. There is no reason for exempting the artist and their arts.

The *Divine Comedy* teaches us and may teach this generation that serial clarity and an evaluating principle steadfastly held and applied are excellences in poetry, by no means at odds with any degree of intensity. One advantage in this, if it should come about, would be in the way of improved relations between poets and other responsible people, as having one large and general criterion in common. It might not in all in-

First published in *The Kenyon Review*, Spring 1952.

stances conduce to the reign of charity nor advance the kingdom of God, for any given poet might detest and be detested by great numbers of his fellow men; but there would be less uncertainty on this as on other points. It would make at least for mutual recognition. We need not conceive this recognition, either, in terms too exalted or remote: merely perhaps as more frequent choice of poetry for vacation reading, more frequent study by poets of the toils and spectacles of the age in politics, war and professional life. Defensive arrogance might abate, or be succeeded by an arrogance more objective and discriminating. These are modest prospects, but desirable. Our various accounts of the "alienation" of the artist imply a vicious circle of social or cultural cause and effect. A circle, however, is the most defenseless of figures, offering the maximum perimeter to intrusion. Capable of entering this one at any point, virtue may in fact enter it through the study, the purely literary study, of Dante.

Whether it does or not, the future will be touch and go, as before. Although the duration of the Dark Ages has been cut down by recent study, they appear to have been indeed dark for most of the laity. Misshapen fortresses still standing in Rome speak repellently of the decline and debasement of classic art. The notion that our own age is moving toward a comparable darkness may not be omitted, and generally is not, from our speculations. But if this is true it is interesting that during the past century the *Divine Comedy* should have won a kind of attention that it never had before. It is as if the poem of the full emergence—the unsurpassable renaissance—became more understandable under the threat of our being again submerged. There is, as always, more to be remarked here than just one more phenomenon; it looks like a sign of healthy response to whatever may impend; as a token of alternatives that we might encompass and should prefer. T. S. Eliot has suggested that we might reach a point at which there would be "an irresistible revulsion of humanity and a readiness to accept the most primitive hardships rather than carry any longer the burden of modern civilization." He was speaking more particularly of the self-consciousness and extreme concern for language that seemed to reach breaking point with Paul Valéry. But Mr. Eliot would contend, as we should, for the salvation of this civilization rather than its abandonment, and Dante's example may serve us in this.

The example is after all only the most remarkable one of many in a tradition that, so far as what we call "fiction" is concerned, has been with us all along. You cannot tell a story effectively without putting it in order, and the range of artistic opportunity in prose narrative has been proved enormous. If the prose artist intends a revelation he will take the trouble to comprehend it and present it distinctly after due preparation; this may be called the classic principle of composition. It is not enough that a vision has been entertained and an emotion suffered, nor is it enough—and this seems to be the crucial point—that the inner powers of language should have been greatly evoked under stress of the vision and the emotion. It remains to lead the reader, by art, out of his remote armchair or bucket seat or sickbed into the world known by the artist and as far within that world as he can go. The preliminary condition, in all the arts, is very nearly impossible: an auditor or spectator half awake, half willing and distracted within an inch of his life; an occasion highly unstable and a relationship highly impure. To master such a condition and occasion for serious ends is perhaps the definition of classic art. The man who works at it cannot afford to neglect any of his resources. Not all artists, it is true, are able to work at it. One writes as one can; there are those who cannot write very well, and there are also those whose spirits, burning but disadvantaged, must deny half of art in order to realize the other half. But an "aesthetic" based upon these cases cannot have philosophic validity because it simply does not meet *the* case. We have been attracted to such an aesthetic, and have seen what comes of it.

The word "classic," with its special overtones, is one that everybody would be happy to exchange for a better one; but there is probably no better one. We can, however, enlarge a little on what it ought to mean. The study of Dante suggests that classic art as here defined, and the classic principle of composition, belong to an ideal we may call *poesia perennis,* related to *philosophia perennis*—ideals that in truth always preside over human art and intellect. "What may be done"—the order realizable—in poetry is something that each poet learns in the first instance from another, or from several others, and in the second instance from himself or from reality itself in the emulation of those others. The critic cannot be too attentive to Dante when he tells us that he had converse with Virgil and that Virgil had not spoken to anyone else in a long time. It is interesting, for the same reason, to note that although Virgil knew Greek literature so well and worked it all so thoroughly, he mentions Sophocles alone by name. These three poets are in fact the strongest hands at classic composition in their respective literatures. Virgil must have known this of Sophocles, and Dante certainly knew it of Virgil and himself. The kind of composition in question is one of progressive revelation, or if you dislike the religious word, simple progression of effect. It is a feat of control. A fine distance runner sees his race as a whole and is able to pace himself, quarter by quarter, putting on a little more pressure in each.

After noting a formal quality it is useful to pause over the act of abstraction we have performed. Our three runners were not on the track to show their form. Why did Sophocles bring progression of effect to the height at which we find it in *Oedipus;* why did Virgil intend that within each unit of the *Aeneid* and in the whole itself we should move always toward ampler and richer or more piercing effects? The answer in each case must surely be that the artist's emotion had such scale that only by degrees could he hope to lead reader or auditor toward the sense of things that moved him. Let us say this and insist upon it: the emotion is primary and indispensable, answering to existence perceived, and by its own magnitude asks the utmost of intelligence in composition. This account of the matter may stand as a translation of statements about "grandeur of imagination and sustained nobility of thought"—qualities in which it is agreed that Dante found Virgil his predecessor. In terms of our translation we discover less to wonder at in Dante's proud and courteous attribution to Virgil of the *bello stile* in which he himself was writing. In the *Aeneid,* known and grasped as a whole, he had found the classic principle of composition—a principle of which earlier medieval poets had been oblivious because they had nothing great to compose. This principle is "style" in the large sense: the manner of doing. Those who wept at Virgil's reading of the Marcellus passage in *Aeneid* VI were not weeping over the twenty-five lines or so there but over the effect these lines had coming after all that had gone before. Nothing is more evident than the fact that Dante understood and adopted this principle. In both cases it is highly conscious and openly alluded to: the *maior opus moveo* of *Aeneid* VII is matched in *Purgatorio* IX by

> lettor, tu vedi ben com'io innalzo
> la mia materia.

> (Reader, well thou seest how I exalt my subject.)

To look to the end, to see the whole, to dispose the parts with economy but without haste in an order that gathers up and carries forward: this is to rule one's art in the general interest. The principle has notable effects on the detail of diction and metric, where we are more prone to think that "style" resides.

If the passage is strictly subordinate to the movement and the phrase or line to the passage, the result is to add just that much more to the exactions under which the phrase or line is formed. This being so, it is no great paradox to find in Sophocles, Virgil, and Dante, respectively, the most beautiful writing, in detail, ever done in Greek, Latin, and Italian. The *bello stile* considered as a matter of the line, the distich or the tercet is derived from and demanded by the *bello stile* considered as a matter of constructive beauty. We may be more specific than this, for we discern in the work of these three poets similarities of texture that suggest a kinship of "speech" in the realm where speech approaches music. A good deal has been said and is generally accepted as to the use of language in each—for example, the tragic "convention" in Sophocles' dialogue, the epic "elaboration" or "ornament" in the *Aeneid,* and the apparently simpler rhetoric of the *Comedy*. If these were not poems, we might be tolerably content with what is said, though we should be dubious always of the imputation of stiltedness in the Greek or Roman work; "plain speech" was no less a resource than "high style" for these poets and in their hands each kind of diction would be transmuted to the distinction required. But *Oedipus*, the *Aeneid,* and the *Comedy* are poems, and therefore besides figure and diction and syntax there is the play of sound to be noticed as essential to their quality.

The fact that in all three this play of sound is so often unobtrusive is perhaps as significant as any other fact about it. Shelley was fond of this line from *Oedipus:*

πολλὰς δ' ὁδοὺς ἐλθόντα φροντίδος πλάνοις

(and in wanderings of thought walked many ways)

but it seems not to have entered his mind that the line depends for its effect on the line preceding:

ἀλλ' ἴοτε πολλὰ μέν με δακρύσαντα δή

(but you know that I have wept for a long while)

for when we take the lines together we find the intensifying sound progressions *pólla, pollás* and *sánta, thónta, phrónti* (the accents here stand for the ictus). Dryden said he was "lost in admiration" of Evander's exhortation in *Aeneid* VIII,

> Aude, hospes. contemnere opes et te quoque dignum
> Finge deo.

but he said nothing to explain the effect it had on him, and we duly notice, on listening hard, the strong rhyming beat of *pes* and *pes* and the echoes and chiastic vowel order in *quoque dignum . . . finge deo*. Until we attend to them these effects are often hidden in Virgil as in Sophocles, enfolded in the stream of speech itself; but when we observe them they seem in both cases audacious in the extreme. Yet we may be sure that they were not sought for themselves but came as a result of the whole stylistic pressure I have described. An incantatory value entered the verse in response to the necessity that it be fluent, meaningful, and memorable. To reverse the process gets you nowhere. Here, for instance, is Tennyson with *ripae ulterioris amore* in his head and the idea of making Virgilian verse:

> Unlaborious earth and oarless sea.

We are aware of a gulf in artistic tact between the Latin and the English cadence—the first softly and appropriately repeating the open-mouthed syllables of longing, the second *ore rotundo*, indeed, but a noise, and irrelevant. Dante's long study and great love of his Virgil book gave him incidentally a better ear. In the opening tercet of the *Divine Comedy* there are formally two rhymes, *vita* and *rita*, but if we listen carefully we hear *ritro* in the second line and *rita* in the third—scarcely audible echoes that bind the lines together in the same key. We might listen, too, to an unpromising specimen, a line that has been quoted more than once to show how utterly different Dante's writing was from the "epic" verse of Virgil even when he derived his image from it. The bleeding and speaking tree trunk in *Inferno* XIII was suggested by the Polydorus incident in *Aeneid* III. As Comparetti puts it, "When he [Dante] says, 'e stetti come l'uom che teme,' he knew well how far he was from reproducing the resonance and grandeur of the Virgilian 'obstipui steteruntque comae et calor ossa reliquit.'" Well, as to resonance it seems unfair to ask nine syllables to resonate as much as seventeen; if we fill up the measure with the preceding 'ond'io lascai la cima / Cadere' we have *la, la, ca* and *scai, ci* and *com e l'uom che*, which together make all the resonance that could be desired. We may observe, besides, that *stetti* echoes Virgil's *steterunt* and *come* his *comae*.

These things should have their place in our appreciation, but to make much of them would be disproportionate, would be to fall into the Alexandrianism, the monumental niggling, that both Virgil and Dante were concerned to put behind them. It is possible that the creative process deserves a little more privacy than it has been getting lately. The "technique" of poetry is something we may be ready to leave mostly to the poets, as we may perhaps leave the mystique of it to them, too. It would be enough for general discussion to define the effect of their work and to extract, with precision, its general relevance, letting the professional curiosities ride for a while. Does not Dante instruct us in a decent reticence about these matters, as he tells of his walk with the great poets in Limbo:

> Cosí andammo infino alla lumiera,
>   parlando cose, che il tacere è bello,
>   sí com'era il parlar colà dov'era.

> (Then we went onwards to the light,
>   speaking things which it is well to pass in silence,
>   as it was well to speak there where I was.)

It is important, however, that we know and distinguish the kind of art Dante was practicing, in company with those others who wore the immortal garland. It is the kind that is most considerate of us, adapted to our condition: we who are anxious, busy and lazy but who wish to read something we can love, and in which we can believe.

Mirroring the *Commedia:*
An Appreciation of
Laurence Binyon's Version

1

One brilliant episode of "the Pound era" has fallen into such obscurity as to remain unregistered in Hugh Kenner's book of that title, marvel of registration though the book is. In telling of Ezra Pound's life in London between 1908 and 1920, Kenner refers once or twice to his friendship with Laurence Binyon, poet and Deputy Keeper of Prints and Drawings in the British Museum. But he says nothing of Pound's interest, years later, in Binyon's translation of the *Divine Comedy*. Now, from early in 1934 to late in 1939, this interest animated a great deal of correspondence between the two men and ended with quite remarkable enthusiasm on the part of Pound. In fact, he all but took a hand in the translation. It would be fair to say that he gave as much time and attention to Binyon's work as he had in other years—in another way—to that of James Joyce, and for the same reason: that he thought the work supremely good. Pound could be wildly wrong about some things but not, I think, about a rendering of Dante in English verse. If anyone's ear and judgment had authority in such matters, his did.

Not only has this whole episode been lost to view, but the translation itself is generally and peculiarly disregarded. Teachers of Dante appear to be only dimly aware of it. And yet the rendering of the *Commedia* that most nearly reproduces the total quality of the original poem is surely Laurence Binyon's. Why is it not likely to be supplied to the student, or the serious reader of English, either at the University or elsewhere? After puzzling over this state of affairs for some time, I have learned enough to realize that it, too—this relative neglect—is a masterpiece in its way, a

First published in *Paideuma*, Winter 1981, and reprinted in *Dante in America: The First Two Centuries*, edited by Bartlett A. Giamatti (Binghamton, N.Y.: Medieval and Renaissance Texts & Studies, 1983).

capolavoro composed by the sheer accidents of history, the fortunes of war and peace.

Here, then, is a story.

2

At Oxford in 1890, Laurence Binyon won the Newdigate Prize with a poem entitled "Persephone." The year and the title combine to bring us the essential fragrance of a period and to suggest the poetic and scholarly tradition that Binyon inherited. Confining to the sensibility though it had certainly become, that tradition had its points, as Binyon's life would demonstrate. He was a studious poet and a sober man. After Oxford he went to work in the print division of the British Museum, where he was to become a pioneer interpreter of the art of the East to the West, author of *Painting in the Far East* (1908) and later a friend of Charles Freer and Langdon Warner. In 1913 Binyon became Deputy Keeper of Prints and Drawings at the Museum. He and young Ezra Pound met one another from time to time and were notably unaffected by each other's work. Binyon's poems, after all, were in the tradition that Pound proposed to shake. One of them became extremely well known: "To the Fallen," first printed in the London *Times* in September 1914. This turned out to be so memorable in the English-speaking world that after 1918 many war memorials throughout Britain and the Commonwealth bore a Simonidean stanza from it, cut in stone: "They shall not grow old, as we who are left grow old, etc."

It is worth remembering that in the Print Division Binyon's eye received an education from the masters of line in East and West. He did a great deal of work on Blake. To an eye so educated, no poetry, probably, could match Dante's in visual fascination. Binyon was not an Italian scholar, but as an amateur, early in the '20s, with the advice and encouragement of his friend Mario Praz, he began translating the *Divine Comedy*. In 1933 *Inferno* was ready, and late in the year Macmillan published it in one volume with the Italian text on facing pages. The book was dedicated to Praz and carried a brief preface.

The modesty of Binyon's prefatory remarks may have veiled the special nature and ambition of this poem. He had tried, he said, to communicate not only the sense of the words but something of Dante's tone and of the rhythm through which that tone was conveyed. This was not merely a matter of matching, with "triple rhyme," Dante's *terza rima*. It involved a more intimate correspondence. So far as English would permit, and in the decasyllabic line native to English, he had imitated the Dantean hendecasyllable, scanning by syllables rather than feet, but through systematic elisions achieving flexibility in syllable count. The result was a regular but very subtle refreshment and quickening of rhythm, e.g., in *Inferno* IV, 49–50:

> "Did ever any of those herein immured
> By his own or other's merit to bliss get free?"

But this was not all, either. By using fine distributions of weight and accent, he had contrived to avoid the beat of pentameters and to even out his stresses on the Italian model. For one conspicuous instance of this he prepared the reader, noting how he had occasionally rhymed on an unaccented syllable (*Inferno* I, 2, "That I had strayed into a dark forest," rhyming with "oppressed")—not intending an abnormal pronunciation, but as "the placing of a heavy or emphatic syllable before the final word seems to have the effect of mitigating the accent on that word, so that it is rather balanced between the two syllables than placed with all its weight on one. Such elasticity of stress seems congenial to Dante's verse. . . ." No doubt Binyon learned the possibility of this, and the advantage of it, from Dante Gabriel Rossetti, who had resorted to it here and there in his translations of Dante's sonnets and *canzoni* in the *Vita Nuova*.

But Binyon went far beyond Rossetti, as he had to, in working out a style adequate to the *Commedia*—a style versatile but consistent, firm but well-wrought, and swift. Drawing on the English of earlier centuries, he would admit old forms and words, but with a selective and measuring ear, so that his archaicisms generally gave body and life to his verses, not quaintness. The diction, thus slightly expanded and elevated, was an accomplishment in itself. It stood, in fact, to twentieth-century English very much as Dante's living Tuscan does to twentieth-century Italian. One brief example may suffice (*Inferno* xxv, 64–66):

> As runneth up before the burning flame
> On paper, a brown colour, not yet black,
> And the white dieth, such their hues became. . . .

Binyon's *Inferno* was published, as I have said, late in 1933. The editor of *The Criterion* in London, at Ezra Pound's request, sent this book to Pound for review. Pound was then living in Rapallo; he had left London thirteen years before, and he had not spent the interval extolling the

English literary establishment, to which Binyon in a quiet way belonged. But a foolish note on Binyon's translation had fallen under his eye and aroused his curiosity. The editor of *The Criterion* must have awaited Pound's review with several kinds of interest. The review appeared in April 1934.

> I state, [wrote Pound], that I have read the work, that for thirty years it never would have occurred to me that it would be possible to read a translation of the *Inferno* from cover to cover, and that this translation has therefore one DEMONSTRATED dimension. . . . The venerable Binyon has, I am glad to say, produced the most interesting English version of Dante that I have seen or expect to see. . . .
>
> The younger generation may have forgotten Binyon's sad youth, poisoned in the cradle by the abominable dogbiscuit of Milton's rhetoric. . . . At any rate, Dante has cured him. If ever demonstration be needed of the virtues of having a good model instead of a rhetorical bustuous rumpus, the life in Binyon's translation can prove it to next century's schoolboys. . . . He has carefully preserved all the faults of his original. This in the circumstances is the most useful thing he could have done.

What these faults were, the reviewer did not expressly say, but it became clear that he meant inversions of word order. Unspeakable syntax had been a *bête noire* to Pound since the days of Imagism, and he now found himself irritated by "Binyon's writing his lines hind side before." But on reflection he had come round to seeing that some of this was appropriate.

> The devil of translating medieval poetry into English is that it is very hard to decide HOW you are to render work done with one set of criteria in a language NOW subject to different criteria. . . . The concept of word order in uninflected or very little inflected language had not developed to anything like twentieth century straightness.

When the reviewer got down to cases, his technical observations were as acute as might have been expected.

> Working on decent basis, Binyon has got rid of magniloquence, of puffed words, I don't remember a single decorative or rhetorical word in his first ten cantos. There are vast numbers of monosyllables, little words. Here a hint from the *De Eloquio* may have put him on the trail. In the matter of rhyme, nearly everyone knows that Dante's rhymes are 'feminine,' i.e. accent on the penultimate, *crucciata, aguzza, volge, maligno*. There are feminine rhymes in English, there are ENOUGH, possibly, to fill the needs of an almost literal version of the *Divina Commedia*, but they are of the wrong

quality; *bloweth, knowing, wasteth*. Binyon has very intelligently avoided a mere pseudo or obvious similarity, in favour of a fundamental, namely the sharp clear quality of the original SOUND as a whole. His *past, admits, checked, kings*, [are] all masculine endings, but all having a residue of vowel sound in state of potential, or latent, as considered by Dante himself in his remarks on troubadour verse.

The fact that this idiom, which was never spoken on sea or land, is NOT fit for use in the new poetry of 1933–34 does not mean that it is unfit for use in a translation of a poem produced in 1321. . . . Coming back to the rhyming, not only are we without strict English equivalents for terminal sounds like *ferrigno, rintoppa, argento, tronca, stagna, feruto*, but any attempt at ornamental rhyme à la Hudibras, or slick epigrammatic rhyme à la Pope or trick rhyme à la Hood, or in fact any kind of rhyming excrescence or ornament would be out of place in the *Commedia*. . . .

One ends with gratitude for [the] demonstration that forty years' honest work do, after all, count for something; that some qualities of writing cannot be attained simply by clever faking, young muscles or a desire to get somewhere in a hurry. The lines move to their end, that is, draw along the eye of the reader, instead of cradling him in a hammock. The main import is not sacrificed to detail. Simple as this appears in bald statement it takes time to learn how to achieve it.[1]

These remarks seem to be valuable above all in that they cast a shrewd—and unique—craftsman's light on the art of the *Divine Comedy* and the task of translating it. Pound obviously felt enticed by the challenge that Binyon had taken up—so much so that he could not stay on the sidelines. In the course of preparing his review, he wrote to Binyon on January 21, 1934.

My dear Laurence Binyon [he said], If any residuum of annoyance remain in yr. mind because of the extremely active nature of the undersigned (it is very difficult for a man to believe anything hard enough for it to matter a damn *what* he believes, without causing annoyance to others)—anyhow. . . . I hope you will forget it long enough to permit me to express my very solid appreciation of yr. translation of the *Inferno*. *Criterion* has asked me for a thousand words by the end of next week, but I am holding out for more space [he got six thousand] which will probably delay publication for heaven knows how long. When and if the review appears and if it strikes you as sufficiently intelligent, I shd. be glad thereafter to send you the rest of the notes I have made. Minutiae, too trifling to print. But at any rate I have gone through the book, I shd. think, syllable by syllable. And as Bridges and Leaf are no longer on the scene, the number of readers possessed of any criteria (however heretical) for the writing of English verse and at the same time knowing the difference between Dante and Dunhill is limited. . . . I was irritated by the inversions during the first 8 to 10 cantos, but having finished the book, I think you have in every (almost every) case chosen the lesser evil in dilemma. For 40 pages I wanted you to revise, after that I wanted you to go on with the Purgatorio and Paradiso before turning back to the black air. And I hope you will. I hope you are surviving the New England winter. . . .[2]

Binyon was surviving it very well. At sixty-five he had retired from his job at the British Museum and had gone to Cambridge, Massachusetts, for the academic year to give the Norton Lectures—he followed Eliot in that chair—lecturing not on poetry but on Oriental art. He replied from the Commander Hotel on February 18:

My dear Ezra Pound, I was very glad to hear from you, and to learn that you had read my Inferno version with so much interest. The difficulties are so immense—often I was in absolute despair—that after surmounting them in a way that didn't seem too bad one was inclined to rate the feat too highly: now, when I turn the pages again a lot of it seems terribly inadequate. (Of course *all of it* is inadequate; that goes without saying; but some passages read well, I think, at any rate apart from the Italian.) When you say 'inversions,' do you mean grammatical inversions or inversions of accent? I shall see when your review appears, if it does appear, as I hope. I shall certainly be very glad of your notes, as I know one can go on improving forever in the matter of details. Shall I go on with the Purgatory and Paradise? I don't know. It takes a devilish amount of time and hard work, but I have done I think 8 cantos of Purgatory so hope to finish that some day. We are having the severest winter on record in the States, but are surviving without any frostbitten members so far. The bright sun is welcome after grey London, which I have now left for good. . . .[3]

So ran the first exchange—friendly if a trifle wary on the part of both men (I hear a reticent gesture of *rapprochement* in Binyon's last remark about London). This led to four or five other exchanges in the course of 1934. Pound's letters were copious and high-spirited, Binyon's briefer and plainer; every now and then he would patiently maintain a point. He enjoyed the *Criterion* review which he found waiting for him in June on his return to England and to his retired farmhouse in Berkshire. He wrote to say that he felt encouraged and grateful, and venerable though he might be he had lots of energy left and hoped to go on. Pound reported in June: "Yeats rumbled in last week / also agreed that you had done a damn good job (my phrase, not his) . . . he assented with noble dignity."[4] As he had promised, Pound sent Binyon his review copy of the book with marginal notations, which Binyon recorded gratefully before returning the book in July. "Of course," he wrote, "in many places you pounce on [things] I should vastly have preferred to be quite plain and direct, but it is devilish hard to get the rhyme, at the same time—as you know. In fact, sometimes impossible. However, you have noted a number of lines wh. I shall try to improve."

In August Binyon wrote to thank Pound for sending him a copy of the Cavalcanti *Rime* in Pound's edition. He said: "I quite see that the having music in view was a gain to the lyric of Campion, etc., necessitating clearness, lightness, a clear contour. But it seems to me that you couldn't go on forever within those limits: and I don't see that the alternative is necessarily rhetorical declamation. Poetry to me is a kind of heavenly speech. . . ." As though by tacit agreement, neither man ever mentioned what each knew the other had in mind: the poetry of Milton. In November Binyon sent Pound versions of the first cantos of the *Purgatorio*. At the end of January 1935, he added a few more and said that at Eliot's request he had sent the Sordello canto (V) to *The Criterion*. Then he went off to Egypt to lecture. Pound continued to think the work over. On the 29th of April he concluded a letter (the last in this series):

> When you get the *Paradiso* done the edition shd. go into use in all university Dante study; at least in America. I don't know WHAT study is committed in England . . . possibly Dante is still considered an exotic. Temple edtn/ was used in my undergrad/ time, but yours sheds so infinitely much more light. . . . And as translation, I don't mean merely of Dante, but in proportion to any translation I can think of, I don't know of any that is more transparent in sense that reader sees the original through it. A translation that really has a critical value, i.e. enlightens one as to the nature of the original. That is rarissima. I don't think my own DO. I have emphasized or dragged into light certain things that matter (to me at any rate) but it is not the same thing. . . . I shall probably do a note on the Purg in Broletto [a new monthly magazine published at Como].[5]

After this there was a long hiatus in correspondence. It was nearly three years later, February 25, 1938, when Binyon wrote again. "I imagine you will be thinking me extinct," he said. "I have at last finished the Purgatorio, and it has gone to the printer. I didn't want to bother you with bits at casual intervals but I wonder if you would care to look through proofs of the whole?" Pound agreed at once. Late in April the proofs were sent. Pound's letters with detailed comments now came thick and fast, more than half a dozen long letters on batches of cantos between April 22nd and May 12th.

Binyon had cautioned him: "But don't take *too* much trouble *now;*

because, as my Inferno was a complete failure from the sales point of view and Macmillan lost over 200 over it, I can't expect them to pay for a heavy lot of corrections, nor can I afford to pay myself." This had not the slightest effect on Pound. Typical of Poundian comments gratefully received and acted on were his remarks on XI, 86–87, *gran disio del eccellenza*, as to which he wrote: " 'desire of excelling or beating someone else' is the meaning, not the 'desire of perfection,' Our 'excellence' is almost a synonym with 'goodness,' As the whole poem is one of fine moral distinctions, this dissociation is worth making."[6]

Wrote Binyon on April 27th: "What I have aimed at above all is getting something like Dante's 'tone of voice,' and my Italian critics and Italian friends all think this is the chief merit of my version. It is the first thing they say. (The English ones say terza rima is un-English, etc.)" Pound's enthusiasm mounted as he read. After Canto XVII he wrote: "MAGNIFI-CENT FINISH! Utterly confounds the apes who told you terza rima isn't English. . . . The beauty here would *only* have been got by using terza rima. Lascia dir gli stolti who don't see it and who have been for two centuries content that *technique* went out of English *metric* with Campion and Waller . . ." At Canto XXI he exclaimed, "Banzai, my dear Bin-Bin. . . ." and at XXVIII, "Bravo, Bravo, Bravo. . . ."

We might listen to a passage from that Canto, XXVIII: the narrator's account of his meeting with Matilda in the *paradiso terrestre*:

> Already my slow steps had borne me on
>   So far within that immemorial wood
>   That I could no more see whence I had gone;
> And lo! a stream that stopped me where I stood;
>   And at the left the ripple in its train
>   Moved on the bank the grasses where it flowed.
> All waters here that are most pure from stain
>   Would qualified with some immixture seem
>   Compared with this, which veils not the least grain,
> Altho' so dark, dark goes the gliding stream
>   Under the eternal shadow, that hides fast
>   Forever there the sun's and the moon's beam.
> With my feet halting, with my eyes I passed
>   That brook, for the regaling of my sight
>   With the fresh blossoms in their full contrast,
> And then appeared (as in a sudden light
>   Something appears which from astonishment
>   Puts suddenly all other thoughts to flight)
> A lady who all alone and singing went,

And as she sang plucked flowers that numberless
All round about her path their colours blent.
'I pray thee, O lovely Lady, if, as I guess,
Thou warm'st thee at the radiance of Love's fire,—
For looks are wont to be the heart's witness,—
I pray thee toward this water to draw near
So far,' said I to her, 'while thou dost sing,
That with my understanding I may hear.
Thou puttest me in remembrance of what thing
Proserpine was, and where, when by mischance
Her mother lost her, and she lost the spring.'

The reader of severe contemporary taste and habituated to contemporary style may find this idiom—one, as Pound put it, "never spoken on sea or land"—at first glance an exercise in the antiquarian. But he will be aware of its clearness and fluency, and as he reads on he will, I believe, begin to feel, as Pound did, the distinction of its fashioning as a medium for the great medieval poem. This cumulative effect cannot be conveyed by quotation, but from the quoted passage the reader may gain an inkling of the means employed. One may notice, for example, in the third tercet the limpid monosyllables of the enclosing lines and the cunning "immixture" of polysyllables in the line enclosed. The fourth tercet is a good one in which to sense the evenness that Binyon achieved in weight of syllables, like musical notes, an effect twice assisted on this page by a flattening-out of the rhyme-word ("contrast" and "witness"). In the final tercet one may hearken not only to subdued alliteration ("puttest," "Proserpine," "mischance," "mother") but to covert internal rhyming ("hear," "where," "her"). Every one of these refinements is a resemblance to the Italian. So controlled and sustained is Binyon's artifice, and so free of any kind of flashiness, that it acquires a life of its own, and this life in the end seems very nearly the life of the original.

In Canto XXXII Pound came upon what he called "the *only* line of really *bad* poetry I have found. . . . 'But when she rolled on me her lustful eye' might be Gilbert and Sullivan. Positively the only line that is out of the sober idiom of the whole of your translation. Like Omerus he SLEPT. Moderate verb and adjective wanted." (Binyon toned it down.) At the end Pound wrote: "Once again my thanks for the translation. And there are damned few pieces of writing that I am thankful for. . . . Nobody has had such a good time of this kind since Landor did his notes on Catullus. . . . And now, Boss, you get RIGHT ALONG with that Paradiso as soon as you've stacked up the dinner dishes. . . ."

Binyon's *Purgatorio* was published in September, with an acknowledgment of Pound's assistance. As he had promised to do three years before, Pound wrote a notice of the book in Italian for *Broletto*. It appeared
in Number 34, for October 1938. This article has to my knowledge never
been translated and has remained forgotten or unknown. Yet it expressed a serious and long meditated judgment, without reserve. It was
headed: "BINYON: we greet a most valuable translation of the Divine
Comedy," and it proceeded (my translation):

> I can repeat all the praises published in *The Criterion* when the transla-
> tion of the *Inferno* appeared; but I must add still others. Constantly devel-
> oping his technique, Binyon in his description of the Terrestrial Paradise
> reaches a true splendor and clarity never achieved before. It seems to me
> that this can be said not only in comparison with the other translations of
> Dante, but perhaps also in comparison with the whole body of translations
> into English of any author whatever . . .

What about Golding's Ovid and Douglas's *Aeneid*, old favorites of
Pound? These were, he observed, works of poetry that had no need of
the originals and served not as interpretations of the originals but as
"comment" of a special kind.

> Binyon [he said], triumphs in another way, he triumphs through an
> honesty that from time to time amounts to genius. His version of Dante
> gives me a clearer sense of the original. It is like a window with glass so
> polished that one is not aware of it, one has the impression of the open
> air. . . .
> My generation in America suffered from the assumption that to under-
> stand Dante it was necessary to suffocate in a pile of commentary. I, at
> least, at seventeen was distracted by the abundance of comments and
> notes and sometimes lost the continuity of the poem. With a prose 'argu-
> ment' of half a page or less for each Canto, Binyon has very clearly shown
> the falsity of this assumption. . . .
> As for *terza rima*, Binyon achieves beauties that he could never have
> attained except by making the effort to employ this form, in which he gets
> a very English flavor with words like *coppices*, or *highlander* for *mon-
> tanaro*. . . .
> The defects of his version are superficial. I see none except in little
> inversions, which could easily disappear in a revision which the translator
> already intends to make as soon as he has finished the whole version of
> the poem. Some defects have already disappeared between the first proofs
> and those passed for the printer. . . .
> But undoubtedly Binyon has already made us a triple gift. First true
> poetry, in his most felicitous pages. Second: a sense of the continuity and

comprehensibility of the poem. Third: an assistance to students. . . . every class for the study of Italian poetry in any foreign university ought to make use of this version to facilitate the comprehension of the *Commedia*.

A decadence begins when attention turns to the ornamental element and is detached little by little from the meaning. In Dante (and in Guido) the meaning is extremely precise; if you doubt it, look at Canto xviii of the *Purgatorio*. The idiom of Binyon's version is the idiom suitable for translating a poet to whom meaning was far more important than ornament. The defects are like nutshells on the table after a magnificent meal.[7]

3

I digress from my story a little, but I'll return to it. The grace of God came to Dante in many forms but in none happier for his poem than the *terza rima*. It was a miraculous formal invention or *trouvaille*. As the formulaic hexameter buoyed and carried the Homeric singer, so that *terza rima* collaborated (it is not too much to say) in the making of the *Commedia*. It gave Dante what he needed for his narrative, a flexible unit beyond the line, capacious enough for description and figure, argument and speech, capable of endless varieties of internal organization, and yet so compact as to make for the famous concision; above all, through the ever-developing rhyme scheme, it gave him continuous movement forward. *Terza rima* is a formal paradigm of Aristotelian Becoming—the latent or "virtual" thing constantly coming into actuality, as each new tercet fulfils with enclosing rhyme the rhyme enclosed in the preceding one. The lyric tercet, moreover, conduced to the design of the poem in cantos or songs of lyric length (the average length in fact nearly conforms to Poe's limit for lyric, reckoned five hundred years after Dante). For these reasons and others, the life of the *Commedia* is inseparable from its form, and a prose rendering alters the nature of the animal even more drastically than usual. Implicit acknowledgment of this is made in the Temple Classics version where the Carlyle-Okey-Wicksteed prose is printed in units or versicles corresponding to Dante's tercets.

The "transparency" valued by Pound in Binyon's version was therefore a formal achievement: Binyon had emulated and matched in English the labor of the original poet in Italian, so that the reader could see through the movement of the English poem the movement of the original composer's invention, working in verse and in verse of just this kind. Of just this kind? Yes, insofar as the Italian hendecasyllable can be matched by decasyllabic lines in English. And in fact the one is closer to the other than may superficially appear. It is close historically, because Chaucer wrote his heroic line with continental syllabic verse, in particular Dante's Italian, in his ear (he was Dante's first translator), and easily every third line in Chaucer is hendecasyllabic because of the nature of Middle English. It is close rhythmically, by virtue of the phenomenon noted by Pound: that in many a "masculine" ending in English the terminal consonant will carry a latent following vowel sound similar at least to the semisyllable of "e muet" if not to the Italian full vowel. The poet and scholar F. T. Prince has been able to argue that it was from the Italian hendecasyllable that Milton derived his line in *Paradise Lost*,[8] and Binyon in turn derived his system of elision from Milton as analyzed by Robert Bridges. By the device he pointed out in his Preface and by other subtle means, he gave his lines the metrical character of the lightly running Italian.

Now twenty years of work on Binyon's part and nearly six years of attentive participation by Ezra Pound led up to nothing less than the miseries and oblivions of the Second Great War. After sending drafts of the first *Paradiso* cantos to Pound and writing to him on December 29, 1939, Laurence Binyon never heard again from his friend in Rapallo. The correspondence they had already had remained in their respective files. No English translation of Pound's *Broletto* article appeared, or was to appear until this writing. Binyon kept his pad on his knee in the wartime evenings; he finished his *Paradiso*. Macmillan published it in 1943. On March 10th of that year Laurence Binyon died in a nursing home in Reading, and his obituary appeared next day in the London *Times*. Along with it appeared news of the Russian armies defending Kharkov and the latest R.A.F. raid on Germany—five hundred tons on Munich. It was not a good year for Italian studies. If Macmillan had lost money on Binyon's *Inferno*, it certainly did not make any on his *Purgatorio* and *Paradiso*. In the event, indeed, all three volumes were allowed to go out of print for long periods and have almost never been in print at the same time.

So matters stood when the war ended in 1945. What trouble had come upon Ezra Pound it is hardly necessary to recall; few people knew or would know for years of his admiration for Binyon's Dante or the reason for it. Some Dantisi remained aware of the Binyon translation. When Paolo Milano edited a *Portable Dante* for Viking in 1947, Macmillan, for a "courtesy fee," allowed him to include Binyon's entire *Divine Comedy*. "Binyon," wrote Milano, "never distorts the original style; he never takes us beyond the range of Dante's own voice." But Binyon's preface, with its clues as to how this great virtue had been worked for, did not appear, nor was it quoted, in the Viking Portable.

W. H. Auden reviewed this book briefly but appreciatively in the New York *Times;* so did Louise Bogan in *The New Yorker.* In the United States the portable sold moderately for a while (bringing nothing, courtesy of Macmillan, to the Binyon heirs), and moderately, again, in a paperback edition (1955), but there was no counterpart in England during the '40s. In those years, however, Penguin Books began to bring out, as "Penguin Classics" under the general editorship of E. V. Rieu, paperback translations, like Rieu's *Odyssey,* priced within range of the railway bookstall trade. For the Penguin Dante, the translator selected was Dorothy Leigh Sayers, and her *Hell* was published in 1949.

It was a formidable work. She, too, had done the poem in English *terza rima.* She quoted Binyon's friend Maurice Hewlett as saying that for the translator of Dante it was *"terza rima* or nothing." With Anglo-Catholic ardor and intellectual bounce, the author of *Gaudy Night* and *The Nine Tailors* provided a long introduction, extremely full notes, and a glossary. In her time Dorothy Sayers had won a first in medieval literature at Somerville College, Oxford, and she wrote with professional skill. Her *Hell* caught on and has been reprinted practically every year. She followed it with a Penguin *Purgatory* in 1955, and after her death in 1957 her friend Barbara Reynolds, General Editor of the *Cambridge Italian Dictionary,* added the concluding dozen or so cantos of *Paradise* for publication in 1962. *Purgatory* and *Paradise* have been reprinted many times. All are to be found in university bookstores in the United States.

One result of these estimable works, however, was not fortunate. If Macmillan had ever intended in the fullness of time to venture a new printing of Binyon's *Divine Comedy,* in the edition with Italian and English on facing pages, the currency of the Sayers version in inexpensive Penguins must have made such a venture seem quixotic. In 1965, in fact, when the question arose, Macmillan pondered a new printing and decided against it. One further development has probably ruled out the possibility forever. In 1972, Chatto and Windus brought out the Viking *Portable Dante* in England, retitled *Dante: The Selected Works.* Remarkably enough, Binyon's name appears neither on the cover nor on the title page of this book, but his version of the *Divine Comedy* is now in print in this form (again minus the preface) in the United Kingdom. Neither there nor in the United States can you buy the bilingual edition that Pound thought should supplant the Temple Classics edition for the undergraduate study of Dante, and the chances are heavily against under-graduates or anyone else ever having it.

This being the case, and admitting the seriousness and utility of Dorothy Sayers' presentation, the quality of her translation, which has already represented the poetry of Dante to several generations of students, invites a little study. When she undertook her work, she was apparently unaware of Pound's *Criterion* review of Binyon's *Inferno*, nor could she have known of the Pound-Binyon correspondence, since none of it appeared in print until eight of Pound's letters were published in D. D. Paige in *The Letters of Ezra Pound* in 1950. If thereafter she became aware of this material, she gave no indication of it in her *Purgatory* or *Paradise*. This may or may not have been to her advantage. Consider the question of feminine rhyming in imitation of the Italian hendecasyllabic line.

"I have used a liberal admixture of feminine rhyme," she wrote in her first introduction. "This is the usual English custom, and I do not know why Dante's translators for the most part fight shy of it." It was perhaps an understandable perplexity, but it had already been resolved by Binyon and Pound. Even without benefit of that solution, the translator might have reflected that a *liberal* admixture of lines that differ in termination from the norm is not like Dante's practice. His *versi tronchi* (accent on the ultima) and *versi sdruccioli* (accent on the antepenult) are rare and exceptional. But once her decision was taken, Sayers went vigorously ahead and allowed herself a good deal of the rhyming "excrescence" that Pound thought out of place in the *Commedia*. At the opening of *Inferno* XXII, for example, she composed four successive tercets with nothing but feminine rhymes and in the fifth added a flourish of the *sdrucciolo* type. It is true that in the Italian of this passage there are subtle irregularities of accent, but the effect of the Sayers English is to carry these to the point of burlesque—and what is true of this passage is true of all too many others.

One might argue that variety of this kind, not only in meter and rhyming but in diction as well (she did the Provençal of Arnaut in *Purgatorio* XXVI in Border Scots), makes the Sayers translation more readable and saves it from monotony. That may be true in this sense: clearheaded and ingenious as she was, but endowed with limited gifts as an English poet or stylist, Dorothy Sayers did well to conceive her work in a way that would utilize her strengths. Her translation is not often dull and is almost always clear—at times clearer than Binyon's. Let one example suffice, *Paradiso* VIII, 49–51:

> Cosí fatta, mi disse: 'Il mondo m'ebbe
> giú poco tempo; e se piú fosse stato,
> molto sarà di mal, che non sarebbe. . . .'

Binyon:

> Transfigured thus, it spoke: 'The world below
> Had me not long; and much would not have happed,
> Had it been longer, that now comes in woe. . . .'

Sayers:

> And shining thus he said: "The earthly scene
> Held me not long: had more time been allowed
> Much ill that now shall happen had not been. . . ."

With her command of workmanlike English and her chosen latitude in rendering, she managed often enough, as in this case, to avoid the "faults of the original"—and of Binyon—in the matter of inverted word order. Without reference to the Italian, as an extended work converting Dante tercet by tercet into English verse, her *Comedy* is a considerable achievement.

Binyon's is simply an achievement of a higher order. His taste is finer. He does not indulge those bright ideas that confuse everything. His style is distinguished and steady, as for all its resources of idiom and invention one feels Dante's style to be. He had indeed caught Dante's "tone of voice." His or any English must be more humid than the dry burning Italian, more muted in sonority, less Latinate and closely knit. But line by line he represents his original with that honesty amounting to genius that Pound remarked. In order fairly to support this judgment, let me examine in both versions a passage of some length, at a point in the poem where each translator after much practice may be supposed capable of his best—the opening of the *Paradiso*.

> La gloria di colui che tutto move
> per l'universo penetra e risplende
> in una parte più e meno altrove.

Sayers:

> The glory of Him who moves all things soe'er
> Impenetrates the universe, and bright
> The splendour burns, more here and lesser there.

Occurring at the end of the first line, "soe'er" could not be a more noticeable archaism. It is also an addition to what the Italian says, and it

concludes the line with a double sibilance following the plural "things."
No less conspicuous in another way is "impenetrates" in line 2, an
uncommon word that seems tautological rather than intensive; in fact, as
it adds nothing to the idea of penetration, it seems forced. In line 3, the
verb "burns" goes beyond the Italian, and does so emphatically through
the position of the verb at the point of caesura.

Binyon:

> The glory of Him who moveth all that is
> Pervades the universe, and glows more bright
> In the one region, and in another less.

Here there is archaism in the old form, "moveth," but the word occurs
midline and is compact, not fluttery. It serves to avoid sibilance, and it
reproduces the disyllabic Italian *move*. "All that is" preserves the singular of the Italian *tutto*. In line 2, "pervades" is the right word to render
penetration by light, and the three syllables of "glows more bright"
follow the contour of *risplende*. Getting in the comparative in this line not
only accords with English idiom but makes it easy for the next line
to retain the chiastic order of the Italian "more . . . in the one region . . . in another . . . less." Moreover, the word *parte* is translated
here, as it is not by Sayers.

> Nel ciel che piú della sua luce prende
> fu'io, e vidi cose che ridire
> né sa né può chi di là sú discende;

Sayers:

> Within that heav'n which most receives His light
> Was I, and saw such things as man nor knows
> Nor skills to tell, returning from that height:

"Most" in line 1 is adverbial with "receives" and barely suggests the
partitive genitive of *più della sua luce*. The verb "receives" connotes more
passivity than *prende*. In line 2, "was I" closely renders the past definite
fu'io, as "saw" does *vidi*, but vagueness begins with "as man nor
knows / nor skills to tell." First of all, this adds a good deal to the Italian
by making the subject generic. The implication that this is an experience
of mankind in general befogs the precision of the singular (though indef-
inite) subject understood and the singular pronoun of the Italian. Sec-
ondly, by pressure of English idiom (we cannot say that one "knows to
tell"), as by the line division here, the alternatives suggested are know-

ing on the one hand and having skill to tell on the other, which misrepresents the original.

Binyon:

> In that heaven which partakes most of His light
> I have been, and have beheld such things as who
> Comes down thence has no wit nor power to write;

"Partakes most of His light" renders the active force of the Italian verb and partitive expression. "I have been," the English perfect, though a looser rendering of *fu'io*, is not only allowable but suitable to the tone of the passage as expressing a more contemplative and less purely narrative time sense. There is concision in "comes down thence," and "has no wit nor power" not only renders the alternatives correctly but unfolds what is latent in the two Italian verbs.

> perché appressando sé al suo disire,
> nostro intelletto si profonda tanto,
> che dietro la memoria non può ire.

Sayers:

> For when our intellect is drawing close
> To its desire, its paths are so profound
> That memory cannot follow where it goes.

The first line and a half closely render the Italian, but the next clause expands the metaphor with an image, "paths," that raises two questions: first, why the plural? and second, why such a degree of concreteness as to make that question arise? In line 3, *dietro ire* is presumed to mean "follow," implying a relationship between intellect and memory that is only superficially plausible.

Binyon:

> Such depth our understanding deepens to
> When it draws near unto its longing's home
> That memory cannot backward with it go.

Here line 1 subtly embodies equivalences to the quality of the Italian: a four-syllable word, "understanding," to match and even chime with the participle *appressando*, and alliteration of four "ds" to match the "s's" and "ds" of the original. In line 3 the Italian is interpreted more precisely than in the Sayers version; here it is not that memory cannot "follow" the intellect but that it cannot return with it, taking *dietro* to mean "back," or indeed "back again," rather than "behind."

Are such points as these mere niggling? Before us on the open page is the philosophical poem of Christendom. It was written, as Ezra Pound once said, to make people think. In every line it exemplifies that activity. The translator's first job is to render Dante's meaning exactly and with delicacy. His second but no less crucial job is to render what he can—and again, with delicacy—of the verbal and metrical form in which the poet did his thinking. It sees that in both respects, again and again, one translation surpasses the other—not a bad one, either— bearing out what Pound said in *Broletto* about Binyon's idiom. But let us continue.

> Veramente quant'io de regno santo
> nella mia mente potei far tesoro,
> sarà ora matera del mio canto.

Sayers:

> Yet now, of the blest realm whate'er is found
> Here in my mind still treasured and possessed
> Must set the strain for all my song to sound.

"Whate'er" in line 1 rarefies the solid *quanto*. The agent *io* and the past action of treasuring up are transposed to a present passive construction. In the monosyllabic line 3, there is insensitive alliteration of four "s's," and the businesslike *sarà ora matera* becomes a tired poeticality, "must set the strain."

Binyon:

> Nevertheless what of the blest kingdom
> Could in my memory, for its treasure, stay
> Shall now the matter of my song become.

The echo of the Latin *verumtamen* in *Veramente* has been perceived and carried into the rendering. *Quanto* is, curtly, "what," and is first the subject of a past action as in the Italian it was the object of one, then the subject of a future statement exactly, and in exactly the same terms, as in the Italian.

> O buono Apollo, all' ultimo lavoro
> fammi del tuo valor sí fatto vaso,
> come dimandi a dar l'amato alloro.

Sayers:

> Gracious Apollo! in this crowning test
> Make me the conduit that thy power runs through!
> Fit me to wear those bays thou lovest best!

Here several displacements have occurred, from *buono* to "gracious" for Apollo, from *ultimo lavoro* to something quite different, a "crowning test," and most interesting of all, from *vaso* to a "conduit" through which the god's power is conceived to run. For the covert and intricate alliterative pattern of the third Italian line (*me . . . man . . . ma . . .* and *di . . . di . . . da*) we have "bays . . . best." In this final phrase a small ambiguity appears: do we understand ("those") bays that among all bays he loves best?

Binyon:

> For the last labour, good Apollo, I pray,
> Make me so apt a vessel of thy power
> As is required for gift of thy loved bay.

Here lines 1 and 2, without obscurity or difficulty, adhere to the vocabulary of the Italian including "vessel" for *vaso*, not less felicitious for not narrowing the conception to an open channel or pipe. The last line lacks any such obvious alliteration as that of the Sayers version, but the closing consonants of "gift" are quietly echoed by those of "loved," and the vowel sound of "required" is echoed by "thy."

4

Though Binyon finished his *Paradiso* without benefit of Pound's criticism, he undoubtedly brought to bear on it what he had absorbed from Pound's notes on the other two *cantiche*. As to the *Inferno*, in recording Pound's marginal notations in 1934 he said he intended some day to bring out a revised edition, and this in fact became a serious undertaking. Using an extra set of clean page proofs of the poem, he went through it canto by canto, making in pen revisions of lines or passages that either he or Pound had found improvable. It is uncertain when most of this work was done; whether he did indeed wait until he had finished the *Paradiso* before returning to the "black air," as Pound suggested, or whether he began at once in 1934 and gave occasional hours to revision over the next eight or nine years. When he died he left among his papers a full set of page proofs of all thirty-four cantos, each bearing a number of revisions, in all more than 500, in almost all cases clear improvements.

The value of this concluding labor was clear to Binyon's widow, who typed out all the revisions and intended to have them incorporated in a new Macmillan printing. This has never taken place. The revisions remained among Binyon's papers until the late '60s when Binyon's daughter, Nicolete (Mrs. Basil Gray), contrived to get them incorporated in the Viking Portable text, in a new edition dated 1969. The very first of these revisions may stand as representative of them all. Canto I, line 1 of the *Inferno* in 1934:

> Midway the journey of this life I was 'ware . . .

In the new edition:

> Midway life's journey I was made aware . . .

The first version announced to the ear at once Binyon's system of elisions (journey of) and his deliberate allowance of a quota of archaism in style ('ware). Evidently to his later judgment, certainly influenced by Pound, these features were not enough to justify such a finicky line. He replaced it with what Pound called "straightness."

NOTES

[1] Ezra Pound, "Hell," *Literary Essays of Ezra Pound*, ed. with an introduction by T. S. Eliot (London, 1954), 201.

[2] Ezra Pound, *The Letters of Ezra Pound*, ed. D. D. Paige (New York, 1950), 251.

[3] This and other letters of Laurence Binyon are quoted by kind permission of Nicolete Gray and The British Society of Authors. I am very grateful to Mrs. Gray for her consideration in placing these and other papers of her father at my disposal.

[4] Quoted from letters in the possession of Nicolete Gray. For permission to use these letters I am grateful to the Literary Executors of Ezra Pound.

[5] From a letter in the possession of Nicolete Gray.

[6] Ezra Pound, *The Letters of Ezra Pound*, 310.

[7] Ezra Pound, "Binyon," *Broletto, Periodico della Città di Como*, 3 (October 1938), 14. For the opportunity of consulting this periodical and copying portions of Pound's article, I am indebted to the kindness of Professor Louis Martz, in 1975 Director of the Beinecke Rare Book Library of Yale University.

[8] F. T. Prince, *The Italian Element in Milton's Verse* (Oxford, 1954), rev. 1962.

APPENDIX

The Art of Translation

INTERVIEWER: First, we thought we'd ask you what made you want to be a writer?

ROBERT FITZGERALD: I don't think it comes on that way . . . wanting to be a writer. You find yourself at a certain point making something in writing, and this seems to be great fun. I guess in high school—this was in Springfield, Illinois—I discovered that I could put words together and the results were pleasing to me. After I had discovered the charms of verse, I wrote verse all the time. Then when I was a senior, a great, kinetic teacher named Elizabeth Graham conducted something called the Scribbler's Club for a few seniors. It was a class, but it called itself a club, and was engaged in writing throughout the year. They put out a little magazine. I guess that was when the whole thing came to a head. I wrote a lot of verse and prose. So it wasn't so much wanting to be a writer as having a knack or fondness for putting things into verse.

INTERVIEWER: Were there any writers whose work you particularly admired at that time?

FITZGERALD: Well, I was greatly taken by a story called "Fifty Grand" in *Scribner's Magazine*, which came into the Scribbler's Club. I thought it was really wonderful. That was Ernest Hemingway's story about the boxer who's offered $50,000 to throw a fight and, though double-crossed and fouled, still goes on to throw it. It's a faultless story. I was also greatly taken at that time by Willa Cather's *Death Comes for the Archbishop*. And in verse, well, you know, you come across the work of William Butler Yeats at a certain point and your head endures fraction.

INTERVIEWER: Where did you go when you left Springfield?

FITZGERALD: I went to the Choate School in Wallingford, Connecticut. When I got out of high school in Springfield, Illinois, in 1928, I had applied for and had been admitted to Yale. My family felt that since I was only seventeen, it would be a little premature to put me in college. So, I went to Choate for a year. While at Choate, I met Dudley Fitts, who was

First published in *The Paris Review*, Winter 1984, then in *Writers at Work, Eighth Series*, by George Plimpton, Editor, Intro. by Joyce Carol Oates. Used by permission of Viking Penguin, a division of Penguin Books USA Inc.

one of the masters there. He had been at Harvard, and I got the idea that where Fitts had gone to college was the place for me to go.

INTERVIEWER: What sort of influence did Fitts have on you?

FITZGERALD: He encouraged me to learn Greek. I would never have gone in for it unless he had dropped the word that it was nice to know a little Greek. So when I got to Harvard, I enrolled in a beginning course. And Fitts was up on Pound and Eliot and Joyce. He read me *The Waste Land*, which changed my life.

INTERVIEWER: Your early poems are full of dislocated, unidentified speakers, images of night and darkness, glinting lights. What drew you to such imagery?

FITZGERALD: I think that the life of the undergraduate, now and certainly in those days, was nocturnal, quite a lot of it.

INTERVIEWER: Do you still feel close to those poems?

FITZGERALD: I recognize them as my own and I don't disown them or feel silly about them. I think some of them are still pretty good, for what they are. I wouldn't have put them in my collection [*Spring Shade*] unless I thought they were worth including.

INTERVIEWER: One of your poems, "Portraits," is a portrait of John Wheelwright. How did you get to know him?

FITZGERALD: It must have been Fitts who introduced me to Wheelwright, and also to Sherry Mangan, a very spectacular literary figure. Both of these gents were socialists and political thinkers. Eventually, Sherry Mangan, whose early poetry was highly stylized and affected, settled into a life of dedication to the Trotskyite cause: socialism without the horrors of Stalinism. Wheelwright, too, was of this persuasion. Well, you probably know something of Wheelwright's place among the eccentrics of Boston of his time. He was always in his great big raccoon-skin coat, and he belonged to the best Boston society of the time. Yet after an evening with friends, wherever the Brahmins of the time congregated, he would go out and do a soapbox turn on the Common, lecturing the cause of socialism in his tux and so on. He was also a devout Anglo-Catholic. These figures, along with B. F. Skinner, who was the white-haired boy of psychology around here at that time, and a physicist named Cuthbert Daniel, were all intellectuals of considerable—what?— presence and audacity and interest. None of them had any money and at that time—this was '32, '33—this country had already felt the very cold grip of the Depression. The mystery of what in the world was going on to deprive people of jobs and prospects, and of what was the matter with American society, occupied these guys constantly. I remember my senior year I went in to see my tutor and I found this man, a tutor in

English, reading *Das Kapital*. When I noticed it, he said, "Yes. I don't intend to spend my life taking care of a sick cat"—by which he meant capitalist society.

INTERVIEWER: Were you sympathetic to revolutionary causes too?

FITZGERALD: Not very, although I had to realize that something was going on. It had been taken for granted in my family that I would go to law school after college. It turned out that the wherewithal to go to law school had vanished, so I had to go to work. I went to work on a New York newspaper, the *Herald Tribune*. But I could never get passionate about revolution, at that time or later—it was a passion that was denied me.

INTERVIEWER: So that when, in the poem about Wheelwright, you speak of "the class machine" . . .

FITZGERALD: I've forgotten.

INTERVIEWER: It goes:

> But [he] saw the heads of death that rode
> Within each scoundrel's limousine,
> Grinning at hunger on the road
> To incorporate the class machine;

FITZGERALD: Those were images drawn from Wheelwright's own work and his way of looking at things.

INTERVIEWER: Do you admire his work?

FITZGERALD: Well, up to a point. I think it extremely peculiar and difficult and always did. The fantasy can be wonderful, figuring "some unworldly sense." Lately, there's been a little fashion of taking it up. John Ashbery, for example, thinks highly of it. A lot of it simply baffles me, and I'd rather not get into it.

INTERVIEWER: Another early poem of yours, "Counselors," is about someone who considers resorting to various professionals for advice, experts in this and that, but decides that on the whole it wouldn't be worth his while. Did you think of Vachel Lindsay, or T. S. Eliot or Yvor Winters, perhaps, as true counselors?

FITZGERALD: I thought that Vachel was a really great fellow, *molto simpatico*, and very good to me. I wrote about him, by the way, in a recent issue of *Poetry*. And later, Winters always seemed to me, crotchety as he was, to have applied himself with great independence and great purity to the literary business. When I was working at *Time*, in New York, I suppose I held him as an exemplar of serious application to the problems of poetry and literature. I remember in June 1940, I was sitting in my office when the office boy came in with the afternoon paper, which was the old *World-Telegram,* and threw it down on the desk. The front page consisted of nothing but one large photograph of the Arc de Triomphe, with German troops marching through it down the Champs Elysées. The headline was: *Ici Repose un Soldat Français Mort pour la Patrie.* That was all. Think of a New York newspaper doing that! That's when I knew that in a year or so we'd be in that affair. There was no question. So, I walked into the managing editor's office and said, "I resign." I'd saved up enough money to live on for a year and I thought I'd do what I could with my own writing until I got swept up in what I knew was coming. They very kindly turned my resignation into a year's leave of absence. I thought, "Now's the time to see Winters." I went to Palo Alto, got a room in a hotel, and called on him. Winters was very kind. He suggested I go to Santa Fe if I were going to make my effort. So, eventually, I'd say in September or October, I found myself, and my then-wife, in Sante Fe, working at poetry, working at Greek—I translated *Oedipus at Colonus*— and spending the year as best I could.

INTERVIEWER: What was your experience of the war?

FITZGERALD: It was very mild. I was in the Navy, and I worked at a shore station in New York. Late in '44, I was assigned to CINCPAC—the Commander-in-Chief Pacific Ocean—at Pearl Harbor, and when that command moved to the Marianas, to Guam, I went along on staff, to do various menial jobs. From, say, February to October of that year, I had nothing to do when I was off-duty but to read. I took three books in my footlocker. One was the Oxford text of the works of Virgil, one was the *Vulgate New Testament,* and the other was a Latin dictionary. I went through Virgil from stem to stern. That's when I first really read the *Aeneid.* I never took a course on Virgil in college or anything like that. I think that's of some interest . . . that with reference to my eventually doing the translation, my first real exposure to the *Aeneid* was hand to hand, with nothing but a dictionary—no instructor, no scholarship, nothing but the text itself, and the choice, evening after evening, of doing that or going to the Officers' Club and getting smashed.

INTERVIEWER: In your memoir of James Agee [which appears as the introduction to Agee's collected short prose], you speak of how difficult it was to write during the '30s and '40s; you seem to mean that it was not only financially difficult to get by as a writer, but also that it was hard to know what to write. Was that so?

FITZGERALD: Well, let's take my first job on the *Herald Tribune.* There was no newspaper guild, no union. It was a six-day work week. For a good part of that year and a half I was coming in, as everybody did, at one-thirty, two o'clock in the afternoon, to pick up assignments—you'd get two or three. Then off you'd go on the subway, up and down the town. From two to six you'd gather the dope. You'd come in around six and knock off, if you could, two or three of these stories and the result would be a couple of paragraphs each, if anything. Then you'd go to the automat, let's say, and eat something, and then you'd come back and get more assignments. You'd be through, with luck, around midnight. It would be a ten-hour day, and you'd have six of these in a row. I can promise you that on your seventh day, what you did, if you could manage to, was to stay in bed. I can remember literally not being able to move with sheer fatigue. How then were you going to arrange to turn out three hundred Spenserian stanzas per year? What added to the difficulty, for me, was that I do not and never could write fast. God knows how I got through it. I really don't. There was the same problem at *Time*, with the additional element that you had to be pretty clever. A *Time* story had to have a good deal of finish, in its way.

INTERVIEWER: Agee and you once planned a magazine. What was it to be like?

FITZGERALD: I have his letters but I didn't keep copies of mine, so I don't know what I was proposing. Anyway, it was to be the perfect magazine.

INTERVIEWER: How did you meet T. S. Eliot?

FITZGERALD: I got to know him earlier, when I was in England in '31–'32. Vachel had written to him, and he wrote me at Cambridge to invite me, saying, "Do drop in." You know, at Faber and Faber. I did. I went to see him and we talked about Cambridge, where I was working in philosophy. He was familiar with the people at Cambridge who were then my teachers or lecturers, C. D. Broad and G. E. Moore. This, of course, was a continuing interest in his life. He had, after all, done his dissertation on Bradley. Had he gone on in that direction, he was going to be a philosopher in the philosophy department here at Harvard. I think on the second or third of my visits I had the courage to hand him a poem. He looked at the poem for a long time. Great silence. He studied it, then he looked up and said, "Is this the best you can do?" *Whoo!* Quite a thing to say! I didn't realize then what I realized later—that it was an editor's question: "Shall I publish this or shall I wait until he does something that shows more confidence?" What I thought at the time, and there was also this about it, was that it was fraternal. Just talking to me as one craftsman to another. A compliment, really.

INTERVIEWER: You've said that *The Waste Land* shook your foundations, and that *Ash Wednesday* always seemed to you something that was beyond literature. How so? Particularly *Ash Wednesday*.

FITZGERALD: Well, the music is unearthly—some of it. It seemed that way to me then, and it still does. And the audacity! "Lady, three white leopards sat under a juniper tree." *Whoo!* Who is the lady? Whose is the juniper tree? What are the leopards doing there? All these questions were completely subordinate to the audacity of the image—and in what would be called a very religious poem. It needs to be said of Eliot that although in the end the whole corpus has settled in people's minds as a work that comes to its climax with the *Four Quartets*, and is definitely religious (Pound in his kidding way referred to him as the "Reverend" Eliot), that the genius was *a fury, a real fury!* Only a fury could have broken the molds of English poetry in those ways at that time. That's what excited us all. *The Waste Land* was a dramatic experience too. It's very hard, in a few words, to get across this particular kind of excitement, but people ought to realize that at its height this gift was the gift of a Fury—capital *F*.

INTERVIEWER: What led you to translate Homer?

FITZGERALD: Now we come to, say, 1950, '51, '52. We were living in Connecticut and having a baby every year, and I was frantically teaching wherever I could, whatever I could, in order to keep everything going. It occurred to me one day—I was teaching at Sarah Lawrence at the time—driving from Ridgefield, Connecticut, to Bronxville, that the best place to get help with the household and the children was overseas. And how could I manage to get abroad? Well, at this time, in the colleges and universities, humanities courses were being developed, and everyone agreed that a good verse translation of the *Odyssey* was something they would love to have. There weren't any. Lattimore had done the *Iliad*, published, I think, in '51. I had reviewed it, admiring it very much. I wrote to Lattimore and I said, "Do you plan to do an *Odyssey* or not?" And he wrote back and said he did not. He had other things he wanted to do. So I thought, "Why don't I try for a Guggenheim with the project of translating this poem?" I felt quite confident I could do something with Homer. Then I went to a publisher, to see if I couldn't set up a contract to do this, maybe entailing advance of a royalty. There was a very bright young man named Jason Epstein, just out of Columbia, who had invented the quality paperback (Anchor Books) at Doubleday, and had made a great killing with these things. So I ended up in the Doubleday office talking to him and, by God, he gave me a contract for an *Odyssey*. This was extraordinary at the time, gambling on me with this contract which assured me of three thousand dollars a year for five years while I was doing the translation. *And* I got the Guggenheim. So, Guggenheim, advance—off we went, to a part of the world where domestic help could be obtained. That's how that worked out. Just a number of favoring circumstances, a concatenation of things, combining to assure me of support, or enough support. We lived very frugally in Italy for several years—no car, no refrigerator, no radio, no telephone—everything was very simple. And so the work began and got done. It was the hand of Providence, something like that, working through these circumstances.

INTERVIEWER: You've said in the past that you came to translate Homer as a kind of amateur or free-lancer, without a full-blown academic background in classics. How did that affect your work?

FITZGERALD: It may have had some ill effects; it wouldn't have done me any harm to have been a better scholar. It wouldn't have done me any harm to have known German. During the whole nineteenth century, you know, German scholars were *it* in Homeric studies. That was a disadvantage.

INTERVIEWER: But don't you think that laboring under that disadvantage perhaps contributed to the immediacy and continuity of your contact with the text?

FITZGERALD: Right. Weighing one thing against the other, I'd rather have had that immediacy than the scholarship. A direct and constant relationship between me and the Greek—that was indispensable. Having the Greek before me and the job of matching the Greek, if I could, from day to day, hour to hour—that was what kept it alive.

INTERVIEWER: Did you set to work with any inviolable principles of translation?

FITZGERALD: Yes, one or two. One was that it didn't matter how long it took. I'd stay with it until I got it right. The other was, roughly, that whoever had composed this poem had imagined people in action and people feeling and saying things out of what they felt; that work of imagining had to be redone. I had to reimagine it, so that it would be alive from start to finish. What had kept it fresh for so many centuries was the sensation you had, when reading it, that *this* was alive.

INTERVIEWER: What considerations went into finding an English equivalent for Homeric Greek?

FITZGERALD: Diction. One wanted the English to be, as I've already said, fully alive. That this should be so, the colloquial register of the language had to enter into it. How far should you go with colloquialism?

Would slang be useful? Answer: practically never. One would avoid what was transient in speech. The test of a given phrase would be: Is it worthy to be immortal? To "make a beeline" for something. That's worthy of being immortal and is immortal in English idiom. "I guess I'll split" is not going to be immortal and is excludable, therefore excluded.

INTERVIEWER: Were there any modern English poets who gave you some insight into what kind of line to take in doing the translation?

FITZGERALD: There was, of course, Ezra Pound and his fondness for the *Odyssey*. He had helped W. H. D. Rouse. Rouse was trying to do a prose version, and there was a correspondence between them. I always felt that Pound was really dissatisfied and disappointed in the end with what Rouse did. Before I went to Europe, I went to see Pound at St. Elizabeths. I wanted to tell him what I was going to try to do. I told him what I felt at the time—which was that there was no point in trying to do every line. I would do what I could. I'd hit the high spots. He said, "Oh no, don't do that. Let him say everything he wanted to say." So I had to rethink it and eventually I did let Homer say everything he wanted to say. I sent Pound the first draft of the first book when I got that done in Italy that fall. I got a postcard back, a wonderful postcard, saying, "Too much iambic will kill any subject matter." After that, I was very careful about getting singsong again. Keep the verse alive, that was the main thing. That's what he meant. And then, at a certain point I came across the *Anathemata*, by David Jones, which I thought was beautiful, like a silvery piece of driftwood that you could carry around with you. I carried it around just because of the texture of parts of it, a wonderful texture. I really couldn't pinpoint or put my finger on anything in my work that was directly attributable to David Jones. It was a kind of talisman that I kept with me.

INTERVIEWER: Did you find your trip to Greece and Ithaca to be useful?

FITZGERALD: That was wonderful. It corroborated my sense of the place. There, for example, was the wine-dark sea.

INTERVIEWER: How did you work on the translations?

FITZGERALD: I had this whole routine worked out while doing the Homer. I wrote out every line of Greek in my own hand, book by book, a big notebook for each book. One line to two blank lines. As I went through the Greek and copied it out in my own hand, I would face the difficulties—any crux that turned up, questions of interpretation—and try to work them out. I accumulated editions with notes and so on as I went along. So before I was through, I had acquired some of the scholarship that was relevant to my problems. But always, in the end, it was simply the Greek facing me, in my own hand, in my own notebook.

INTERVIEWER: How different is it when you compose your own verse?

FITZGERALD: You don't have any lines of Greek. And you're not riding the ground swell of another imagination as you are in translating. You have your own imagination.

INTERVIEWER: Would you revise as you went along, book by book, or did you wait until it was over with?

FITZGERALD: Both. It was heavily revised before I got the typescript more or less as I wanted it. Then the routine was for me to send in to the publisher what I had done during that year and at the same time send revisions for what had been submitted the year before. Then at the end, I spent a summer going through the whole damn thing from start to finish. Revising was interminable.

INTERVIEWER: How long did it take altogether?

FITZGERALD: Seven years of elapsed time. I'd say six full *working* years went into this poem.

INTERVIEWER: What were the peculiar satisfactions of translation?

FITZGERALD: Well, this is exaggerating a little bit, but one could say that I eventually felt that I had him, the composer, looking over my shoulder, and that I could refer everything to him. After all, it was being done for his sake, and one could raise the question with him, "Will this do or won't it?" Often the answer would be no. But, when the answer was yes, when you *felt* that it was yes—that is the great satisfaction in writing. It's very precious. Writing is very difficult. It's pure hell, in fact, quite often. But when it does really click, then your little boon is at hand. So that happened sometimes.

INTERVIEWER: Your own poems seem to have fallen off since you began translating Homer.

FITZGERALD: I wonder if they did. I don't know. I think that what roughly happened with my own poems was that, indeed, I had taken on a very large job. The magnitude of that job did rather put in the shade the adventure of making a wonderful page, which is, as I would put it, the pleasure and satisfaction of making a poem: to make which really has about it something wonderful, as a good lyric poem has. On the scale of what I was trying to do, that rather faded away, and I guess I would no longer feel the complete satisfaction that in the old days had come of making a poem. I must have begun to feel that there was a slightness in comparison with the big thing. That's one way of looking at it. And then I think that when I got to Harvard and began teaching, and putting a lot into the teaching, that also took care of a certain amount of what had been taken care of in the old days by making a poem. Instead of making a poem, I was helping other people make poems, and on quite a steady basis too. I was handing it out to other people instead of keeping it. Maybe, anyway. That's possible.

INTERVIEWER: After you finished the *Iliad*, you said that you weren't going to do any more translations. What led you to take up Virgil?

FITZGERALD: Well, the circumstances are really very clear. My first teaching job after the war, at Sarah Lawrence, was to give a course in poetry. I could do anything I liked, so I devised a little course called "Virgil and Dante." Each year I would take a small group of students through the *Aeneid* and through the *Divine Comedy*, using the original languages. When I moved to Harvard after the long interval with Homer, I devised a little course called "Studies in Homer, Virgil, and Dante." That kept the Virgil, so to speak, abreast of the Homer. Kept it alive in my mind. So, in 1978, four years after the completion of the *Iliad*, I was sitting in Boston's South Station waiting to get a train, and going over in my mind the Latin of certain lines at the beginning of Book Two of the *Aeneid*. I found these Latin lines taking English shape in my mind. Aeneas is beginning his remarks to Dido, the queen: a little story of the fall of Troy. So, he says:

> Infandum, regina, iubes renovare dolorem,
> Troianas ut opes et lamentabile regnum
> Eruerint Danai . . .

And he goes on:

> Et iam nox humida caelo
> Praecipitat suadentque cadentia sidera somnos.

"The humid night is going down the sky . . . and the sloping stars are persuading slumber"—a literal translation, the sort of translation that a kid would make in class. So, I found myself uttering *this* sort of thing:

> Now, too, the night is well along, with dewfall
> Out of heaven, and setting stars weigh down
> Our heads toward sleep.

Well, I said to myself, "My God, I've got that!" *Now, too: dewfall*—the end of the line is symmetrical with the beginning of the line. *Out of heaven, and setting stars weigh down: Out* at the beginning of the line; *down* at the end. The secrets of music in this business are very subtle and strange; I did not see these sound patterns at the time, but eventually I realized that what I had had that kind of quality to it. Having done that, I said to myself, "Hmm, if I can do a few lines with pleasure, why don't I do the whole thing?" And so I did.

INTERVIEWER: Translating Homer, you avoided Latinisms as much as possible and made words of Anglo-Saxon origin the backbone of your language. But in the Virgil you seem to have employed a more Latinate vocabulary. Is the effect of Latin words in Latin really akin to that of Latin-derived words in English, where they've developed new connotations?

FITZGERALD: It's absolutely true that I avoided Latinisms in doing Homer; the Latin forms of the names of people and places were avoided in favor of the Greek. I wanted the *Greekness* of the thing to come across, and a lot of Latinate phrases would irresistibly have taken you back to the neoclassical, which I wanted utterly to skip . . . I wanted to skip Pope and Chapman because they all came to Greek so much through Latin. Their trots were in Latin, and kids in school, of course, learned Latin so thoroughly. Greek was always second for educated people in the seventeenth and eighteenth centuries. I wanted to skip all that and, if possible, to make it a transaction between Homer, 700 B.C., and Fitzgerald, 19-whatever. Between that language at that time and our language at this time. I don't think that these criteria were very much altered in doing the Virgil. A living English in our time had better be careful about Latinisms. Latinisms are so associated with mandarin English, with the English of Englishmen, not of Americans.

INTERVIEWER: In your introduction to Dryden's translation of the *Aeneid*, you speak of Dryden's clear perception of the difficulties any translator of Virgil faces. In Latin words there are, on the whole, as many vowels as consonants, whereas English words are cluttered with the latter. Latin is inflected, English is not, so that Virgil could rearrange word-order at will for musical effect. Virgil exploits a nearly endless stock of figurative terms. How did you grapple with these problems?

FITZGERALD: Well, Dryden's despair, you know. I wouldn't say that I was overthrown very often by it, though it is true, toward the end of the poem, that more and more of what Dryden calls "figurative, elegant, and sounding words" keep coming in. The vocabulary is freshened. One copes with that. One keeps on doing the best one can with the problem of the moment, whether it be in speeches or in narrative, always, first of all, making sure that it's idiomatic English . . . that it's not muscle-bound or stiff.

INTERVIEWER: Arnold said that the distinguishing feature of Homer's verse is its rapidity. What quality of the *Aeneid* did you consistently try to bring over into English?

FITZGERALD: Well, I ventured to put as an epigraph to the book the line *"Aeternum dictis da diva leporem,"* from *De Rerum Natura* of Lucretius. This is a plea that the goddess (whom we may understand as Venus in Lucretius' case, or indeed as the Muse) should give eternal charm. Charm to the work. That the product should have an incantatory quality, as a charm, pronounced in the enchanter's way. Insofar as one can make a conscious effort to achieve this kind of thing, I suppose that here and there I've made it. "And setting stars weigh down / Our heads toward sleep" is an example.

INTERVIEWER: When you speak of the music of poetry, what exactly do you mean?

FITZGERALD: Well, take from *Ash Wednesday:*

> A pasture scene
> And the broadbacked figure drest in blue and green
> Enchanted the Maytime with an antique flute . . .

That's music. And one notices in the sounds. "Enchanted the Maytime with an antique flute"—*ant, ant, flute.* What comes into the Maytime thing, the colors blue and green, what the air is like on a day in mid-May, under the magnolias, the lilacs. The little echoing in the line—that's a kind of music, it seems to me. *"Formosam resonare doces Amaryllida silvas."* This is from the First Eclogue. *Ryllida, silvas*—again an echoing, like a note in the bass on the piano, although in fact the right hand is carrying another melody, so you have this repetition in the left hand which insists on doing a second melody there. What the line is saying is one melody. What in counterpoint these little repetitions of sound are doing is another. The music is enriched as the music in a fugue is enriched by two things going on at once.

INTERVIEWER: In translating, do you try to mimic the music of the original?

FITZGERALD: That, or make an equivalent. It's what I meant when I said in the afterword to the *Odyssey* that translating the Greek of Homer into English is no more possible than translating rhododendron into dogwood. On the other hand, suppose you make dogwood?

INTERVIEWER: But wouldn't you want some relation?

FITZGERALD: You would like to convey as exactly as possible what is being conveyed in the Latin narrative. You want what is happening to be exactly what's happening in Homer's imagination, if you can, and then you want an English equivalent of the Latin music. The Latin music is very elaborate. Listen to this:

> Vertitur interea coelum, et ruit oceano nox,
> Involvens umbra magna terramque polumque
> Myrmidonumque dolos.

That's the full orchestra, really, the full orchestra. Let's see what the Latin turns out to be in English:

> As heaven turned, Night from the Ocean stream
> Came on, profound in gloom on earth and sky
> And Myrmidons in hiding.

There is at least the matching of the series of long vowels—*night, ocean, stream, came, profound, gloom, sky, hiding*—long open vowels that by their succession and echoing give something like the effect of the Latin. But it's English, it's carrying the story on. You don't have to listen to this music. If what you want to hear is the story, read the story.

INTERVIEWER: Robert Lowell wrote a little piece on epics in which he said, "Homer is blinding Greek sunlight. Virgil is dark, narrow, morbid, mysterious, and artistic. He fades in translation." What do you think of those adjectives Lowell racks up?

FITZGERALD: Well, too much has been made of texture. One of the things that I tried to bring out more fully, as I went along, was the pure narrative interest of this thing as a story. It's Aeneas's story, some of which he tells himself, and most of which he doesn't. The narrative, if it's properly rendered, is extremely interesting and exciting. What happened to Virgil (partly because of the curse of his being a text in the fourth year of secondary school, and also because of his having supplied so many tags for speakers in the House of Lords) is that the poem has been fragmented. The arc, the really quite magnificent arc of the original narrative, has been rather lost to view. Nobody ever reads the entire *Aeneid*. They read in school, if they read anything, Books Two, Four, Six, *maybe*, if they're lucky. That's it. Nobody ever reads the last six books. Yet in the last six books the whole thing happens, really. That's the man at war. That's the *arma* and the *virum*. I would love to think that the whole story will be restored to view. People can read it, and will read it, because it turns out to be readable.

INTERVIEWER: It certainly seems that in the first half, Aeneas is an oddly stunned sort of hero, while in the second half he is commanding, even horrifyingly so.

FITZGERALD: Exactly. The tragic import of all this is what happens to a man wielding power, especially in hostilities of that kind. He goes as berserk as anybody. The point is very abundantly made that the Roman state was founded on war, on their being very good at war. I happened to reread Caesar, *The Battle for Gaul*, during the composition of the last six books, to see what, in fact, war was like in the generation preceding Virgil. Virgil certainly knew, as every Roman did, what it cost, and the exertion that was made to defeat these hordes of extremely hard-fighting Germans and Gauls. No doubt about the carnage, the incredible carnage: field after field left absolutely soaked in blood, with dismembered individuals for miles. The scene was one of great terror and desolation, all of this in order that Julius should become first consul and have his career. One does sense throughout the *Aeneid* the tragic import of Roman power, of what they were proudest of: their ability to defeat the tribes that came against them and then to create some kind of civil order in the provinces they conquered. But the cost of that, and the dreadful effects of these encounters of armed men, is very vividly brought out, and is one of the things that Virgil meant to bring out, along with the *pro forma* praises of the Roman heroes. A Roman *gladius*, or short sword, honed on both edges, was like a cleaver! A two-edged cleaver! Just imagine turning twenty thousand men with two-edged cleavers loose on the opposition!

INTERVIEWER: You once said that English poetry "hungers for a sound metaphysic," but that its history is largely a record of a failure of supply. What did you mean?

FITZGERALD: English poetry "hungers for a sound metaphysic"? I was, I think, at the time, interested in the superior precision of Aristotle's *De Anima* as contrasted with Coleridge. I was thinking in particular of the difference between the Aristotelian and the Coleridgean views of what happens in creative work of the mind. I made my remarks, that's it. I never went out to argue.

INTERVIEWER: In the Agee memoir you speak of your brotherhood in the arts with him. Did you have a similar relationship with Lowell or Berryman or Auden? Did you consult them when you were working on your translations?

FITZGERALD: I certainly did. Not W. H. Auden, though, because we met so rarely. John Berryman saw what I was working on at the time and made a suggestion or two on word order which I adopted. Randall Jarrell also saw what I was working on one summer. He had an excellent notion. His notion, to put it briefly, was that if you're going to be collo-quial, you can achieve the colloquial thing by gradation. You depart from the formality a little bit and then a little bit more, and then you're collo-quial, and then you modulate away from it—modulate toward and mod-ulate away from it. Such a beautiful idea! I don't know whether I really obeyed this or not. And Cal Lowell just said, "You've got it! This is a bulls-eye!" There is, after all, a brotherhood among people who are working at the same craft, who show each other what they're doing from time to time. The result's likely to be more helpful if your pal simply runs his hand down the page and stops, and does not say a word. Just stops. You see something's wrong where the finger's pointing, and that's enough.

INTERVIEWER: How did you get to know Lowell?

FITZGERALD: I met him through Randall Jarrell. Jarrell was teaching at Sarah Lawrence the first year I taught there, and we therefore saw one another every week and got to be friends. He brought Lowell along some evening or other and we had the evening together.

INTERVIEWER: Nowadays people tend to praise Jarrell's criticism and downplay his poetry. Do you think that's fair to his work?

FITZGERALD: No, I don't. I think quite a few of his poems are very good indeed. No one ever did anything remotely like what he did for the Air Force, for the carrier pilots, and all the rest of that.

INTERVIEWER: You've often said that you think poetry should be "chiefly hair-raising." At the same time, however, you've spoken of the desirability of a strong bond between the poet and the community he lives in—a bond that you seem to believe has been broken in modern times. Do you see any contradiction or tension between such social concern and the requirement that poetry be, above all, hair-raising?

FITZGERALD: Well, don't we have Emily Dickinson, the wondrous lady of Amherst, as an authority for that: "It's a poem if it makes you feel as though your head were taken off"? And A. E. Housman: "If while I am shaving a line of poetry strays into my mind, my beard bristles so that I can't cut it"? This is an extreme, and this kind of poetry is part of the extreme literary experience—extreme both for the maker and for the reader. That's at one end of the spectrum. At the other end there is Dryden, sitting in his coffeehouse, turning out couplets to insult some-one whom he feels like insulting. So, one has the gamut between what is essentially a private, we might say a metaphysical experience, and the other which is simply a refinement of prose—verse devoted to wit, or to the quotidian purpose of making something clear or making somebody ashamed, of exposing somebody, of putting into a witty form someone's foibles . . . which can be read with amusement and without a touch of the other extreme, which is private and rare and precious. I don't see why we can't live with a decent consciousness of these two poles of poetic experience. I once said, too, that poetry is at least an elegance and at most a revelation. That says it pretty well—"is at least an elegance"— something that is well formed, readable, and then again something that takes you *up*.

INTERVIEWER: How close is the revelation of poetry to the religious experience of revelation?

FITZGERALD: Very close, I think. Very close indeed.

INTERVIEWER: You've spoken of a "third kind of knowledge" that came out of moments of vision you had as a young man. How important were they?

FITZGERALD: Terribly important. I don't think that anything could be more important than to be reminded that, as Flannery O'Connor used to say, "The church is custodian of the sense of life as a mystery." We get so used to it that we lose the sense. To have the sense restored to us— which the religious experience does and which the poetic experience at its extreme does as well—is a great boon.

INTERVIEWER: You say that you came back to the Church with a "terrific bump." What brought you back?

FITZGERALD: Well, a number of things that I really don't think I can satisfactorily speak of in this context.

INTERVIEWER: Do you think that the integration of poetry and the university since World War II has been harmful?

FITZGERALD: Maybe. At Harvard in my time there was Robert Hillyer's course in versification, and beyond that, very little indeed in the way of writing courses. An exceptional teacher at that time would be *au courant* with what was living and exciting about writing. Hillyer was exceptionally the other way. He was deliberately blind, deaf, and dumb to what was going on in the avant-garde. I think one felt, in general, one wasn't going to get much attention from the faculty. If you wanted to put things in the undergraduate literary magazine, *The Advocate*, okay. *The Advocate* was . . . *The Advocate*. I don't think that people on the faculty paid much attention to these half-baked manifestations of literary ambition on the part of the undergraduates.

INTERVIEWER: Can we ask you about Flannery O'Connor and how you came to know her?

FITZGERALD: Flannery O'Connor came with Cal Lowell. Lowell and she and Elizabeth Hardwick turned up in New York together. They'd been at Yaddo, and there was a dustup at Yaddo in which I'm afraid Lowell had begun to go off his trolley. At that point nobody really understood that this was the case, but we all understood it before it was over, very thoroughly. It was one of Lowell's very early, maybe his earliest breakdown. We met Flannery in the course of that, really, and then, of course, we went on independently of Lowell.

INTERVIEWER: You seem to have been something of a counselor to her. She would send her work to you, seeking your comments.

FITZGERALD: I wouldn't want to build myself up. No, no, she knew what she was about. Owed nothing, I don't think, to me so far as the essence of these things was concerned. I supplied her with one title, "The Life You Save May Be Your Own." I'd been driving through the South, and it just happened this was something one saw on the road signs. And I supplied her with some reasons for undertaking a revision of her novel, *The Violent Bear It Away*, which she did. I think she was better pleased with it after she'd done the revision. Those would be practically the only instances in which I had any effect on what she did. She was a good friend. One liked to see what she was working on. That was always great fun to see.

INTERVIEWER: Has your career so far differed from your early expectations of it? Or didn't you have any expectations?

FITZGERALD: I don't know that I had any. I just hoped to keep on. I suppose I'd have been amazed when I was twenty to hear that before I was through, I would have translated Homer and the *Aeneid*. The notion that I should go in for these gigantic labors would have been completely out of this world. As I remember, when I was signing Elizabeth Bishop's *Iliad* for her, her only remark was, *"My,* all that *work!"*